*To my mom, Sallie Chapman, who told me I could do anything
I set my mind to, and to my dad, Wayne Slocum, who never quite figured out
what I actually do but was proud of me nonetheless.*

More Praise for *Building the Skills-Based Organization*

"Koreen Pagano cuts through the buzzwords and delivers a smart, grounded guide that helps organizations actually do the work of becoming skills-based. This book is a must-read—it's full of clarity, examples, and actionable steps."
—David Kelly, former Chairman and CEO, the Learning Guild

"Koreen's blueprint illuminates the path for L&D leaders navigating the workforce transformation driven by AI augmentation and agents. It's essential reading for understanding the landscape of skills data, harnessing task intelligence, and building a future-ready, skills-based organization that fosters human-machine collaboration."
—Josh Cavalier, Founder and CEO, JoshCavalier.ai

"This book is a blueprint for leaders serious about building a future-ready workforce."
—David Blake, Founder and Co-CEO, Degreed

"The growing influence of skills is necessary but confusing. In this book, Koreen Pagano leverages her extensive experience to provide a thorough and cogent look at the what, why, and how to make the journey comprehensible and compelling. Highly recommended!"
—Clark Quinn, Executive Director, Quinnovation

"For anyone navigating the shift to a skills-based organization, this is the guide. It's written in a beautifully clear way and is full of invaluable case studies from the organizations already on the path."
—Julie Dirksen, Author, *Design for How People Learn*

"If you are struggling with how to build a skills-based organization, then I strongly urge you to read this book as it provides not only the blueprint, but the broader context and influence you'll need. Invaluable to any transformational leader."
—Helen Marshall, Chief Learning Officer, Thrive

"This is an era in which shifting the skills of people, and not just machines, is the key for unlocking for strategic agility. Pagano delivers a pragmatic guide that captures the imperative, context, and tactical requirements of skills transformation as a competitive advantage for building tomorrow's workforce today."
—Vidya Krishnan, former Global Chief Learning Officer, Ericsson

Building the Skills-Based Organization

A Blueprint for Transformation

Koreen Pagano

PRESS

ALEXANDRIA, VA

© 2025 ASTD DBA the Association for Talent Development (ATD)
All rights reserved.

28 27 26 25   1 2 3 4 5

No part of this publication may be reproduced, distributed, or transmitted in any form or by any means, including photocopying, recording, information storage and retrieval systems, or other electronic or mechanical methods, without the prior written permission of the publisher, except in the case of brief quotations embodied in critical reviews and certain other noncommercial uses permitted by copyright law. For permission requests, please go to copyright.com, or contact Copyright Clearance Center (CCC), 222 Rosewood Drive, Danvers, MA 01923 (telephone: 978.750.8400; fax: 978.646.8600).

ATD Press is an internationally renowned source of insightful and practical information on talent development, training, and professional development.

ATD Press
1640 King Street
Alexandria, VA 22314 USA

Ordering information: Books published by ATD Press can be purchased by visiting ATD's website at td.org/books or by calling 800.628.2783 or 703.683.8100.

Library of Congress Control Number: 2025936313

ISBN-10: 1-960231-74-X
ISBN-13: 978-1-960231-74-1
e-ISBN: 978-1-963392-08-1

ATD Press Editorial Staff
Director: Sarah Halgas
Manager: Melissa Jones
Content Manager: Bianca Woods
Developmental Editor: Jack Harlow
Production Editor: Katy Wiley Stewts
Text Designer: Shirley E.M. Raybuck
Cover Designer: Rose Richey

Text Layout by PerfecType, Nashville, TN

Contents

Foreword by Kelly Palmer vii
Preface xi
Introduction xv
    Contribution by Sandra Loughlin xxvii

Part 1. Laying the Groundwork

Chapter 1. Making the Case 3
    Contribution by Lori Niles-Hofmann 10
Chapter 2. Understanding the Current Landscape 15
    Contribution by JD Dillon 40
Chapter 3. Deciding How to Start 47
    Contribution by Oli Meager 54
    Contribution by Jeroen Van Hautte and Cedric Vandamme 58
Chapter 4. Assessing Organizational Readiness 61
    Contribution by Matt Hayward 78

Part 2. Planning and Strategizing for Skills

Chapter 5. Defining Skills Data 85
    Contribution by Matthew J. Daniel 103
Chapter 6. Planning for Skills-Data Collection and Analysis 107
    Contribution by Dani Johnson 133
    Contribution by Sarah Mullens and Maria Chrastka 136
Chapter 7. Preparing the Skills Infrastructure 141
    Contribution by Paul Turner 142
    Contribution by Angela Le Mathon 164

Part 3. Developing Your Blueprint

Chapter 8. Transforming Hiring Practices 171
    Contribution by Rosellen Beck 189

Chapter 9. Fostering a Learning Culture 193
    Contribution by Gina Jeneroux 211
Chapter 10. Implementing Skills-Based Talent Management 217
    Contribution by Asi DeGani 234
    Contribution by Emily Anderson, Jennifer Tucker,
        Allison R. Suerdieck, and Katie Gunther 238
Chapter 11. Empowering Employees 243
    Contribution by Kristi Bloom 258
    Contribution by Matthew J. Daniel 262
Chapter 12. Measuring Impact and Sustaining Your Skills-Based
    Organization 267
    Contribution by Aaron Silvers 285

Conclusion. A Skills-Based Future: What's to Come 289

Acknowledgments 299

References 303

About the Contributors 307

Index 315

About the Author 325

About ATD 327

Foreword

Kelly Palmer

What if I told you that the greatest risk to your company's success isn't your competitors or the market, but a failure to invest in your people's skills?

It might seem counterintuitive, but in today's world, the difference between thriving and merely surviving often comes down to how prepared your workforce is for change. According to recent studies, more than a billion people—more than 60 percent of the global workforce—will need to learn new skills by 2030 (Zahidi 2020). Let that sink in for a moment. Organizations are up against a challenge they've never faced before: preparing for an uncertain future by focusing on skills we can't fully predict. How do you build a workforce ready for such rapid evolution?

It wasn't long ago that a college degree and years of experience were the ultimate indicators of expertise. But today, as the world changes at a pace no one could have predicted, skills have become the new currency. The question now is not *if* organizations should focus on upskilling their workforce but *how* they can do it effectively in a landscape that evolves so rapidly.

For the past few decades, I've been captivated by the complexities of learning. I've asked myself questions that are deceptively simple yet endlessly challenging: How do people really learn? What motivates them to seek knowledge and develop new capabilities? How can we measure learning in ways that truly affect performance? The science of learning has revealed that it's not just about lectures and exams; it's about engaging the brain, fostering curiosity, and designing experiences that lead to genuine growth. As technology, especially artificial intelligence, reshapes our world, the way we learn must evolve too.

But in recent years, one thing has become increasingly clear: It's not enough to just learn. In today's fast-changing world, learning must translate into real, applicable skills. This book takes that next step, guiding organizations to bridge the gap between knowledge and capability, ensuring that learning is purposeful and that employees are equipped with the skills needed to succeed. This shift—from focusing on learning alone to building relevant, adaptable skills—is the foundation of a thriving, future-ready workforce.

In *The Expertise Economy*, I explored the transformative power of continuous learning and upskilling to prepare organizations for the challenges of a rapidly changing world. Now, several years after the book's publication, the urgency around this mission has only intensified. The world of work is evolving faster than ever before, fueled by technological advances, shifting market demands, and the emerging priorities of a new generation. In this environment, the ability to continuously develop and adapt skills is no longer just beneficial—it is essential for both individual and organizational resilience.

As someone who has devoted much of my career to understanding learning and skills development, I deeply appreciate the expertise and dedication that Koreen Pagano brings to this book. As the author of *Immersive Learning*, Koreen has been at the forefront of innovative learning design and development, and we share a commitment to building a more skilled, adaptable workforce. I am honored to support Koreen's work and am confident that readers will gain invaluable insights from her perspective and experience.

This book arrives at a crucial time, offering a road map for building a workforce equipped to meet today's demands and tomorrow's unknowns. Its insights guide us toward a future in which skills serve as the foundation of decision making, organizational structure, and individual growth. Within these pages, you will find strategies for creating an environment where skills are measured, nurtured, and celebrated; where data-driven insights inform development pathways; and where upskilling and reskilling become integral parts of everyday operations.

But this book also speaks to something more profound: the value of making skills a core part of an organization's culture. By investing in skills, organizations aren't just preparing for immediate challenges—they're committing to long-term adaptability and innovation. This shift requires buy-in at every level—from executives to individual contributors, who together create a dynamic, skills-focused culture that can weather disruption and seize opportunity.

In a world that refuses to stand still, the insights in this book will empower organizations to turn skills development into a lasting competitive advantage. It is a must-read for leaders, practitioners, and learners who understand that the future of work belongs to those who can continuously grow, adapt, and lead through change. With this resource as a guide, I am confident that organizations everywhere will be better equipped to meet the challenges of our time and thrive in the expertise economy.

Preface

When I first meet someone, they typically ask, "Do you have kids?"

Most people are really shocked when I say I have seven.

This inevitably results in a series of follow-up questions about their origin stories, their genders, and their ages. By the time this book is published, the youngest will have graduated from high school, and I will officially have seven kids in early adulthood, ranging in age from late teens to mid-20s.

One of the things I've learned as a parent of so many kids is that the world of work they are all entering is very different from the one I entered. A college degree is not a golden ticket anymore. Many of the jobs that exist today I couldn't have imagined when I was thinking about my future career, and the rate of change is accelerating. Young people now entering the workforce will be unlikely to map a single career path to a future retirement. Technology is evolving so fast that we can only imagine the role that humans will play in the future.

As a mom trying to advise and support my brood of fledgling workers, it often feels like the experiences that shaped my career path are somewhat obsolete in today's landscape, with entry-level jobs becoming increasingly automated. That raises some weighty questions: How will my kids learn and grow in their careers? How will they develop expertise? How will they find opportunities that bring them joy and fulfillment?

Believe me when I say the potential of centering the future of work around skills is deeply personal to me.

The world evolving to become skills-based means my kids will have deeper insights into how their unique strengths and interests can align with work opportunities. It means organizations might see potential in my kids' skills to meet their business needs. It means that there will be more transparency, ideally more equity, and more intention finding jobs and being hired, promoted, or put to work on projects that match my kids' abilities and interests.

Skills aren't a nebulous concept to me. They're a data-driven approach to handling the rapidly evolving pace of innovation, which is putting demands on the workforce to adapt and respond to constant change. Without the transparency and insights that skills data can provide to help us weather persistent change, I worry how my kids will navigate their career journeys. And so, this book is as much for my kids as it is for organizations who want to better understand what it means to be skills-based. If we want to chart a future path forward together, let's do it by building a common language and talking to one another about the skills we have and the skills we need.

For the last nine years, I've been immersed in this idea of creating a common language and measurement system of what someone can do. It started while I was a product leader at D2L; I was asked to form a small team to think about how to address the challenge of helping educators and employers to bridge the communication gap when talking about what skills are needed in the workforce. It continued in my very short stint at ETS, doing market validation for a potential skills assessment product (and my subsequent disappointment that the company seemed to be looking for a standardized test for skills). Then, I took a job at Degreed (with the cool title vice president of skills) and learned more about the opportunities and challenges of skills ontologies, measurement, and analytics before I expanded my role across products and thought about the connections to skills development and internal mobility. When I later joined Wiley, I dug into the deeply different ways to assess and develop human skills versus technical skills, working on the problem of how you can best develop different types of skills at different proficiency levels. And today, I'm working with several different skills assessment and validation products, including my own, to solve for skills validation, skills proficiency, and the value proposition for employees.

I've worked with dozens of different companies that are all at different levels of maturity in their journeys to become skills-based. Many of them are just at the beginning of the journey.

It's a complex problem to solve. Most organizations see only a glimmer of what evolving to a skills-based organization would mean for their culture. Nor do they see the effort it would take. Yet, everywhere you turn, you hear about skills and how organizations need to embrace them (even though the definition of a skill is still so inconsistent from person to person and organization to organization). The question remains: If you've only ever seen a caterpillar, how can you imagine a butterfly?

I wrote this book to share what I know: There are clear steps to becoming a skills-based organization and common obstacles along the way that you can anticipate. This book is not a road map to a single destination. It is a blueprint for a process you can adapt to diverse needs. No two organizations will transform in the same way. I'm describing one version of a butterfly emerging from the process so you can imagine what your organization might look like in the end.

Introduction

Gamers who play role-playing games (RPGs) understand the importance of skills data.

If you've never played Dungeons & Dragons (D&D) or World of Warcraft—or any other RPG in which you align with other players to fight battles and win rewards—you might miss the parallels between the gaming world and the real-life world of work (Kaufman 2019). In many ways, these games are enormous and complex simulations of how effective teams work.

One of the key features of RPGs are the skills that your character has, and at what proficiency level. This data helps determine how successful you might be in fighting against any particular enemy. It also helps determine if you have a strong, balanced team to go into battle with. As scenarios play out, each player's unique skills can be used strategically in collaboration with the skills of their teammates to navigate seemingly insurmountable odds. The more you play, the more experience you gain, and the stronger your skills become. Some players may lean into their strength, others their agility, their intelligence, or their magic. Each player also has weaknesses, because no one can be good at everything. Diverse teams become successful teams. Understanding how your skills complement others' skills is a key advantage in the game.

Maybe because of my love of games and my background as a game designer, skills data has always made sense to me. When I explain game design to others, particularly for scenario-based games, I explain it as a big data engine—players make decisions that have consequences (sometimes good, sometimes bad) and those decisions are heavily influenced by their skills. In sophisticated design, game play adjusts to your experience and skill level, continuing to challenge you as you get better and better by making things harder and harder.

Game designers (or, in the case of D&D, Dungeon Masters) have figured this out: The more you know about your players, the better you can adapt the game. Players also know that the more you know about your skills, the better you can use them to play the game.

The same is true of organizations, business leaders, and employees—the more you know about the skills you have, the more you can leverage that knowledge to your advantage.

The Questions

For the decades I've been working in professional learning (and I'm sure for decades before that), organizations have been trying to figure out key questions about their people:

- Who is capable of doing the work that we need to do?
- Who is ready to be promoted to the next step in their career?
- If we develop or train our employees, will it positively affect our business?
- Are we hiring the right people to help us succeed?

These questions have challenged organizations to seek answers in all sorts of ways, mainly focused on assessment and measurement in relationship to not only individual job performance, but also business performance. Organizations have sought creative solutions for measuring employee capabilities, some of them individually focused (such as 360-degree performance reviews) and others broad-spectrum (such as competency models). Some of these models have persisted, others have evolved, but none have fully solved the critical questions organizations have about their workforces.

The Strategies

To understand why attempts to measure capabilities have failed, let's review the strategies that companies have used to try to answer these questions.

Degrees

Besides apprenticeships, which develop job capabilities and prove expertise with hands-on experience, degrees were the earliest qualifications for working in a job or role that companies leveraged to make people decisions. Degrees have long been considered a hallmark of expertise, but the traditional view of a college education as a reliable indicator of professional competence has been increasingly challenged. There is a growing gap between what graduates know and the skills employers require for effective job performance, particularly as higher education often lags in adapting its curriculum to reflect cutting-edge industry standards and technologies. Additionally, many degrees do not require practical experience, leaving graduates unprepared for professional demands. While fields such as medicine and teaching mandate hands-on training, most disciplines do not, leading to a workforce that is academically qualified but practically inexperienced. Last, only 47 percent of graduates are working in their fields of study, which undermines the assumed correlation between academic study and professional expertise (Haller 2022). I received my undergraduate degree in speech pathology and audiology and my master's degree in curriculum and instruction, but work neither as a speech pathologist nor a teacher; instead, I am a product executive. All told, employers find themselves needing to invest in training new graduates, shifting the burden of developing job-ready skills from educational institutions to the workplace.

Certifications

While degrees are often regarded as the foundational entry point for establishing expertise and capabilities, certifications serve as both a benchmark and a continuous indication of a professional's abilities and knowledge. Certifications are prevalent across various professions, including accountancy, law, teaching, nursing, and more; many require completion before you can commence work in the field. Certifications typically require not just theoretical knowledge but also practical experience, along with ongoing education and recertification to demonstrate a commitment to maintaining relevance in the field. However, the credentialing system faces significant challenges. Only a small fraction of jobs actually require formal certifications or licenses, and the governance surrounding the definition, award, and maintenance of credentials must continually evolve to remain relevant. The process of obtaining certifications can be costly and time-consuming. This situation is exacerbated when employers do not support (either financially, with time, or both) attainment or maintenance of credentials, potentially skewing the demographic makeup of those who are certified. For credentials to be useful as a measure of job capabilities, they must be more broadly adopted and easier to access.

Microcredentials and Badges

Microcredentials and badges have emerged as flexible alternatives to traditional degrees, certifications, and other credentials, aiming to verify focused learning achievements and competencies. In 2022, UNESCO defined *microcredentials* as records that confirm specific knowledge or skills, include an assessment based on clear standards, and are awarded by trusted providers. These can stand alone or complement further credentials through recognition of prior learning, all while adhering to stringent quality assurance standards.

Digital badges, on the other hand, serve as verifiable symbols of an award or a skill; they are earned in diverse environments and used to demonstrate competencies. However, the lack of consistency in the meanings and requirements of badges and microcredentials leads to uncertainty among employers regarding their value. Some employers issue their own badges, but many hold little meaning outside that specific context. Ultimately, although microcredentials show signs of possible broader recognition and implementation, they are still not widely accepted or understood as reliable indicators of expertise in the wider workforce.

Self-Reported Expertise

As organizations recognize the visibility gap regarding the expertise within their workforce, many have turned to directly asking employees as a quick method of collecting data about their capabilities. This approach, akin to the models we use daily (such as resumes, CVs, and LinkedIn profiles), leverages self-reporting to gather insights on education, work experience, and professional accomplishments. However, self-reported data relies on inherent biases, such as the social desirability response bias, which occurs when individuals portray themselves in a favorable light. While resumes, which are also largely based on self-reported data, are a common basis for hiring decisions, studies indicate a high incidence of dishonesty, with a notable percentage of individuals admitting to falsifying information. This skepticism is even more pronounced when assessing self-reported expertise, which is harder to verify compared with employment or educational history. Without a standardized method to evaluate skill levels, the validity of self-reported expertise remains questionable, making it a less reliable source for assessing true competency.

Social Validation of Expertise and 360-Degree Reviews

Many organizations seeking a more reliable alternative to self-reported expertise turn to social validation, using the insights of managers, peers, and direct reports to offer a more objective view of an individual's abilities based on shared work experiences. This method can help mitigate the bias typically associated with self-reports, as colleagues and supervisors are more likely to have accurate perceptions of a person's skills in their day-to-day activities. For instance, everyone in the office may know that for expert advice on market data analysis, "Ask Carol," or on handling difficult customers, "Ask Chris." But social validation, too, suffers from challenges and limitations (Peiperl 2001). Peers can struggle to be objective judges. It can be difficult to separate individual performance from the group's. And managers may express biases toward employees who align with their own or the company's values, which can skew perceptions of expertise. Despite these pitfalls, when managed carefully, social validation still serves as a common tool in recognizing and affirming expertise, particularly when combined with other data sources and indicators.

Competency Models

In the 1970s and 1980s, organizations began to focus on *competency models*—a collection of the competencies needed to perform successfully in a particular work setting—as a way of better understanding what people needed to be able to do to complete their work for the organization. Undertaking a competency-based approach meant digging deep into two sides of the equation: what competencies are needed to do the work or to be successful in a role, and what competencies employees have.

The idea of competencies made sense, but the mechanism to identify which ones were needed simply did not evolve fast enough to be cost-effective or relevant. Many leaders felt burned, having spent extensive time and money to finally answer those key questions about their organization's workforce. The need remained, and while competency models hadn't worked, organizations still wanted and needed, more than ever, to better understand four key questions:

- Who is capable of doing the work?
- Who is ready to be promoted?
- Are our development investments affecting the business?
- Are we hiring the right people to help us succeed?

The Move to Skills

The speed of change and innovation in technology is not only what caused competency models to ultimately fail, but also what led to the emergence of skills and skills data as the leading solution to answer critical questions to map people to the work they do. It was really the convergence of technological innovation and data that created the environment for skills to take hold. How was this possible when it wasn't before? Large pools of data—in particular, job data—were finally captured, searched, and analyzed in different ways.

Job data—through job descriptions posted in online recruitment sites, job postings listed on company websites, and publicly available digital databases published by global governments—was finally available, and the internet and evolution of data science and analytics enabled organizations to determine the requirements for the jobs within their companies. Those requirements were labeled "skills," and companies quickly realized that skills were not a static concept like competencies, but a constantly evolving set of requirements. Large companies began to talk about upskilling and reskilling initiatives and investments. They recognized that the evolution of their businesses required new skills, and that the fastest way to build those new skills was by developing their existing employees, in part because replacing them was expensive, but also because the availability of workers with these new skills was scarce. The chasm between what higher education prepares students for and what employers need has been growing to the point of crisis, and everyone is looking for solutions. Skills have potentially become the data that could provide visibility into the answers for those critical workforce questions, and organizations globally have acknowledged that skills and skills data may finally do what competencies and every other initiative could not: allow them to connect people to work in data-informed ways.

As the focus on skills has gained traction, challenges have inevitably arisen. Significantly, the difficulty of measuring and assessing skills has created questions around trusting skills data. Disagreement about the definition of a skill, particularly in relation to competencies, has created discrepancies in how skills data might be relevant from education to employment, and from employer to employer—especially for companies that haven't abandoned their competency models. Vendors that provide technology and data solutions across the HR and learning ecosystems have begun to build features and systems to find point solutions in the process. New use cases for leveraging skills data have emerged, from coaching and mentoring to succession planning. Differences in how skills are developed have also become clear, separating soft (or human) skills from technical (or job) skills. With artificial intelligence (AI) helping drive even more demand to evolve new skills faster, companies are left asking how to solve this complex problem of becoming a skills-based organization but have few clear answers.

Everyone is only beginning to figure this out. There isn't one path, and there is no right answer. Skills are not a panacea for making good people decisions; they are simply a new and better source of data for making those decisions. I'll be including a lot of qualifying language in this book to emphasize that skills present a possibility, not a guarantee. Just like any data, skills are only as good as the bias they reduce and the purposes for which they are used. I am optimistic that skills will help us all be better informed and armed with more data to make critical decisions about hiring, learning, and career pathways; it's up to us to ensure that we also understand their limitations.

The Skills-Based Organization: A Vision for the Future

Many organizations have started down the path of becoming skills-based to help resolve this issue with a higher level of confidence by making data-driven decisions (WEF 2024). But the journey to becoming a skills-based organization is complicated, and most organizations struggle to get started or stall out at points of complexity in the journey.

A skills-based organization prioritizes the practical skills of its employees, and how they contribute to the organization's goals and challenges, over traditional credentials such as degrees and job titles when making decisions about hiring, promotions, and project assignments. It's critical to have a holistic vision of the future potential and benefits of becoming a skills-based organization if you want to create an effective blueprint to evolve into one. Let's look at skills-based organizations through the lenses of people, processes, and systems.

People

Empowering your people, both employees and managers, is a critical component of a skills-based organization. Here are some ways in which a skills-based organization can evolve its current methods of employee engagement.

- **Transparent skills mapping and career pathways:**
  - *Visibility of skills.* A skills-based organization provides clear visibility of the skills employees currently possess and those skills required for various roles within the organization.

Visibility can be achieved through a detailed skills inventory that is accessible to all employees.
- *Clear career pathways.* A skills-based organization develops and communicates clear career pathways that show how employees can progress within the organization based on skills acquisition and development. This helps employees understand how they can grow and what they need to learn to reach their career goals.

- **Coaching:**
  - *Goal-oriented and skills-focused.* In a skills-based organization, coaches work with employees to identify specific skills that need development and align these skills with both the individual's career aspirations and the organization's strategic goals. Coaching sessions are highly personalized, focusing on short-term objectives and long-term skills acquisition plans.
  - *Regular and structured sessions.* Coaching in a skills-based organization is an ongoing process, with regular sessions to discuss progress, hurdles, and strategies for skills improvement. These sessions provide an opportunity for real-time feedback based on recent projects or tasks, making the guidance timely and relevant.
  - *Performance and development integration.* In a skills-based organization, coaches help integrate performance management with skills development, ensuring that employees not only meet their current job requirements but are also prepared for future roles and challenges. They use tools such as 360-degree feedback to gather comprehensive insights into the employees' skills from various stakeholders, which informs the coaching process.
  - *Use of technology.* A skills-based organization leverages technology platforms to track skills development and coaching progress. This can include digital tools for setting goals and receiving feedback, and even AI-driven platforms that suggest tailored learning paths based on skills gaps.

- **Mentoring:**
  - *Long-term relationship building.* Mentoring in a skills-based organization often involves longer-term relationships compared with coaching. Mentors provide guidance and support based on their own experiences within or outside the organization. Mentors help mentees navigate not only technical skills but also organizational culture and politics, which are crucial for career advancement.
  - *Career and skills pathway guidance.* In a skills-based organization, mentors assist in mapping out a career pathway, which includes necessary skills acquisitions, potential roles, and projects that align with the mentee's interests and the organization's needs. They share their own career experiences and the skills that have been most beneficial to their success, providing a practical, real-world context to the guidance.
  - *Cross-functional skills exposure.* In a skills-based organization, mentors can come from different parts of the organization, exposing mentees to a variety of skills and perspectives. This cross-functional mentoring helps break down silos and fosters a broader understanding of different roles and the skills they require.
  - *Encouraging innovation and experimentation.* In a skills-based organization, mentors encourage mentees to experiment with new skills and take on challenging projects that can lead to innovative solutions and personal growth. They provide a safety net by offering advice and insights, which can reduce the risk associated with trying new approaches.

Processes

One of the most important ways your organization evolves while becoming skills-based is by introducing skills data into people-focused decision making. Here are key areas where skills data can help bring more visibility into these decisions.

- **Recruitment and hiring:**
  - *Skills-focused job descriptions.* In a skills-based organization, job postings are designed around specific skills required for the role rather than emphasizing certain degrees or career backgrounds. This approach opens opportunities to a broader range of candidates, including those from nontraditional backgrounds but with relevant skills.
  - *Skills-based interviews.* In a skills-based organization, hiring processes often include practical assessments, such as work samples or simulation exercises, to evaluate candidates' skills in real-world scenarios. Interviews focus on understanding how a candidate has applied their skills in various situations rather than merely discussing their qualifications.
- **Performance management:**
  - *Skills inventories.* A skills-based organization maintains detailed records of employees' skills and competencies. This helps in understanding existing capabilities and identifying skills gaps within the workforce.
  - *Performance reviews.* Employee evaluations in a skills-based organization are based on skills application and development. Goals are set not just to meet job requirements but also to advance an employee's skill set and adaptability.
- **Work allocation:**
  - *Project assignments.* Project leaders in a skills-based organization choose team members based on the specific skills needed for the project rather than seniority or departmental lines. This often leads to cross-functional teams with diverse skill sets working together.
  - *Task rotation.* To broaden skills exposure, employees may rotate through different roles or projects in a skills-based organization. This not only enhances individual capabilities but also promotes a deeper understanding of the organization.

- **Decision making:**
  - *Data-driven.* A skills-based organization makes decisions regarding talent management and project management using data analytics that assess skills distribution and organizational needs. This approach reduces bias and improves strategic alignment with business objectives.

Systems

Finally, full systems in your organization will evolve as it becomes skills-based. This journey truly creates opportunities for your entire culture to become more data-driven, and your systems will change as a result. Here are key areas where skills data can highlight organizational systems.

- **Emphasis on skills development:**
  - *Continuous learning.* A skills-based organization heavily invests in the continuous professional development of its employees. It typically offers access to a variety of learning content and experiences to ensure that employees can keep up with industry trends and expand their skill sets.
  - *Career paths.* A skills-based organization encourages employees to develop skills that align with their career aspirations and the organization's needs. Many career paths are flexible, allowing individuals to move laterally across different roles or upskill to take on new challenges, in either new roles or new projects.
- **Culture and values:**
  - *Meritocracy.* A skills-based organization bases promotions and rewards on demonstrated skills and the impact of an employee's work, rather than tenure or past credentials. A merit-based system helps foster a culture of fairness and motivation.
  - *Inclusivity.* By focusing on skills rather than pedigree, a skills-based organization becomes more inclusive, providing equal opportunities to individuals regardless of their educational background or personal connections.

- **Innovation:**
  - *Encouragement of skill diversity.* A skills-based organization values diverse perspectives and novel problem-solving approaches, which are crucial for fostering creativity and innovation within the organization.
- **Robust feedback and recognition systems:**
  - *Regular feedback.* A skills-based organization implements a system of regular and constructive feedback that helps employees understand their performance in relation to their skills and areas for improvement.
  - *Recognition programs.* A skills-based organization develops recognition programs that reward skills development and application. This could include awards for mastering new skills or for innovative uses of existing skills in new projects.

In essence, a skills-based organization is designed to maximize the potential of its workforce by focusing on the practical abilities that directly contribute to achieving business outcomes. This not only enhances organizational performance but also improves employee satisfaction and retention by aligning work more closely with personal skills and interests.

A Skills-Based Organization: EPAM as a North Star

Contributed by Sandra Loughlin, Chief Learning Scientist, EPAM Systems

Being a skills-based organization is part of the DNA at EPAM Systems—it's just something that's always been there for the roughly three decades of the company's existence. And not because focusing on skills was trendy 30 years ago or because HR needed something to justify compensation plans. EPAM oriented around skills early on because it was the best way the founders could think of to solve problems and do business.

EPAM is a professional services company focused on digital platform engineering and technology-driven business transformation, with more than 50,000 employees, including some of the world's brightest AI, software, data, and product experts. Founded in 1993 and headquartered in Newtown, Pennsylvania, EPAM got its start helping digital native firms—now some of the world's most valuable companies—build the disruptive technology platforms that changed how the world shops, communicates, travels, and relaxes today. Over the years, EPAM's portfolio of work has evolved several times and now combines strategy advising with technology implementation to help global enterprises create business and societal value in a world dominated by technology.

What has remained constant for EPAM is being a company that delivers value to clients through people. As a professional services firm, it can only achieve differentiation and competitive advantage by having the right people with the right skills in the right locations at the right time in the right configurations. In other words, EPAM is in the business of matching work to people.

As a startup, matching was relatively easy for EPAM to do because there were only a few people and projects—whatever skills clients needed, EPAM employees had to have or quickly learn. But as the company grew and new people joined, it became harder and harder to remember who was good at what. EPAM's early leaders dealt with this in a way that made sense to them: by treating it as a data problem.

Skills were selected as the common unit of analysis because the construct was easily understood and helped to both describe the work and the people available to do it. From the outset, EPAM's leaders thought about skills as a fraction: The denominator represented the skills required to do the work and the numerator represented the skills of the available talent. To arrive at the denominator, work was divided into discrete tasks and then into the skills required to complete each task, while the numerator represented the skills of any single employee. The goal was to get the highest match between the denominator and the numerator to find the best person for the job, project by project.

To do this, EPAM developed rudimentary methods to identify the denominator and numerator for each client engagement. Project leaders were tasked with breaking work into tasks and then skills, people managers were responsible for documenting each employee's skills, and both were expected to keep the information up to date in spreadsheets. Task and skill documentation also occurred at the job level with the creation of taxonomies for roles, which were used as reference material for job leveling, hiring, compensation, and promotion decisions, and also served as the foundation for EPAM to tag training resources and suggest them to employees.

Spreadsheets and databases solved the documentation and matching problem for a while, but eventually expanded services and continued headcount growth made it too cumbersome, particularly as new data features were demanded by the business (like skills proficiency and recency, industry context, and project type). So, EPAM did what it does best: Build custom software to efficiently match work that needed to be done with people who could do it.

The desire for a cutting-edge, skills-based staffing tool confirmed the EPAM's founders' early decision to build, not buy, software to power the business. Initially, the orientation toward homegrown technology stemmed from the need to be lean. Why buy software with a cadre of top-notch software engineers at the ready? However, as the infrastructure was slowly built out, EPAM's executives began to realize the value of having access to all business data and a technology infrastructure that evolved on demand. These considerations set EPAM on a trajectory that would define it to this day: a business powered by fit-for-purpose technology, optimized for data insights, and grounded in a desire to maximize the fit between people and work.

By 2012, the year of EPAM's initial public offering, the company had a digital profile for each of its roughly 10,000 employees that included skills, project and task history, learning and training experience, documentation from hiring and all project interviews, 360-degree feedback, and many other data points. Critically, the digital profiles were automatically populated by data feeds from EPAM's homegrown systems of record and work, made visible to employees and managers, and referenced in performance management conversations. The company had also begun gleaning insights from almost 20 years of data to build strategic workforce planning tools to close the gap between skills needed by the business and skills in the pipeline.

Bringing employees' digital profiles into performance management conversations created the need to solve an issue that had been slowly building—leaders were becoming less confident that the skills listed in every employee's profile reflected what the individuals could really do on the job. This was a critical issue as EPAM had, by that time, developed a reputation for best-in-class engineering talent and was leaning on that reputation to attract new clients and secure top engineering talent in a highly competitive market.

Realizing its talent-related digital platforms were useless without accurate skills data, the next task was to figure out skills validation. Degrees were deemed helpful but ultimately insufficient indicators because technology was moving faster than university curricula. Moreover, as the geographic footprint of the company continued to expand, there was less known about, and therefore more uncertainty in, the quality of the engineering programs new hires were coming from.

After some trial and error, EPAM found an effective, albeit labor intensive, solution to the skills verification problem it called "assessment," which is still a core part of the company's performance management practices today. The solution was designed as a skills-verification gateway to promotion. It goes something like this:

- Sandra, a solution architect II, indicates that she wants to be considered for promotion.
- A random selection of solution architect III peers, all trained assessors, is chosen to assess Sandra's skills and a meeting is convened.
- Prior to the meeting, Sandra is told about the mandatory meeting and what she needs to bring as evidence of her skills. Evidence can include things like certifications, a portfolio of work, reports from project manager and clients,

and performance tasks specifically created by EPAM for the assessment process.
- During the meeting, Sandra presents her evidence and answers her peers' questions about her work.
- After Sandra leaves the meeting, her peers decide together whether she is ready for promotion and prepare a rationale.
- Sandra is informed by her manager of the assessment committee's recommendation: pass; pass contingent upon targeted and minor skill development; or no pass with recommendations for significant skill development, suggestions for formal and informal learning and practical application, and an invitation to return for re-assessment in six months.

Notably, individual managers have a minor role in the assessment process to reduce bias and limit the practice of talent hoarding. While managers can theoretically overrule the decision of the committee, this rarely happens in practice because deviation from the committee's guidance requires justification to senior leadership.

The assessment process—elements of which were quickly applied to the hiring process—did more than offer a means to verify skills; it helped EPAM crack one of the most pervasive challenges in business: motivating employees to learn continuously and build necessary skills. By operationally defining skills and linking skill demonstration to promotion, employees were oriented toward the right skills for the business and given a reason to develop them.

This realization came at a critical time as EPAM was moving aggressively into new geographies and industries, expanding into digital solutions and emerging technologies, and seeing rapid growth in revenue and headcount. Because leaders could rely on good data on the supply of skills and had a powerful mechanism to ensure employees would develop new skills, EPAM succeeded in stretch projects with clients and was able to outcompete other service providers in delivering results on innovative, business-critical assignments. Having a consistent standard for hiring and promotion also helped EPAM maintain its incredibly high employment standards and reputation for engineering quality as its footprint and headcount grew rapidly.

The latter half of 2010s saw a dramatic and rapid development of EPAM's ability to capture, validate, and use skills data at scale by leveraging its expertise in areas like architecture, the cloud, API and microservices, data, machine learning, and AI. EPAM made significant investments in its proprietary suite of digital platforms—which by now were collectively called Telescope—as leaders began to appreciate the tremendous value to the business afforded by broad and deep workforce and work intelligence. By 2020, EPAM had developed a host of new skills-related capabilities and tools including:

- A skills ontology leveraging natural language processing and other AI models to synthesize internal and external data, including crowdsourced skill forecasting from internal and academic subject matter experts
- Dozens of AI and data products to support task and skill inference from systems of record and work and to match skills of people (employees, prospectives, and gig workers) to work
- A suite of tools for direct skills verification
- More than 25 specialty platforms to support skills-based talent practices including hiring, staffing, internal mobility, feedback, performance management, learning, career pathing, mentoring, and workforce planning

More recently, EPAM has been applying GenAI to the ecosystem and further streamlining the integration of HR processes into the employee experience by the extensive use of automation and AI agents.

Today, EPAM uses millions of internal and external data points and a suite of proprietary, best-in-class AI-powered digital platforms to maintain verified skill profiles of individuals, understand the tasks needed to complete projects and fulfill jobs, and use this data to gain insights and operate the business efficiently. Verified skills data is used to make decisions across the entire talent life cycle to plan for, hire, develop, engage, and retain some of the world's most sought-after technical talent.

If you ask EPAM leaders to explain the value of skills to the business, they quickly get to the heart of the matter: being a skills-based organization is about creating business agility. Having rich, current, verified data about the work and who can do it has allowed EPAM to grow organically and evolve as a business while being one of the industry's fastest-growing companies for decades. In a world dominated by AI, EPAM leaders are counting on its skills DNA to help successful propel the company into the future, emerging stronger than ever.

Are You Ready to Get Started?

Now it's time to get working to crack the potential of skills data for your organization. You may have a role in HR, learning, or talent. You may be a leader, looking to understand how skills could help you better grow and evolve your team. You may be an executive, trying to cut through the hype and gain clarity on the work your organization needs to do to become skills-based. You may even be one of the growing number of people who have roles or titles specifically focused on unlocking the potential for skills. And while this book isn't necessarily written for individual employees in the workforce, if you are part of an organization that has stated a goal of becoming skills-based, this book will provide context about what that means both for the organization and for you. Truly, the success of becoming a skills-based organization means bringing everyone along, from job candidates to recruiters, from managers to their teams, from HR and L&D to the C-suite. This book aims to bring clarity to what a skills-based organization is and what the journey to becoming one entails.

To that end, examples from organizations that are on the journey to becoming skills-based will be highlighted throughout this book. EPAM provides an organizational model of what a skills-based organization can be and the potential for skills to drive more informed decisions about people at work. But admittedly, most organizations didn't start out and evolve around data as EPAM did, and because this isn't a linear path, different organizations have started from different places and have different metrics that are demonstrating the impact of skills. This book will include stories, struggles, and successes to show how companies are progressing on unique paths to becoming skills-based, including upskilling and reskilling efforts; companies working to improve recruiting and hiring, internal mobility, coaching, and mentoring; and those who are leveraging skills to plan for the future needs of their organizations.

While a true skills-based organization may be rare today, many companies are well on their way in the journey. As you read this book, note where your organization is, where you have opportunities to progress, and what lessons you can take from others to help you create your own blueprint for transformation.

PART 1
Laying the Groundwork

I wish there was a clear plan with step-by-step instructions I could provide for how to start your journey to creating a skills-based organization. Instead, the start of this journey requires you to build your own map, depending on where your organization is and where you want to go. The chapters in part 1 focus on how to do the analysis necessary to build that map, who needs to come along for the journey, and what results will indicate success.

CHAPTER 1
Making the Case

In this chapter, we'll cover:
- Unpacking why skills matter for organizations
- Addressing possible objections to skills

Why Skills?

In the introduction, I offered ways skills can improve the people-centered functions, processes, and systems of your business, and so it might seem silly to ask, "Why skills?" But it is necessary, because skills are complex—it's important to understand the implications of effort versus impact. While there are ways to get started quickly and relatively easily, the true shift to becoming a skills-based organization is multifaceted, and can be expensive from both a time and financial perspective. You can't push for commitment without also being able to articulate the expected benefits and impact of prioritizing skills.

In making the case for skills, no matter the audience, there are some core beliefs: namely, that skills, and the evolution of organizations to be skills-based, are not only a strategic imperative, but also a moral and economic necessity. This manifests in three critical areas. First, skills can unlock human potential. Second, becoming skills-based helps organizations foster innovation. Last, evolving into a skills-based organization ensures long-term organizational resilience. Let's look at these one by one.

Unleashing Human Potential: Better for People

Skills-based organizations prioritize identifying and using an individual's skills over traditional job descriptions and qualifications. This approach allows companies to fully leverage the unique talents and capabilities of their workers. By focusing on skills, organizations can break down artificial barriers created by rigid job roles and hierarchies. Employees are empowered to contribute in areas they are most skilled in and passionate about, leading to increased job satisfaction and engagement.

A skills-based framework promotes inclusivity by recognizing a broader range of capabilities beyond formal education and previous job titles. It opens doors for individuals from diverse backgrounds, including those who may not have had access to traditional career paths. This inclusivity not only enriches the talent pool but also helps organizations tap into underutilized potential, driving creativity and innovation.

Fostering Innovation and Agility: Better Products

In a world where the pace of change is accelerating, the ability to adapt quickly is crucial. A skills-based organization is inherently more agile and adaptable than one anchored in static job roles. By continually assessing and cataloging the skills within the organization, companies can rapidly deploy talent to meet emerging challenges and opportunities. This flexibility enables organizations to pivot in response to market shifts, technological disruptions, and changing consumer demands.

A skills-based approach also encourages a culture of continuous learning and development. Employees are incentivized to acquire new skills and deepen existing ones, knowing that their value is recognized and rewarded based on their capabilities rather than their tenure or position. This culture of lifelong learning is essential in fostering an innovative mindset because employees are more likely to experiment, take risks, and collaborate across disciplines when they are not confined by traditional role boundaries.

Organizational Resilience: Better Processes

Organizational resilience lies in the business's economic strength. We all want to do what's right, and do what's right for our organization's bottom line.

By implementing skills-based hiring and promotion practices, organizations can mitigate unconscious biases and ensure that all employees have equal opportunities to progress based on their abilities. This not only enhances diversity within the organization but also strengthens the company's reputation as a fair and equitable employer, attracting top talent who value inclusivity.

Beyond the ethical and strategic advantages, a skills-based organization can also realize significant economic benefits. By optimizing the deployment of talent, companies can reduce inefficiencies and increase productivity. Employees who are engaged and working in roles that align with their skills are more likely to perform at a higher level, contributing to better business outcomes.

A focus on skills can lead to more efficient talent acquisition and development processes. Organizations can precisely identify the skills they need and tailor their training and development programs accordingly, reducing the time and costs associated with traditional recruitment and training methods. By promoting internal mobility and upskilling, companies can retain valuable employees, reducing turnover and the money spent recruiting and onboarding new staff.

In the end, the question "Why skills?" is as much about the future of work as it is about the specific needs and potential impact of your organization. In truth, if the world is moving toward skills data as the currency of work, and you resist the movement, your organization will be left behind. You won't have visibility into the skills your organization has or needs. You will have less-informed hiring and mobility practices. Your teams may be less diverse. You will have less-informed and focused investments in learning and development, less personalization of learning, and less focus on skills development. It may be harder to measure the impact of learning. Your managers will have less data to manage and coach their teams. Employees will be less empowered to drive their career development. You will have less-informed workforce management and succession planning. And it will be harder to attract and keep top talent.

While the promise of skills is appealing, in the end, the consequences of not having skills data may actually be the most meaningful answer to "Why skills?" If you don't begin thinking about how to evolve your business to be skills-based, the risk and impact of being left behind are very real.

Getting Past the Hype

There are some trends and buzzwords that peak and then fizzle, some that morph as reality sets limitations and challenges, and some that stand the test of time (although I would argue that very few trends live up to their original hype). So, where do skills fall on that continuum?

It's critical to not fall so in love with the idea of skills that the complex reality is lost. The evolution to becoming skills-based is not simple or easy. You will meet questions along the way, from others and likely from yourself—is it worth it? There has also been debate across industries and experts on whether the investment and effort are worth the potential impact on and benefits to an organization. Let's examine some common resistance, with counterpoints that you may use to respond to objections to becoming a skills-based organization.

Lack of a Clear Definition of Skills

There is no consensus on what constitutes a "skill." Different organizations and consulting firms define skills in various ways, often including broad elements such as personality traits and interests. This lack of clarity can make it challenging to structure a company around skills.

Counterpoint: There are many emerging ontologies that seek to shortcut the challenge of defining what a skill is, and there are lots of definitions that are all directionally similar. I often posit to skeptics, does it matter if there is a clear definition of skills? If two different organizations define skills differently, but they both are able to define what skills means within their organizations, collect data on their definition of skills, and make more-informed decisions based on that data—does it matter if their definitions don't align?

It is still early days for skills, and our collective agreement on what a skill is will become more aligned over time. Maybe standards will emerge that will align across companies and industries, and maybe they won't. In the meantime, prioritizing skills in your organization will help you take steps toward making more-informed decisions that can be beneficial to your business. Maybe it's not all that important to have a clear definition to still have an impact.

Uncertain Benefits Versus High Costs

The costs of transitioning to a skills-based organization can be substantial, potentially reaching tens or hundreds of millions of dollars. These include reorganizing company structures, changing staffing methods, retraining employees, and revising compensation systems. Meanwhile, the benefits, such as increased retention, more diverse hiring, and improved organizational agility, are often vague and unquantified.

Counterpoint: While it is impossible to predict the exact impact skills data might have on your bottom line, there is no requirement that you make a massive investment to start gauging impact. In fact, please don't! The best way to start evaluating skills data in your organization is by starting small and expanding your skills footprint over time.

Using skills data to make more-informed people decisions should result in a positive impact, the extent of which should be evaluated and measured. Businesses often invest in initiatives that have uncertain benefits, but with skills, it is clear how the data is intended to improve processes. It is possible to set milestone objectives and map progress and investment against those goals so you don't overinvest for the return on investment of skills.

Challenges in Efficient Skills Matching

There is skepticism about the potential for a skills-based approach to efficiently match people with jobs—after all, just because individuals have additional skills, it doesn't mean they want to use them in a professional context. Moreover, even if people have extra skills, they may not match the market's needs. Additionally, those with more experience in a specific skill will likely be favored over those with less experience, even if they possess the skill.

Counterpoint: Matching people to the work that needs to be done is both an art and a science. There will never be a perfect solution, but there can be more-informed solutions. By thinking about the work in terms of skills, and by better understanding what skills people have, it is possible to have more-informed recommendations for skills matching.

Skills should also not be the only data used to match people to work! In fact, in some cases, people may be assigned to a project in order to develop their skill, not because they already possess it. Skills are just an additional data point to consider, not a panacea for matching people to work.

Solution in Search of a Problem

Frequently, I'll run into someone who wonders if the problems that a skills-based approach aims to address, such as removing unnecessary degree requirements, could be resolved with simpler solutions. For instance, organizations could just eliminate degree requirements from job descriptions instead of restructuring around skills.

Counterpoint: It's true; if degrees aren't a good measure of someone's capabilities, then degree requirements for a role should be dropped. But what should take their place so hiring managers aren't flying blind and recruiters know how to narrow a candidate pool appropriately?

Skills data provides another way to understand someone's capabilities, but it does not replace job history, educational background, professional accomplishments, and many other types of data that can inform job readiness or capability. Don't ignore existing solutions if they are effective in solving the problem at hand, but consider whether skills will solve your problem more effectively.

Persistence of Credentialing Needs

Even if degree requirements are removed, some form of credentialing or assessment will still be necessary to verify skills. This indicates that completely moving away from traditional qualifications may not be feasible or beneficial.

Counterpoint: When I hear this critique, I like to counter with a question—does the current way of credentialing or assessment provide you with enough data, or the right data, to make informed people decisions in your organization? If the answer is yes, then investing in skills may be unnecessary. But if the answer is no, or not completely, then evaluating skills as either a replacement or an additional solution is worth the effort.

Validating skills is not necessarily a simple task; we'll do a deep dive into skills data and trust in part 2. But it is possible to create new ways of assessing skills, beyond current certifications and assessments, that can unlock the value of skills data.

Concerns About Equity and Networking

Finally, what about the role and benefits of networking? A skills-based approach could create a more equitable job market by focusing on "what you know" rather than "who you know," but personal networks will always play a role in hiring.

Counterpoint: Skills data will not eliminate the impact of relationships or networking on someone's career path. What it can do is provide more data to consider in people decisions than simply who you know. Today, when evaluating candidates for a job, relationships and prior experience play an oversized role because they're some of the only data about skills that we have beyond a job history on a resume. What if we had more data to compare candidates?

I look forward to a world in which we can compare known candidates' skills against unknown candidates. Will that change our decision making? Maybe not, but being able to compare candidates' skills profiles will certainly force us to concede when we are hiring less-qualified candidates based on relationships, and make those decisions more visible. The hope that skills data will reduce bias depends on uncovering the data that is being used to make hiring or promotion decisions; skills data is a mechanism to make the data used for those decisions more transparent.

The Path to Becoming Skills-Based

Making your case and addressing objections like these and others will be common along your path to becoming a skills-based organization. There is some truth in all these objections, and it's important to consider a measured approach to any investment of time and resources to evolve an organization's culture. As organizations have become increasingly data driven, skills data should be viewed from this perspective. Will more specific data about skills help your organization make better people decisions? If the answer is yes, then embarking on the process is worth a thoughtful plan forward.

The Supply Chain Management of Skills

Contributed by Lori Niles-Hofmann, EdTech and AI Transformation Strategist, 8Levers

In the ever-evolving landscape of organizational L&D, we've witnessed a remarkable transformation in how many companies approach skills acquisition and management. This journey, from traditional classroom-based training to our current era of strategic skills management, mirrors the broader shifts in our understanding of work, learning, and organizational success.

The Classroom Era: A Trip Down Memory Lane

If we take a trip in the way-back time machine, we find ourselves in an era when the classroom was the de facto delivery channel for learning. Upskilling was a carved-out event from day-to-day work, a special occasion that required physical presence and dedicated time away from the job. In this bygone era, people managers were the gatekeepers to these coveted learning opportunities. The prevailing hypothesis was that these managers, with their insight into both individual and organizational needs, would send the right people to the right courses at the right time.

The classroom catalogue, limited by physical and logistical constraints, offered a curated selection of courses. This limitation, while restrictive, had a silver lining: The odds were likely that people would be pointed in the right direction for their careers and what the business needed. It was a system that, while not perfect, had a certain logic to it.

The E-Learning Revolution: A Buffet of Knowledge

As technology marched on, the early 2000s saw the introduction of e-learning, heralding a new era in corporate learning. Suddenly, every learning department thought they were doing right by their people by offering them the biggest, most diverse buffet of learning options we could muster. The digital nature of e-learning meant that physical limitations were no longer a concern. Companies could offer courses on everything from coding to creative writing, from Lean Six Sigma to Latvian.

Unfortunately, this "spray and pray" approach to learning wasn't quite hitting the mark. While people were indeed learning, a crucial question remained: Were they learning the right things? Were they developing the skills our organizations actually needed?

A good analogy here is hosting a potluck to which everyone brought dessert—sure, it's all delicious, but it's not exactly a balanced meal, is it? We had created a smorgasbord of learning content, but without strategic direction, it was akin to nutritional chaos. If your company isn't opening an office in Riga or doesn't need an army of Six Sigma Black Belts, then courses in Latvian or advanced process improvement might not be the best use of your employees' time and your organization's resources.

The Present Day: A Paradigm Shift

Fast forward to the present day, and the goalposts have shifted even further. Technical skills are evolving at an unprecedented pace, while deep knowledge in niche areas can be incredibly valuable to an organization. In this context, our approach to learning and development needs a radical rethink.

What if we started thinking about skills the way a factory thinks about its supply chain? It can seem cold and corporate to compare human skills to widgets on an assembly line, but there are some applicable synergies that can revolutionize how we approach learning and development.

The Supply Chain of Skills: A New Paradigm

Imagine you're running a pizza factory. Your most crucial ingredient is tomatoes. Now, you've got two options: you can either buy tomatoes from suppliers, or grow them yourself. Each option has its pros and cons, costs and benefits. You need to consider factors such as quality control, cost-effectiveness, and how quickly you can get those tomatoes when you need them.

Now, replace tomatoes with skills, and you've got the beginnings of a whole new way to think about L&D and skills management. Just like our hypothetical pizza factory, organizations need to make strategic decisions about whether to "buy" skills (through hiring) or "grow" them (through internal development).

This is where the concept of "supply chain management of skills" comes into play. It's about being precise, strategic, and efficient in how we develop and acquire the skills our organizations need. No more throwing courses at people and hoping something sticks. Instead, we need to get surgical about identifying skills gaps, deciding how to fill them, and measuring the impact of our efforts.

Precision Learning: Tailoring Development to Needs

In this new paradigm, broad-brush programs for new managers are replaced with targeted interventions based on individual and organizational needs. A company looks at the specific skills the person has already demonstrated, the individual skills gaps for that person, and the skills that business unit in that area of the organization needs to meet its future key performance indicators.

Rather than lengthy generic pathways of content consumption on emerging skills, L&D works with the business to define precisely how many individuals need a new skill, who has adjacent skills, the full cost of upskilling versus procuring the skill in a new hire, and how much one person with this skill will affect the company.

This approach represents a deliberate movement toward learning as a precious resource within a company, meant to be deployed for maximum benefit. To do this right, we need to break down silos and create an ecosystem that extends far beyond the traditional boundaries of L&D. This might mean integrating HR tech, talent marketplaces, skills intelligence platforms, and artificial-intelligence-based simulators for safe skills practice. It's a whole new landscape, and it's changing the very nature of how we think about learning in organizations for the better.

Beyond the Bottom Line: The Human Element
The reasons for this shift are not to simply commoditize employees, skills, and learning, down to a basic cost versus benefit equation. While we cannot ignore that a business exists to generate revenue, there are individual considerations as well that make this approach not just financially sound, but ethically imperative.

Learning takes time and energy. A lot of it. When we ask our people to learn, we're essentially imposing a "tax" on them. Every hour spent watching a training video or attending a workshop is an hour not spent on their actual job or prioritizing family and friends. Employees are too often standing on unstable foundations, and upskilling is the real difference between career advancement and stagnation. We are irresponsible to leave it to chance that they stumble on the right e-learning module, or force them to rely solely on a savvy people manager.

By adopting a strategic approach to skills management, we're not just optimizing our organizational capabilities; we're providing our employees with clear, purposeful development paths. We're saying, "We value your time and effort, and we want to ensure that your learning journey is meaningful and impactful."

The Road Ahead: Challenges and Opportunities
Implementing a supply chain approach to skills management is not without its challenges. It requires a significant shift in mindset, from viewing learning as a nice-to-have perk to seeing it as a critical business function. It demands sophisticated data analytics capabilities to

accurately forecast skills needs and measure the impact of learning interventions. And it necessitates a level of collaboration among L&D, HR, and business units that many organizations may find challenging to achieve.

However, the potential benefits far outweigh these challenges. Organizations that successfully implement this approach can expect to see improved agility in responding to market changes, enhanced employee engagement and retention, and a more efficient use of learning and development resources.

Moreover, this approach positions L&D as a strategic partner in achieving business objectives, elevating its role within the organization. It transforms L&D from a cost center into a value creator, directly contributing to the organization's bottom line and competitive advantage.

In conclusion, the supply chain management of skills represents a paradigm shift in how we approach learning and development in organizations. It's a move from abundance without direction to precision with purpose. As we navigate the complexities of the modern business landscape, this approach offers a promising path forward, one that aligns organizational needs with individual growth, creating a win-win scenario for businesses and employees alike. The future of work demands nothing less than this level of strategic thinking about our most valuable asset: our people's skills and capabilities.

CHAPTER 2
Understanding the Current Landscape

In this chapter, we'll cover:
- Evaluating the effects that skills can have in an organization on recruitment and hiring, learning and development, people management, employee engagement, and workforce management

To plan for the future, you need to understand your organization's starting point. And planning for a future when your organization considers skills its lifeblood means understanding how decisions are being made. In all the areas that could benefit from skills data, decisions are already being made with different types of data. There are some variations from organization to organization, but for the purposes of this book, I'll refer to *traditional approaches* and *skills-based approaches* to highlight the differences you'll see after you begin to include skills data in decision making. Understanding the current landscape in the market, and in your specific organization, will provide you with a more-informed starting point for beginning a needs analysis and strengthen the case for skills. Let's look at the traditional and skills-based models of recruitment and hiring, L&D, people management, employee engagement, and workforce management.

Recruitment and Hiring

The way you bring people into your organization and fill gaps in your workforce has an enormous impact on your business, yet in many cases, recruitment and hiring are managed with very little data or potentially biased data. How do you know that a candidate is the right match for a job? Understanding your current state will help identify where skills data would have an impact.

External Talent Acquisition

Let's talk about the elephants in the room: job descriptions, resumes (or CVs or LinkedIn profiles), and interviews.

Most organizations have created a system of applying for, and awarding, jobs based on these three types of data, and each has inherent disadvantages and limitations. So, let's break each of them down into what works, and what doesn't, in the recruitment and hiring process.

Job Descriptions

Do you think the job descriptions in your organization are an accurate representation of the work that needs to be done? Do they clearly articulate your needs as a hiring manager, or the organization's needs in context of the team? Are they regularly updated and reviewed for accuracy? Do you have a standard template, or do you create a new job description for each role?

Every time I talk to someone in a business unit about the quality and accuracy of their job descriptions, they give me a "deer in the headlights" look in response. I've never had someone tell me they were confident that the job descriptions they post are relevant, accurate, and up-to-date. Most often, I am told that they typically copy and paste previous job descriptions, make some adjustments, and make more adjustments if a job is posted and they don't get enough applicants who fit the profile.

Job descriptions aren't just used for candidate recruitment; they are also used to set expectations for performance and achievement once someone is in a role. Tell me—are you doing the job as described in your job description?

And so job descriptions are the first challenging part of the traditional recruitment and hiring process. Because organizations are pretty bad at describing the work that needs to be done accurately, they seldom update the description for a role once someone is in it and the work evolves.

One of the biggest shifts for organizations in becoming skills-based is to begin thinking about work in terms of skills, not job roles. The challenge in being job-role centric is the assumption that career paths are primarily a linear progression, and that once you're working in a specific type of role, your next role will build on that specific experience.

The truth is, technology is changing work so rapidly that job roles that exist today may not exist five years from now. So, if jobs are changing faster than people's careers are progressing, organizing work around job roles will prevent agile systems and thinking from mapping the right people to the work that needs to be done. Skills and skills data will allow organizations to adapt more quickly, creating and deprecating job roles in a way that will make traditional resumes and job histories obsolete. The future will necessarily be job descriptions centered on the skills needed to do the work, and potential applicants will match the skills they have to the skills needed for any particular job. This approach not only allows organizations to change more quickly, but it also begins to reduce job history bias and opens opportunities to more diverse candidates who have the necessary skills.

Do we lose something if we no longer center work on job roles and instead look at how to match skills to work? Possibly—we lose some of the potential continuity of career pathing, and perhaps make it harder for someone to build highly contextualized expertise. But in the long term, a system focused on job roles and titles prevents us from adapting quickly to new ways of working, and a skills-based approach supports a system that requires agility.

Resumes

In the introduction, I discussed how organizations have relied on self-reported data on expertise and experience to make decisions, and the limitations of self-reporting because of inaccuracies and bias. Why are resumes, and their digital evolution in the form of LinkedIn profiles, still so widely used if they can't really be trusted?

The short answer is organizations just haven't replaced them with something better, so they manage through the issues, knowing that the system is imperfect but not having a better option.

Essentially, a resume focuses on your experience first, organized around the companies you worked for, when and how long you worked there, the roles you held, and your summarized achievements. Other information, including your educational background, can be helpful to bolster your job history, especially if you're either very early in your career or have extensive expertise in a field.

When I'm hiring someone, their resume serves a validation function—has this person done the work that I need to have done? How long have they done that kind of work? And it doesn't hurt if I recognize the company names where they've worked, which can bolster my biased perception of their capabilities, even before I meet them.

Things I don't typically learn, or even have an inkling of, while reviewing a resume are what someone is particularly good at and how well they performed in a role. In short, the resume is a great jumping-off point for a recruiter or hiring manager to make a lot of assumptions.

Automated resume screeners review applicants' resumes and rely on keywords to identify the candidates who are most qualified. It's not surprising at all that the potential for bias with this type of automation is extremely high—if AI is meant to match an applicant's resume (with self-reporting bias and inaccuracies) to a job description (that's out-of-date and not specific), it will certainly make mistakes in screening. Even organizations that rely on testing as a data input for hiring decisions may not be offering the assessment opportunity to the best candidates if applicants are erroneously filtered out before the assessment stage.

I firmly believe that resumes will slowly fade in importance and become a supplemental lens on work history that supports the headlining story of your skills. If job roles no longer exist in the way they do today and skills become the primary driver of hiring decisions, then resumes evolve to simply become evidence of someone's skills and expertise. In the short term, creating a more skills-focused overlay as a companion piece to a resume will help individuals and organizations better communicate about what skills they have (applicants) and what skills they need (organizations). Long term? I could see job history being infused with skills evidence, or a section called "Skills Profile" that mirrors how we detail our educational history today.

This acknowledgment may be slow to take form, but evidence of this transition is already happening in many of the learning, skills, and talent platforms that companies are using today. Many have some form of a skills profile that attempts to bring skills forward. The challenge is the data to power it—until skills assessment and validation are easier and more universally recognized, skills profiles will still mainly be self-reported, and less trusted and recognizable than the resume format we're using today. Until skills data is a requirement for applying to a role, and until people have a way to share their skills with a higher level of validity, resumes will likely retain their foothold as the primary data point reviewed by hiring teams.

Interviews

The last piece of data in the hiring trifecta is the information collected through the interview process. If you think job descriptions and resumes have flaws, add in personal variations in style and communication and our own internal biases, and you have a perfect storm for making bad hiring decisions.

Some organizations have recognized that personal opinions on candidates are at best circumstantial and at worst significantly biased, so they have built accountability systems, committee reviews, rating scales, and other products or technologies intended to level the playing field and create fairer evaluations of candidate pools. But many have not. Because interviews are usually the last gate before hiring, personal opinions often trump data and can create teams with homogenous profiles, show bias toward applicants with personal connections to the company, or a preference for less-qualified candidates with stronger interviewing skills.

In high-volume recruitment teams that need to screen thousands of applicants week after week, the challenges of using job descriptions, resumes, and interview feedback data as the tools for hiring become amplified. Organizations need better, more consistent data at scale to make more-informed hiring decisions.

Skills-based interviewing has the potential to supersede the resume in the hiring process. Why? Because, frankly, our interviewing systems are so inconsistent, they are ripe for innovation and becoming more data driven.

First, skills assessments as part of the interviewing process are likely to become much more common, if not an expected part. Skills-based portfolio assessments, video assessments of work scenarios that can be leveraged to evaluate skills, and simulations and labs that allow candidates to demonstrate skills (whether technical skills or human skills) are all on the immediate horizon.

I don't believe that the interviewing process of meeting with candidates and getting to know them before inviting them to work with you will go away. However, those conversations will be better informed with data, and both candidates and hiring managers will have more data to evaluate one another. The interview process being infused with skills data will help level the playing field, and highlight critical data for making hiring decisions that might be otherwise lost in an awkward conversation or by a bad interviewer. Creating a lens that helps hiring teams understand not only the skills someone has, but how they have applied them, will lead to more informative and structured data for decision making than saying, "Tell me the story behind your resume."

Internal Mobility

While current methods for recruiting and hiring external talent are fairly consistent from organization to organization, the same cannot be said for sourcing and hiring talent internally. Companies vary in their openness to and sophistication in hiring from within, and even when they are building internal career paths and encouraging employees to set career goals, they often struggle to apply the same level of focus in finding internal candidates that they do to marketing open roles to external candidates.

Many organizations do want to retain top talent, and promotions are expected and common for top performers. Often this happens along linear career paths, but when someone is interested in moving in a different direction, the path—and opportunities—is less straightforward.

Some organizations have begun to create talent pools to support internal mobility, as well as other decisions related to work opportunities. *Talent pools* refer to groups of employees who are identified based on their skills, experiences, and potential to fill specific roles or take on particular projects. These pools are used for succession planning, project assignments, and internal mobility to ensure that the right talent is available when needed.

Skills data can significantly enhance the effectiveness of talent pools by more accurately identifying who has the skills to qualify for any particular talent pool. For example, if you have skills data for employees across your organization, you could more easily identify pockets of expertise in project management or AI to leverage for emerging roles or projects. Skills data can also help you look at talent pools through multiple lenses to better target potential candidates for specific opportunities. What if you didn't need someone with project management or AI skills, but someone with project management *and* AI skills? Talent pools allow organizations to cluster people with direct and adjacent skills to better source candidates internally.

If organizations make talent pools visible, employees can identify which skills they have and which talent pools they belong to, or they can target which talent pools they would like to be a part of and focus on developing those skills. Internal job marketplaces are an example of how transparent talent pools can help shape employee goals to prepare them for the next step in their career.

Skills data can make talent pools more relevant and meaningful while also enabling more effective talent mapping to new roles and opportunities. As talent marketplaces emerge to help organizations make internal mobility more transparent and effective, skills data becomes the connector between people and available jobs. Sometimes, talent mapping is to new roles; other times, it is for projects or assignments. Skills can be the connection between skills supply and demand.

Skills data transforms talent pools from static groups into dynamic and strategic resources that drive organizational success. By ensuring that the right people are in the right roles at the right time, organizations can enhance their agility, competitiveness, and ability to respond to changing business needs.

And it's not just about visibility into talent pools—skills data can also create a stronger meritocracy within organizations. Promotions and rewards can be based on demonstrated skills and the impact of an employee's work, rather than tenure or past credentials. This merit-based system helps foster a culture of fairness and motivation, and ensures that internal hires know exactly why they, or someone else, were selected for an opportunity. This also helps avoid the problem of "it's not what you know; it's who you know," which often influences hiring or promotion decisions. By focusing on skills rather than pedigree, organizations become more inclusive, providing equal opportunities to individuals regardless of their educational background or personal connections.

Learning and Development

L&D faces three common challenges:
- How do you make learning meaningful to employees?
- How do you use the best strategies to help employees learn and build expertise?
- How do you show the impact of the learning programs and systems that you create?

Many organizations see L&D as a cost center and a necessary but nonstrategic investment. As the global market shifts, the importance of upskilling, reskilling, and making more meaningful learning investments means leaning into skills as a way of demonstrating L&D's strategic importance to the business.

Personalized Learning

Personalized learning in traditional L&D models is, in short, difficult. To create personalized experiences, you need to understand where people are starting from, what progress they are making, and where they want to go. For organizations striving to deliver more personalized learning, some options exist, with limitations, to try to attain this goal:

- **Manager assessments.** A lot of traditional personalized learning relies on manual assessments conducted by managers, mentors, or HR professionals. These assessments involve evaluating employees' performance, skills, and career goals through observations, reviews, and interviews.
- **Employee self-assessments.** Employees may be asked to complete self-assessments to identify their own strengths, weaknesses, and areas for development. Goal-setting can be part of self-assessments as well. These assessments help tailor learning experiences but are subjective and can be inconsistent.
- **Performance reviews.** Annual or semiannual performance reviews can be used to discuss employee progress and identify areas for development. These reviews help you plan future learning activities but may not provide real-time or detailed insights.

Learning content and programs can also be personalized in traditional methods, albeit in limited ways:

- **Choice of training programs.** Companies often offer standardized training programs that employees can choose from based on their perceived needs. While these programs aim to address common skills gaps, they may not be tailored to individual requirements.
- **Career pathing and mentorship.** Personalized learning experiences are sometimes created through career pathing and mentorship programs. Recommendations for things such as leadership development programs or project assignments to achieve specific goals can be suggested and facilitated by managers and mentors to help an employee build skills that they may lack in their current role, or that they may need to take the next step in their career. Managers and mentors guide employees based on their understanding of individual goals and organizational needs.

Although it's been difficult to implement personalized learning in traditional models, skills data is the catalyst to make personalized learning a reality. While education, experience, and goals are still relevant to understanding a person so you can make more meaningful individual recommendations, skills data is the supercharger of personalization, from setting a baseline, showing progress, and indicating job readiness. Here are some ways to leverage skills data:

- **Skills assessments.** With skills data, personalized learning experiences are based on assessments of employees' skills and competencies. This data is collected through various means, such as performance metrics and peer reviews.
- **Skill tracking.** Skills data allows for real-time tracking of employees' skill development. This continuous monitoring provides up-to-date insights into skills gaps and learning progress, enabling more timely and relevant solutions.
- **Tailored learning paths.** Using skills data, companies can create highly tailored learning paths that align with individual employee needs and career goals. These paths are customizable based on precise skills profiles, ensuring that learning activities are relevant and effective.
- **Adaptive learning.** Future learning management systems powered by skills data could adapt content and learning activities to the specific needs of each employee. These systems could use algorithms to recommend courses, modules, and resources that match individual skill levels and learning preferences.
- **Predictive analytics.** Skills data mapped with other data sources, such as job trends or typical career paths, enables the use of predictive analytics to anticipate future skills needs and identify employees who are likely to benefit from specific learning experiences. This proactive approach ensures that employees are prepared for upcoming challenges and opportunities.
- **Enhanced feedback mechanisms.** With detailed skills data, feedback mechanisms become more precise and actionable.

Employees receive specific feedback on their skills development, along with recommendations for targeted learning activities.
- **Integration with career development plans.** Skills data can be seamlessly integrated into employees' career development plans, ensuring that learning experiences are directly linked to career progression. This alignment fosters a more strategic approach to personal and professional growth.
- **Personalized content delivery.** Skills data enables the delivery of personalized learning content through various platforms, including e-learning modules, workshops, webinars, and on-the-job training. With advances in AI, personalized videos or interactive practices could be powered by skills data. This would ensure that employees receive the right content at the right time, in the format that best suits their preferences.

By leveraging skills data, organizations can move beyond traditional, one-size-fits-all approaches to learning and development. They can offer highly personalized, data-driven learning experiences that are more effective and engaging, and aligned with both individual and organizational goals.

Learning and Skill Building

To describe the impact of skills on L&D, it's important to understand the difference between learning how to do something and building skill in doing that something. Most L&D teams develop a mix of learning and skill-building activities, but perhaps didn't think about it in quite that way.

Learning is a dynamic and multifaceted process that encompasses the acquisition of knowledge, understanding, and insights. It often begins with exposure to new information through reading, social learning activities, classroom models of learning from an expert, or engaging with multimedia content. Learning involves cognitive activities such as memorization, comprehension, analysis, and synthesis of information. In a workplace setting, learning often focuses on exposure to and interaction with new content areas related to the needs of the business.

Skill building, on the other hand, is a targeted process focused on developing specific competencies and abilities through active practice and repetition. This process often involves hands-on activities, training sessions, simulations, and real-world application of techniques to refine and perfect particular skills. For example, a machinist learning how to build a new component for a piece of equipment will iterate and improve the application of their skills until the component meets their needs. Skill building requires regular feedback and incremental adjustments to enhance performance, best coming from an expert. The outcomes are tangible and observable improvements in performing tasks with greater accuracy, efficiency, and effectiveness. In a workplace setting, skill building might involve employees participating in workshops or on-the-job training to master software tools, improve customer service techniques, or develop project management capabilities, directly affecting their job performance and productivity.

While learning content and activities play a role in preparing people to build skills, in a skills-based organization, activities that allow people to build skills are the primary focus. There are two ways to build skills—simulated practice and real practice—and determining which is more appropriate depends on the skill.

Some skills lend themselves to simulated practice. Most human skills can be practiced in simulated environments, as can many technical or job skills. Think scenario-based simulations or virtual labs for technical skills. New technologies such as AI, augmented reality, and virtual reality are creating even more options for simulated practice and assessment of skills by broadening the options for what skills can be developed through designed experiences.

Other skills simply can't be simulated. I could learn a lot about baking from reading and watching experts, but until I actually bake a cake, it's hard to simulate the experience. This is also true of many skills that require kinesthetic practice. Knitting, driving, and public speaking are all experiences that require real practice, and organizations need to consider how to provide real opportunities for people to practice those types of skills.

Continuous learning and practice are also hallmarks of skills-based organizations and shouldn't be overlooked in importance. While some organizations that aren't skills-based have embraced the concept of continuous learning, it's often at the point of need, or without clear direction or focus. In a skills-based organization, continuous learning and practicing new skills become the norm because there is more transparency around the skills the organization needs. With new skills constantly emerging, employees can ask themselves, "Do I have the skills I need?" and focus their development on emerging gaps or future skills needs.

Impact of Learning

The impact of learning is traditionally measured through qualitative and indirect methods. This can include self-assessments, during which learners reflect on their perceived growth and understanding, as well as surveys and feedback forms that capture learners' satisfaction and engagement. Observations by instructors or managers can also provide insights into behavior changes and application of new knowledge. Additionally, exams, quizzes, and assignments evaluate the retention and comprehension of the material.

Organizations and L&D departments sometimes also use performance metrics to measure the impact of learning or skills development, but for more complex goals, such as customer satisfaction or sales numbers, it is harder to show a direct relationship between learning activities and performance results. Organizations can draw correlations between learning and performance, but it is more difficult to measure specific impact.

With skills data, measuring the impact of learning becomes more precise and actionable. Skills data provides a baseline of employees' competencies and skills before and after learning solutions, allowing for a clear comparison. Organizations can collect this data through performance metrics, skills assessments, and real-time tracking of specific abilities. For instance, if an employee undergoes training in project management, skills data can reveal improvements in project completion rates, adherence to deadlines, and quality of deliverables. Advanced analytics can also identify patterns and correlations between learning activities and skills enhancements, offering deeper insights into the effectiveness of various training programs. By integrating skills data, organizations can quantify the direct impact of learning on job performance and productivity, enabling more targeted and effective development initiatives.

People Management

People management keeps an organization running successfully, or not. Yet people management is one of the most challenging jobs because it requires a multitude of skills itself. If your organization has inconsistent results across people leaders, skills data can help inform people management in ways that make the whole organization, and especially its managers, more effective.

Coaching and Mentoring

Coaching and mentoring relationships are most successful when both the employee and their coach or mentor have clear expectations of the relationship's goals and how to make progress toward those goals. While coaching and mentoring relationships are different in their form and function, for the purposes of this discussion, I'm grouping them together because of similarities in how they function today from a data perspective, and how they could evolve to be more skills-based in the future.

Traditionally, coaching and mentoring relationships start out with a goal-setting objective: What does the employee want to achieve, and how can the coach or mentor contribute to the achievement of that goal? In both types of relationships, there is an expectation of growth and development in the employee, and that the coach or mentor will support the employee in opening doors to potential opportunities.

Organizations establish these relationships to help employees grow in their career, whether to move to the next level in their current career path, or to help explore other, adjacent opportunities. Coaching and mentoring typically include a strong element of relationship development in addition to career support. And while different programs may have different parameters, there are often elements of progress tracking toward goal achievement to help structure conversations, recommendations, and referrals. Because of this, most models offer some variation on setting SMART (specific, measurable, attainable, relevant, and time-bound) goals around which to structure the relationship. An example of a SMART goal for a junior sales associate who is interested in building a career in sales might be:

> Develop leadership skills to prepare for a promotion to sales associate within the next 12 months.

In this example, the junior sales associate and her coach could explore a variety of different ways to develop leadership skills that may or may not result in her receiving a promotion.

Coaching and mentoring aligned with and powered by skills data adds an additional layer to progress measurement and focus. Let's take the previous SMART goal example and consider the difference in an organization that is skills-based and actively measures skills.

Skills data can help the junior sales associate *develop leadership skills*. If the organization has already defined the skills that correspond to leadership, she and her coach can review the specific skills she could consider developing. Looking at existing skills data on the junior sales associate's leadership skills, or assessing those skills if baseline data isn't already available, would help her and her coach better target skill areas for growth, such as written communication, relationship building, and collaboration.

Once they've established the junior sales associate's baseline skills data and selected the skills to focus on, then the organization can monitor progress by collecting additional skills signals or by conducting reassessments at planned intervals. The processes she uses to develop her skills may vary, but skills data enables the coaching (or mentoring) relationship to be based on data that can help focus the development and monitor progress.

Performance Management

Performance management is mainly driven by a mix of performance data and qualitative opinions from 360-degree reviews and feedback. Some organizations leverage objectives and key results (OKRs) or team-level metrics (such as key performance indicators or dashboards) to benchmark performance and show progress over a period, sometimes annually or quarterly. Some organizations have well-defined processes for performance management across the organization, but others leave much up to a manager's discretion.

Continuous formal feedback is rare in traditional models but is often shared informally or in haphazard ways and timeframes. Because informal feedback isn't often documented, it is rarely tied to development goals, learning recommendations, or broader personal development or organizational needs.

Similarly, many recognition programs depend on peer or manager recommendations or acknowledgment of positive contribution to the team or business, but that feedback isn't usually tied to broader performance management systems. If it is, it is often in the form of a statement like "This person received seven kudos"—recognition without specific details of what the person did to be recognized.

In a skills-based organization, performance management can be framed around goals, performance milestones, or activity data, but it can also include real insight into skills development. Recommendations for ongoing performance improvement can be skills-based as well, with an employee's overall skill set and agility reviewed as part of the performance management process in the context of the organization's skills needs.

These types of skills-based conversations can better ensure a longer-term relationship between employees and employers, simply by having conversations that focus on what skills employees have and what skills the organization needs. Any gaps or opportunities can then be the focus for recommendations provided during performance management conversations.

Continuous feedback on employee performance is a key part of skills-based organizations. Employees are aware of the skills they are applying at work or developing, and feedback on their performance is tied to those skills, signaling when skills are developing or when skills haven't been applied in a while and might be waning. Skills-based feedback raises employees' awareness of the skills they use every day, and their proficiency in applying those skills. With this level of insight, annual performance conversations should yield no surprises regarding their skills.

Recognition programs can also evolve to include skills application or development. Imagine a kudos system that lets people not only recognize someone for good work, but specifically acknowledge the skills that deserve recognition. This additional layer of data provides deeper insight for a broader audience about an employee's skills on the job.

Employee Engagement

Employees are the lifeblood of any company, yet many of the decisions that are most personally meaningful are made with limited data. A person's ability to progress their career, set meaningful goals, and market their expertise can have a significant impact on employee engagement, satisfaction, and retention metrics.

Career Progression

First, it's worth noting that fewer than half of organizations have career pathways outlined for employees, either traditional (linear progression pathways) or nontraditional (alternative career paths; Dewar 2023). This lack of visibility into how an employee can grow their career within an organization contributes to employees looking outside their current employer for their next opportunity, affecting metrics for employee retention. Most companies that do offer career progression models and pathways are job-role based, with some expectation of performance milestones achieved or behavioral maturity demonstrated. For example, a product manager career pathway at a SaaS company might look something like Table 2-1.

Table 2-1. Example Career Pathway for a Product Manager

Career Stage	Job Title	Typical Responsibilities	Required Qualifications	Potential Next Steps
Entry level	Associate product manager	• Assist with product development and management • Conduct market research • Gather user feedback	• Bachelor's degree in business or related field • Analytical skills • Communication skills	• Product manager • Project manager
Midlevel	Product manager	• Lead product development • Define product strategy • Manage product life cycle • Collaborate with cross-functional teams	• Three to five years of experience • Strong project management skills • Technical understanding • Leadership skills	• Senior product manager • Product lead
Senior level	Senior product manager	• Oversee multiple products or a product line • Develop and implement product strategies • Mentor junior product managers	• Five to eight years of experience • Advanced strategic thinking • Strong leadership and mentorship abilities	• Product director • Head of product
Leadership	Product director	• Lead the product management team • Set product vision and goals • Align product strategy with business objectives	• Eight to 10 years of experience • Proven track record of successful product launches • Excellent leadership skills	• Vice president of product • Chief product officer
Executive	Vice president of product	• Drive overall product strategy and vision • Oversee entire product portfolio • Represent product strategy at the executive level	• 10 or more years of experience • Exceptional leadership and strategic thinking • Strong business acumen	• CEO (with broader business responsibilities) • Board member

While some of the qualifications for progression in this pathway are clear, such as years of experience expectations, some are very vague, such as "technical understanding." This traditional model of career progression introduces a great deal of subjectivity and risks confusion and bias for employees and for managers on the front lines of career progression.

Consider the same career progression for a product manager, now with the inclusion of skills (Table 2-2).

Now, imagine you are an employee looking to move to the next step in your career as a product manager. By simply looking at the list of skills required, you can identify whether you have demonstrated those skills or if you need to seek out opportunities to develop and demonstrate them before moving to the next step.

Creating visible skills expectations and having a mechanism for assessing, validating, or demonstrating those skills not only helps set appropriate expectations for employees about where they are in their career progression, but also helps managers and internal mobility specialists identify who is ready for the next step in their career. Even better, setting skills expectations alongside proficiency levels truly allows employees, managers, and hiring managers to have more transparent and informed conversations about promotions and internal mobility.

Goal Setting

While not all organizations leverage goal-setting as part of an employee engagement model (some use it as part of performance management, which implies that goals should be in the interest of the business objectives, not the employee's personal career aspirations), more and more are realizing that asking the employee for their input in goal setting helps drive motivation and answers the question "What's in it for me?"

For organizations that aren't skills-based, goals can be tied to a person's career (*I want to become a vice president of engineering*), professional advancement (*I want to get a certification in Amazon Web Services*), or development (*I want to improve my coding skills*). While understanding development context and motivation is good, organizations may then struggle to

Table 2-2. Example Career Pathway for a Product Manager With Required Skills Identified

Career Stage	Job Title	Typical Responsibilities	Required Experience	Required Skills	Potential Next Steps
Entry level	Associate product manager	• Assist with product development and management • Conduct market research • Gather user feedback	• Bachelor's degree in business or related field	• Analytical skills • Communication skills • Basic understanding of product management • Teamwork	• Product manager • Project manager
Midlevel	Product manager	• Lead product development • Define product strategy • Manage product life cycle • Collaborate with cross-functional teams	• Three to five years of experience	• Strong project management skills • Technical understanding • Leadership skills • Analytical and problem-solving skills • User-centric mindset	• Senior product manager • Product lead
Senior level	Senior product manager	• Oversee multiple products or a product line • Develop and implement product strategies • Mentor junior product managers	• Five to eight years of experience	• Advanced strategic thinking • Strong leadership and mentorship abilities • Market analysis • Stakeholder management • Advanced product life cycle management	• Product director • Head of product
Leadership	Product director	• Lead the product management team • Set product vision and goals • Align product strategy with business objectives	• Eight to 10 years of experience	• Proven track record of successful product launches • Excellent leadership skills • Strategic planning • Budget management • Cross-functional team leadership	• Vice president of product • Chief product officer
Executive	Vice president of product	• Drive overall product strategy and vision • Oversee entire product portfolio • Represent product strategy at the executive level	• 10 or more years of experience	• Exceptional leadership and strategic thinking • Strong business acumen • Visionary thinking • Influence and negotiation skills • Corporate governance	• CEO (with broader business responsibilities) • Board member

find the appropriate opportunities to help an employee develop, leaving it up to the individual and their manager to map a path to achieve the employee's goals.

In skills-based organizations, goal setting—whether career, professional, or developmental—can be more precise by aligning with skills. For career goals, identifying the skills needed to achieve the goal can clarify the path forward. For professional and developmental goals, the development of skills themselves can be the focus of the goal. For example, if my professional goal is to obtain a coach to improve my executive communication, I can find a coach with that particular expertise and then identify the particular skills I need to focus on to improve.

Not only does the path to goal achievement become more obvious, but you can track your progress by measuring your skills over time. And organizations that have built learning or internal mobility systems based on skills can suddenly map goals to learning, project, or job recommendations, which will help employees achieve their goals more quickly. Skills become the connective tissue between your aspirations and your activity, ensuring that you know what to do to make your goals a reality.

Marketing Their Expertise

Employees really have a heavy lift in most organizations, relying on word of mouth and reputation to be considered for internal opportunities. Unfortunately, even strong employees aren't recommended for or supported in taking on new roles if their manager puts personal needs or the needs of the current team ahead of the employee's aspirations. In these cases, employees must network and keep an eye out for job postings or hope that they are recommended for opportunities they might not know about. Employees still rely on resumes, job descriptions, and—most important within an organization—recommendations as the main marketing tools for their expertise.

In skills-based organizations, employees can develop skills profiles that allow them to match their skills to opportunities, whether projects or roles. Employees can show the development of their skills over time and see how their skills align with desired opportunities to better advocate for themselves. Some skills-based organizations are developing internal talent marketplaces and talent pools; their employees can see if they have the right skills for an opportunity—and if they don't, they can develop those skills for future consideration. Skills-based organizations take the guesswork out of understanding whether you have the skills you need, and give you the tools to market yourself for opportunities.

Workforce Management

Your internal processes related to people and people management are some of the most effective areas for introducing skills data, by both bringing value to employees, which can drive retention metrics, and helping managers and hiring managers make more-informed decisions. Skills data has the potential to reduce bias; used incorrectly, it could also introduce bias. Let's look at traditional methods of workforce management processes and how those processes could evolve with skills data.

Work Allocation and Project Staffing

Most organizations organize work around job roles. It's one of the reasons resumes have persisted for as long as they have—a business needs a job to be done, so it looks for someone who has done that type of work before (sometimes within the organization and sometimes for someone new to join the company).

The nature of work is changing, however, to be more initiative- or project-based, not necessarily role-based. In some industries, such as consulting, the entire business model is project-based. In other organizations, work initiatives and projects spin up and wind down as needed to support the needs of the business, including launching innovation initiatives and product lines or addressing specific opportunities or challenges that can improve the trajectory of the business.

Staffing projects for organizations is nuanced, but it often comes down to two factors: availability and skills.

Let's avoid trying to determine someone's availability and focus on how to allocate work based on skills. The same balance is needed for assigning projects and hiring for a job. First, what skills do you need? Then, who has those skills? For many projects, you likely need a mix of skills, and no one person likely possesses all of them. Considerations for skills-based project staffing include:

- **Diversity in teams.** By evaluating the skills needed for a project and the candidates available to do the work, you can create teams made up of people with diverse skills, expertise, and backgrounds. Research has shown that diverse teams are better at decision making, and skills data can add an extra layer of insight into diversity as you're building a team (Rock and Grant 2016).
- **Prioritizing skills.** If you have limited resources for staffing a project (and let's be honest, that's typically the case), then knowing what skills need to be prioritized will allow you to determine which people are most needed for your team. It will also allow you to assess your project for risks, identifying any critical skills gaps that could affect success.
- **Expertise levels.** Similar to prioritizing skills, you also need to understand what level of skill, or expertise, is required to do the work. For some projects, deep expertise is needed; for others, an intermediate skill level is sufficient. Expertise level alongside skill priority will help determine whether your project is set up for success from a skills perspective.
- **Job skills and human skills.** Successful project teams typically require not just the technical skills to do the work, but also the human skills needed to work well as a team. How often have you been part of a team that struggled, not because of the work, but because of how team members weren't working together? Analyzing the human skills will better set up a project team for success.
- **Stretch opportunities.** It is important to know whether you are staffing a project for expertise or staffing some team members to have an opportunity to learn or practice a skill. Some projects may require prior experience or expertise but in many cases,

working on a project is an opportunity to build skill sets. Clearly identifying what is needed for a project will provide context for whether someone could build required skills as they work on the project.

Adding skills data into the mix to allow for better decision making can empower organizations to consistently build more effective teams.

Succession Planning

In traditional succession-planning models, organizations typically rely on hierarchical structures and tenure-based promotions to identify and prepare future leaders. This process typically involves periodic performance reviews, subjective assessments by senior management, and a focus on employees who have been with the company the longest or who exhibit leadership potential based on observable behaviors and past achievements. While effective to some extent, these methods can be limited by bias, lack of comprehensive data, and an over-reliance on a narrow set of criteria. Consequently, organizations may overlook high-potential employees and leave skills gaps unaddressed, leading to leadership shortages or mismatches that can hinder organizational growth and resilience.

Many traditional models simply rely on a recommendation from the previous person in that role, and therefore incorporate whatever biases that person possesses. People tend to prefer people who are like them, both in style and in broader characteristics. For example, if you are a leader who values people who work long hours, you will be biased toward those who come in early and work late. If you are a leader who values speed over accuracy, you will recommend people with a bias toward speed. This also illustrates how bias infiltrates across gender, race, and other demographics. Organizations have struggled with evaluating performance and merit for succession planning equitably and with placing business needs above personal biases.

Integrating skills data into succession planning revolutionizes this traditional approach by providing a more objective, comprehensive, and dynamic understanding of employee capabilities. Skills data allows organizations to identify the precise competencies required for various leadership roles and assess employees against these criteria using data-driven insights. This enables the identification of high-potential candidates based not only on tenure or past performance but also on their current skill sets, potential for growth, and readiness to take on new challenges. Additionally, skills data can highlight skills gaps and inform targeted development programs, ensuring that future leaders are well prepared. This data-driven approach reduces bias, enhances transparency, and aligns succession planning with the strategic goals of the organization, fostering a more agile and prepared leadership pipeline.

Workforce Planning

The key to effective workforce planning is having the data available to look at an organization as a system, and plan for what the system needs today and tomorrow. If the key is in the data, then your workforce planning can be only as good as the data you have. Many traditional workforce-management models revolve around static job descriptions, rigid organizational hierarchies, and generalized performance reviews. Organizations typically assign employees roles based on their job titles and previous experiences, with little consideration for their evolving skills and potential beyond their current positions. Workforce planning in this context is primarily reactive, addressing immediate needs rather than anticipating future demands.

In traditional models, data points such as tenure and past credentials are often used to plan for the future. These data points contribute to a backward-looking view of success, increasing the risk that future planning is based on irrelevant data not predictive of the needs of the future.

Integrating skills data into workforce management transforms this traditional approach by fostering a dynamic, responsive, and personalized system. Skills data provides detailed insights into each employee's capabilities, enabling managers to assign tasks and roles based on current skills and potential growth rather than static job descriptions. This is another area where job descriptions (similar to hiring and internal mobility) offer less relevant data, and where skills (and, where appropriate, proficiency levels) aligned to roles can create a more fluid system that can change as business needs do.

A skills-based approach also facilitates more strategic workforce planning, allowing organizations to proactively address future skills needs and align talent with business objectives. By leveraging skills data, organizations can create a more flexible and agile workforce view that's better prepared to adapt to changing market conditions and innovate, ultimately driving sustained competitive advantage.

Conclusion

Before your organization can plan the path ahead for skills, you need to understand where you're starting from. Getting an accurate picture of how people-related decisions are currently made in your organization and where there are friction points will help you to pick a meaningful starting point for your skills journey.

The Front Line Runs on Skills

Contributed by JD Dillon, Chief Learning Officer, Axonify

Who can do what? This was the most important info I needed to be an effective operations manager. Early in my career, I managed the world's busiest roller coaster. More than 2,000 guests per hour stopped by to experience the "wildest ride in the wilderness." My frontline team was responsible for safely and efficiently managing queues, loading guests into ride vehicles, and monitoring operations. Creating magic takes lots of know-how, technical proficiency, and teamwork!

My job was to make sure the front line had the resources needed to run a safe, courteous, and efficient operation. This included critical tasks such as managing technical downtimes, responding to guest concerns, and closing staffing gaps. I had to put the right people in the right places to get the job done. And if four people called out sick one day, I had to find staff to cover their spots so the guest experience wasn't interrupted.

To make decisions like this on the fly, I had to know what every person on my team could do. Putting someone without the necessary capability in the wrong position could not only interrupt the operation (and make our guests wait longer), but also put our guests, employees, and the business at risk. Thankfully, we tracked all this information; we just didn't call it "skills data." We kept records of every team member's certifications, including when they were trained, who completed the assessment, and when the certification expired (if applicable). If I tried to assign a position or task to someone who didn't have the required "skills," the system stopped me. If I needed to find someone to fill a shift, I could pull a list of qualified employees to figure out whom to call first.

We may not have realized it at the time, but we were applying a skills-based approach to people operations—15 years before it became such a hot topic in L&D.

The Tangibility of Frontline Skills

Frontline work is different, and it's these differences that make the front line especially suitable for a skills-based approach. First, the skills required to complete common tasks are well defined. For example, distribution center managers know exactly what skills people need to be safe and efficient lift-truck drivers. To meet regulatory scrutiny, these requirements are documented in standard operating procedures and serve as the basis for job training. They're also consistent across locations—so lift-truck drivers in Canton, Ohio, have identical skills as those working with the same company in La Crosse, Wisconsin.

Skills also scale more effectively on the front line than in other parts of the business. In a corporate office, a few hundred people may do a few hundred different jobs. After all, a company only needs so many directors of environmental health and safety. This makes it harder to define skill requirements for each individual role. But the skills math changes on the front line, where thousands—or tens of thousands—of people do the same jobs. A regional grocer may have 35,000 employees across 500 locations, but 2,800 of those people work in the produce department. Even unique frontline roles have significant skills overlap. Deli clerks and front-end cashiers handle different tasks, but they're both expected to possess skills in customer service, math, communication, upselling, and so on.

Frontline skills are also easier to measure. Critical job tasks—and related skills requirements—are connected to specific business metrics. Call center interactions are scored based on the agent's ability to execute against a rubric of customer service standards. Cashier efficiency in retail is measured based on point of sale scans per minute. These skills are also easily observed and evaluated. Trainers must assess an employee's readiness to perform the job based on these standards. Otherwise, the employee may negatively affect operational outcomes. Plus, managers regularly observe job performance and review key performance indicators (KPIs) to determine if an employee is meeting expectations. This reduces the need to apply less reliable skills measurement tactics, such as inference or self-evaluation.

This combination of definition, consistency, scale, and measurability makes frontline skills more tangible and manageable when compared with those for corporate teams.

Applying Frontline Skills

When it comes to talent management, frontline skills strategies offer similar value to their corporate counterparts. HR teams can proactively identify skills needs and adjust hiring and development plans to fill gaps (in addition to roles). Employees can leverage skills-based training catalogs and talent marketplaces to find relevant opportunities. Managers can apply skills insights to inform talent decisions, such as promotions and performance evaluations, rather than solely relying on subjective observations and KPIs.

But the utility of frontline skills extends beyond traditional use cases. Managers apply this data every day to answer a plethora of important operations questions, including:
- Is it OK for Anika and Diego to swap shifts?
- What's Tyler's hourly pay rate?
- Is Meaghan allowed to operate this machinery?
- Should Omar be able to access this part of the facility?
- Can Sam be assigned this task?

Each answer is based—at least in part—on the employees' skills. Frontline workers are scheduled for shifts, assigned tasks, and authorized to use company resources based on their verified capabilities. In some cases, employees may be paid different hourly rates based on their accumulated skills. Managers can also leverage skills data to improve operational efficiency while controlling costs. In particular, cross-trained employees are highly regarded because they can help fill multiple roles during a single shift without the need to schedule more people.

Adopting a skills-based approach within a corporate workforce often requires a significant organizational mindset shift along with adjustments to job descriptions, skills taxonomies, and data collection practices. Meanwhile, most frontline teams already understand the importance of this approach, because it's what they've been doing for years. Now it's a matter of finding new ways to gain value from a frontline skills strategy.

Enabling Frontline Skills

The front line may already run on skills, but L&D has an important role to play in making this approach work. Many organizations still apply manual processes to track and apply skills-related insights. While they may record training completions and certifications in a learning management system, managers often transfer this "who can do what" data into other systems by hand. In some cases, employee skills are tracked using even more antiquated methods, such as spreadsheets and managers' memories.

L&D can help reduce administrative burden, minimize manager effort, and simplify the employee experience—all in service of improved operational efficiency, frontline engagement, and business outcomes.

- **Clarify skill requirements.** Many third-party skills taxonomies are too generic or missing specific job functions that apply to frontline workers. L&D must partner with operational stakeholders to clarify job expectations and translate everyday work tasks into a list of well-defined, measurable skills.
- **Codify skills data.** Just because someone completes training doesn't mean they have the related skills. L&D must embed real-world skills evaluation within training programs to make sure people are ready to apply what they've learned. L&D must also simplify this data in the form of credentials and certifications so it's easy to access, understand, and share.
- **Automate skills processes.** L&D must reduce administrative effort and improve data reliability to maximize the impact of skills-based talent strategies. Besides skills clouds and talent marketplaces, L&D must integrate learning data with frontline-focused HR and operations tools, such as scheduling software, task management tools, payroll systems, and property management systems. Plus, managers must be able to access up-to-date information on employees' current skills in the workflow. This includes any potential expiration or recertification requirements so they can proactively manage their teams' capabilities.
- **Build for common skills.** A capable, confident frontline team is vital to business success. However, managers have limited labor hours with which to get the job done. L&D must get people up to speed quickly while limiting training time so people can focus on essential job tasks. Taking a skills-based approach can help L&D deliver right-fit training and accelerate development. By breaking content down to focus on specific skills, L&D can use assessments and adaptive learning technology to deliver

only the training each employee needs. This microlearning approach also enables cross-training by reducing the amount of redundant content between roles.

Organizations have a lot to learn from the skills-forward nature of frontline work. Generic taxonomies and inconsistent measurement practices will only get you so far. To boost operational efficiency while fostering employee opportunities, organizations must clearly define skills so they can be observed, measured, and applied. Otherwise, you'll never really know who can do what.

CHAPTER 3
Deciding How to Start

In this chapter, we'll cover:
- Identifying the right first steps in your organization's skills journey
- Creating a vision statement for your skills-based journey
- Developing your skills-based organization blueprint

Once you have determined that skills can be a catalyst for making better people-related decisions in your organization, the biggest question is how to get started. Different organizations may start at different places, and every organization will have their own pace and metrics for what "good" looks like. Here are some parameters for your organization to consider in your first step toward becoming skills-based:

- **Business problem to solve.** When embarking on the journey to become a skills-based organization, start by identifying a small, measurable, and meaningful business problem that skills data could significantly affect. This could be a high-turnover position that you could improve retention for by understanding specific skills gaps, or a project consistently missing deadlines because of skill mismatches. By focusing on a clear and narrow problem, you can more easily demonstrate the value of skills data and create a compelling case for broader adoption. This targeted approach allows for tangible results that can be scaled up once the initial success is proven.
- **Success metrics identified.** After selecting the business problem to solve, identifying success metrics is crucial for measuring the impact of becoming a skills-based organization. Determine what amount of change would be meaningful for your organization,

such as a 1 percent improvement in productivity equating to $X in savings or revenue growth. Clearly defining these metrics helps set realistic expectations and provides a benchmark against which progress can be measured. For example, if reducing employee turnover by 5 percent translates to $100,000 in savings, this quantifiable goal can guide efforts and help you evaluate the effectiveness of skills-based initiatives.

- **Baseline data.** Establishing baseline data is essential to measure the impact of skills-based strategies. Analyze how the problem is currently measured and how you would like it to be measured in the future. Determine if the necessary data exists; if not, develop a method to start collecting and tracking this information. For instance, if improving project completion rates is the goal, you need baseline data on current completion rates, reasons for delays, and perceived skills gaps. This initial data collection sets the stage for comparison and highlights areas needing attention.
- **Capability to measure impact.** To effectively transition to a skills-based organization, ensure you have the capability to continuously measure and demonstrate changes over time. This involves setting up systems to track skills development and performance metrics consistently. Being able to show the delta from the baseline is critical; for example, if you initially measured project completion rates at 70 percent, and they rise to 85 percent post-initiative, this quantifiable improvement underscores the success of the skills-based approach. Continuous measurement also helps iterate and refine strategies to achieve better outcomes, or to identify when no further action is needed.
- **Executive buy-in.** Gaining executive buy-in is pivotal for a successful transition to a skills-based organization. Skills-based initiatives must address problems that matter to senior leadership, such as improving profitability, enhancing productivity, or reducing turnover. Presenting a clear connection between skills data and solving these high-priority issues can capture their interest and support. Executives are more likely

to endorse changes when they see how skills-focused strategies align with the organization's strategic goals and deliver measurable business benefits.

- **Broad versus deep.** Decide whether to adopt a broad or deep approach when implementing skills-based strategies. A broad approach focused on enhancing a few critical skills across the entire organization can foster general competency improvements. Conversely, a deep approach targets all skills required for a high-importance or strategic role, ensuring that those employees are highly proficient in their specialized areas. For instance, deeply developing the skills of your sales team could yield significant revenue increases while broadly enhancing digital literacy across the organization might improve overall efficiency and adaptability.
- **Timeboxing.** Timeboxing is an important consideration to ensure that the transition to a skills-based organization shows meaningful impact within a specific timeframe. Define a clear period, such as six months or a year, to implement and evaluate your initial investment in skills-based initiatives. This creates urgency and focus, enabling you to assess progress and make necessary adjustments promptly. If, for example, the goal is to reduce technical bugs by 20 percent within a year, regular check-ins and evaluations during this period will help keep efforts on track and demonstrate interim successes.
- **Resources needed.** Assess the resources required to test and fully embed skills-based solutions within your organization. This includes determining whether additional personnel or systems are necessary to support the transition. For instance, you may need a dedicated team to manage skills-data collection and analysis or new software to track skills development and performance metrics. Identifying these needs up front ensures that you have the infrastructure and support to sustain skills-based initiatives and achieve long-term success. Proper resourcing is critical to avoid overburdening existing staff and

to maintain momentum in your skills-based transformation. But remember to start small. Over-investment too early in your skills journey will put pressure on your outcomes. Keep the initiatives and outcomes focused; investments should match the scale and scope of your first step. Investments can grow over time as results are shown.

Skills Tip

For most skill initiative starting points, you'll need to identify not only the skills, but also the tasks involved. Keeping your scope simple and narrow will help prevent you from getting bogged down in defining whole systems of skills or tasks before you've shown the value of skills data to the business.

Setting the Vision

Maybe your organization has already answered the "Why skills?" question from chapter 1—it's not an *if*; it's more of a *how*. One strategy to gain organizational support for becoming skills-based is to create a vision statement.

Let's address some caveats here. First, creating a vision statement doesn't have to be an exhaustive effort! Don't let this be the step that holds you up from actually starting the journey. I've seen organizations spend more time trying to agree on a vision statement than on defining the actual business need and expected impact of prioritizing skills. So don't believe that this has to be perfect! And second, don't assume that the vision statement will be static—it may (and probably should) evolve as you learn more through the process. That said, a clear vision statement can be a grounding and uniting artifact to help kick off your journey, and allow you to give context as you communicate what you're doing across your organization.

A skills vision statement should articulate the company's commitment to leveraging skills to achieve its strategic goals, foster innovation, and enhance employee growth. Focusing on the intended business impact and what's in it for employees will ensure that your skills vision statement resonates with different audiences. Here's an example:

Skills Vision Statement

Our organization envisions a future in which our success is driven by the unique skills and potential of our people. We are committed to creating a dynamic and inclusive workplace that recognizes and nurtures individual talents, aligns them with organizational goals, and continuously evolves to meet the demands of a rapidly changing world. Through a skills-based approach, we will:

- Empower our employees to thrive by identifying, developing, and using their diverse skills.
- Build a culture of continuous learning and adaptability, enabling our workforce to respond swiftly to emerging opportunities and challenges.
- Foster innovation and excellence by connecting people with the roles and projects that best match their skills, interests, and aspirations.
- Ensure fair and equitable access to opportunities, promoting a workforce that reflects the diverse skills and backgrounds of our society.

We believe that by focusing on skills, we can unlock the full potential of our talent, drive organizational growth, and create value for our customers, employees, and stakeholders.

This vision statement emphasizes the organization's commitment to leveraging skills for personal and organizational growth, innovation, and equity. It sets a clear direction for building a skills-based culture while aligning with broader strategic objectives.

Now, you could spend a lot of time building a vision statement, or maybe you could start with this one. I've also found that leveraging AI to generate examples is a great starting point if you have specific elements or language to include. The goal is not to overthink it, but to create a touchstone that everyone in your organization can align with, and that will guide specific skills initiatives.

Developing a Skills-Based Organization Blueprint

You're committed to (or at least ready to explore) the journey to becoming a skills-based organization. You're ready, but is the rest of your organization?

While there is no linear path, there are many different aspects of this evolution to consider and to evaluate your organization against. In no particular order, here are the components of a skills-based organization blueprint:

- Organizational needs analysis and buy-in from stakeholders (chapter 4)
- Skills definitions, grouping, and proficiency levels (chapter 5)
- Skills measurement, validation, and data collection (chapter 6)
- Skills-data infrastructure and technologies (chapter 7)
- Skills-based hiring and internal mobility (chapter 8)
- Skills development, upskilling, and reskilling (chapter 9)
- Skills data for enhancing people management (chapter 10)
- Employee value of skills (chapter 11)
- Skills-based business processes and decision making (chapter 12)

Imagine a skills-based organization as a house (Figure 3-1). The foundation is the skills-data architecture and technology infrastructure. Can you build a house without a foundation? Yes, but if you want the house to stay sturdy, you'll eventually need to ensure that you have a foundation.

Figure 3-1. Example Blueprint of a Skills-Based Organization

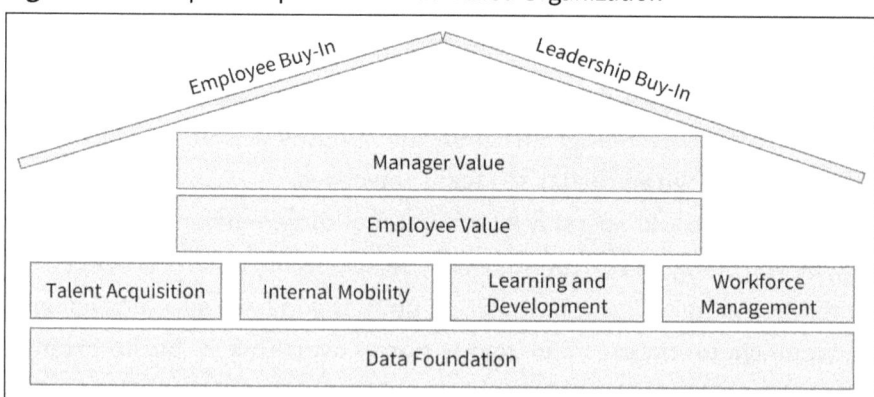

Your business use cases (such as talent acquisition, internal mobility, L&D, workforce management, and succession planning) are the rooms that you build on top of the foundation. Your house could have one room or many—you could build them all at once, or you could add one room at a time. The roof is your employees and executive stakeholders—without their buy-in and engagement, the building will eventually crumble from lack of investment.

To assess your organizational path to becoming skills-based, each of these areas must be evaluated. Depending on your organization, you might have matured in some areas but be totally lacking in others. To map a journey for your organization, it's important to understand where you are starting from in each potential area to leverage skills.

This is not to say that every organization will infuse skills data in every aspect of its business—many will not, at least not right away. And that's OK—not every organization will have the same level of need, urgency, or ability to invest into their skills "house." Every organization will take a different path and approach to becoming skills-based, even if the North Star is the same. Throughout the rest of this book, we'll explore how to look at each area to build an effective skills-based organization.

Conclusion

> "A journey of a thousand miles begins with a single step."
> —Lao Tzu, *Tao Te Ching*

This quote is attributed to lots of different types of journeys and is appropriate advice for organizations getting started with skills. It's important to know where you want to go, but it's also important to not get so bogged down in planning that you don't get started. By identifying your first step, you start the journey and can learn and adjust along the way to reach your desired destination with skills.

Building the Right Foundation for Skills and Experimentation

Contributed by Oli Meager, Co-Founder and Managing Partner, Skill Collective

When transitioning to a skills-based model, organizations need to prioritize creating a solid foundation first. A well-established foundation supports not only the identification and development of essential skills but also the alignment of talent with business objectives, fostering both organizational growth and employee development. At the heart of this foundation is creating a common language of skills that enables consistent understanding and application of skills across departments and functions.

A shared language ensures that you recognize, categorize, and evaluate skills consistently, reducing the risk of fragmentation and misalignment. This process begins by identifying the most critical skills that drive the organization's current and future objectives. This step requires collaboration across different functions, from human resources to operations and leadership, ensuring that the organization remains competitive in its industry and can respond quickly to shifts in demand.

Once you've identified the skills, the next step is to standardize how they are communicated across platforms and tools. Modern organizations use a variety of talent management systems, making it essential to ensure data interoperability among these systems. This allows for seamless integration of skills data and facilitates talent mobility, learning and development opportunities, and workforce planning. Where the common language begins is often overlooked. Skills data in the job architecture layer (typically job descriptions) is the most logical place for creating the right foundation. It may not have bells and whistles, or even be something that is visible, but that is the purpose of having the right foundation—it is the unseen elements or below-the-surface activity that results in success.

Another key consideration in building this foundation is data governance. It is crucial to have clear ownership over the skills data, ensuring it remains accurate and up to date. Without proper custodianship, organizations may struggle with inaccurate or outdated skills profiles, leading to inefficient decision making. This governance framework should align with business goals, ensuring that skills data drives the broader talent and organizational strategies.

Once the foundation is set, experimentation can play a pivotal role in refining and enhancing the skills ecosystem. Experimentation allows organizations to test new strategies, tools, and processes to ensure that their skills framework remains adaptable to evolving business requirements.

Defining the Focus of the Experiment

The key to any successful experiment is ensuring alignment with business objectives. Before initiating an experiment, it is essential to clearly define the problem or opportunity that the experiment seeks to address. For instance, an organization might decide to test how upskilling specific teams in emerging technologies can lead to better decision making or innovation. The focus of the experiment should be tightly connected to the organization's overall goals, ensuring that outcomes contribute to both immediate and long-term objectives. This business alignment will help ensure buy-in from stakeholders outside HR.

To define the scope of the experiment, organizations should start by identifying the specific skills or roles they aim to address. This may include determining which departments or business functions are involved, what tools and data will be used, and how progress will be tracked. Clearly defining the focus ensures that resources are used efficiently, and the experiment is set up for success.

Execution and Alignment

Effective execution of a skills experiment requires collaboration across different functions, such as HR, operations, and technology teams. This cross-functional collaboration ensures that you consider all necessary perspectives and can execute the experiment in a comprehensive manner. Starting with a small-scale pilot group allows the organization to minimize risks, gather insights quickly, and iterate if needed.

During the execution phase, leveraging the right tools and technologies is critical. For instance, using data analytics platforms to monitor skills development or track talent mobility can provide valuable insights into the effectiveness of the experiment. These tools also enable real-time adjustments, allowing organizations to respond to challenges or opportunities as they arise.

Additionally, aligning with business processes is essential for successful execution. A pilot program should be seen not as an isolated initiative but as an integral part of the organization's broader talent and business strategy. Cross-departmental buy-in is key to ensuring the experiment's success and scalability. So, although monitoring skills development or tracking talent mobility is valuable, ensuring these metrics are linked to the applicable business objectives is even more important when articulating the impact of any skills initiative.

Measuring Success

To gauge the effectiveness of a skills experiment, organizations must establish clear success metrics from the outset. These metrics should be directly tied to the experiment's objectives and the organization's broader business goals. Some common metrics might include:

- **Skills development**—tracking how many employees have acquired new or enhanced skills
- **Talent mobility**—measuring the internal movement of employees into roles that align with the newly developed skills
- **Business impact**—assessing whether the experiment led to measurable improvements in performance, innovation, or operational efficiency

It's important to focus on both quantitative and qualitative data when measuring success. While metrics such as the number of upskilled employees or internal hires can provide valuable insights, gathering qualitative feedback from participants and stakeholders will offer deeper insights into how the experiment affected overall business objectives.

The success of a skills experiment also depends on its ability to drive cultural change. Organizations that can embed a culture of continuous learning and adaptability are better positioned to respond to future challenges. Successful experimentation should not only lead to the desired outcomes but also foster a mindset of agility and innovation.

Organizational Alignment Around Experimentation

For experimentation to succeed, there must be alignment across all levels of the organization, from leadership to individual contributors. This alignment requires clear communication channels and a governance framework that supports innovation and experimentation.

In many cases, leadership plays a critical role in championing experimentation efforts, ensuring they are adequately resourced and aligned with the organization's strategic goals. However, engagement should not be limited to leadership alone. Encouraging a bottom-up approach by actively involving employees and teams in the experimentation process helps create buy-in and drives participation.

Building an experimentation-friendly culture requires a combination of leadership vision, organizational structure, and employee engagement. Experimentation should be framed as an opportunity to learn and grow, rather than a high-stakes initiative. By creating an environment in which teams feel empowered to test new ideas and learn from failures, organizations can foster innovation and make significant strides toward their skills-based objectives.

Conclusion

Building the right foundation for skills is a critical step for any organization looking to develop a competitive and agile workforce. By creating a common language of skills, ensuring data interoperability, and fostering governance structures, organizations lay the groundwork for long-term success.

Once the foundation is in place, experimentation can help refine and enhance the skills ecosystem. By starting with small, focused experiments aligned with business goals, organizations can test new strategies and measure their effectiveness. Successful experiments not only drive immediate business impact but also contribute to a culture of learning, agility, and continuous improvement.

Ultimately, the combination of a well-established skills foundation and a willingness to experiment ensures that organizations remain flexible, resilient, and prepared for the future.

Treat Skills as a Data Problem

Contributed by Jeroen Van Hautte, Co-Founder and CTO, TechWolf, and Cedric Vandamme, Vice President, Professional Services, TechWolf

Most companies attempting to become skills-based start by implementing a tool of some sort. Many of these tools add to the long list of applications competing for employees' attention. In fact, many existing HR and learning systems already have some skills-based functionality. Each system has its own perspective on skills. For one, skills are about learning; for another, they are key to internal mobility or strategic workforce planning. These silos create different skill profiles, leading to a fragmented and exhausting experience. This situation creates challenges that scale as you try to do more with skills. If every use case adds more complexity and we can't reuse what was previously done, how can we ever expect skills to make a tangible difference?

To unlock the full potential of skills, we need a different approach. Instead of treating skills as just a feature in various products, we should see them as a data problem. The challenge is to create a sustainable, accurate, and trusted dataset of skills across the organization, and then connect this data to the systems and processes that need it. This requires infrastructure where skills data is produced and refined centrally for distributed consumption.

Many infrastructure projects involve significant up-front investments, but they pay off by making individual uses far more efficient. You wouldn't build a massive power plant for just one device; you'd use a small generator instead. In this line of thinking, many skills-based systems offer limited solutions to the skills-data problem. However, unlike power generators, these small implementations don't truly replace high-quality skills data, even for their own narrow use cases.

One key reason for this is that the systems needing skills information differ from those that people actually use to demonstrate skills. We don't often interact with core HR systems, but we use tools such as Microsoft Teams, Slack, and Jira all the time. Even with advanced AI, skills-based systems still lack a true understanding of relevant skills without actual data from these day-to-day tools. This leads to an over-reliance on employees manually entering their skills, resulting in incomplete profiles. A data-first approach, which leverages external data and ensures that signals propagate throughout all systems, addresses this issue.

A data-first approach also allows organizations to manage and govern skills data centrally, ensuring that it stays accurate, up-to-date, and consistent across all systems. Centralized management supports governance frameworks, data quality standards, and real-time updates as the business evolves. This way, every application—whether focused on learning, workforce planning, or internal mobility—relies on a single source of truth rather than conflicting views scattered across systems.

Historically, relying on individuals to maintain skills data manually has proved ineffective. Previous efforts, such as competency management, often failed, with frameworks left to gather dust in HR cabinets. Fortunately, recent advances in AI, combined with the exponential increase in digital data from our work, make maintaining a good baseline of skills data feasible across the organization.

For the first time, all the elements for a successful skills-based approach are available, including advanced technology, data infrastructure, and AI capabilities that can integrate skills data at scale. But not every approach will succeed. The key is to build solutions in the right places and address skills as a data problem from the outset. By treating skills as core data infrastructure—not just a feature in tools—organizations can fully realize the benefits of a skills-based approach. This means investing in centralized systems to manage and govern skills data while allowing it to flow seamlessly to the tools and processes that need it. Only then can the true value of a skills-based approach be unlocked.

CHAPTER 4
Assessing Organizational Readiness

In this chapter, we'll cover:
- Assessing your organization against the skills-based organization blueprint
- Identifying where skills data can have an impact in your organization
- Securing buy-in from leadership, managers, and employees
- Overcoming resistance

If you're thinking, "We need to be a skills-based organization," you're already thinking about this journey the wrong way. Instead, think about what business challenges your organization is facing. Which of those challenges are related to your workforce? Now you're on the right track.

Because becoming a skills-based organization is a major organizational change, and in many cases, a major culture shift for your organization as well, you need to ensure that you are focused on the problems that will be solved with deeper insights into your employees' skills, and that those problems are significant enough to warrant the investment of time and resources to enable the change. And not only do you need to understand the journey, goals, and benefits—your stakeholders need to understand as well.

> **Skills Tip**
> Start small and prove value as you go. One of the biggest obstacles organizations face in starting their skills journey is trying to "eat the whole elephant in one sitting." In most cases, that's a recipe for disaster. Set

expectations early so people know that evolving to becoming a skills-based organization is a multiphase journey with milestones along the way to measure progress and success. And, in getting started, select a problem to solve that's meaningful to the organization, allowing you to demonstrate the value of skills data and generate support to keep going.

Conducting a Needs Analysis

Your organizational needs analysis is important to clearly establish the business problems to solve with skills data in a way that connects with all the stakeholders across your organization. This section includes steps to follow when conducting a needs analysis.

1. Define Objectives

Imagine your skills evolution in its end state. What are you hoping to achieve? Smaller milestones or initiatives might be improving business or employee performance, preparing for a project, or addressing skills deficiencies identified in performance reviews. Larger objectives may focus on increasing employee retention, improving employee performance and business performance, or growing your organization's customer base or market share. The key to defining objectives is to clearly identify the problems to solve and what success looks like.

2. Identify Stakeholders and Participants

List the key roles and responsibilities of the people related to the problem to solve in your organization, department, or team. These are the people you will focus on to generate buy-in. Identify whether this problem affects them directly or indirectly, and what role they have in solving the problem. What have they already tried? What was the outcome of those attempts?

Just as important as identifying the stakeholders involved is understanding their motivation and the data they care about. For C-level executives, their motivation may be more closely tied to business-related outcomes and data; for individual contributors, it may be more closely related to compensation or career progression.

3. Determine Required and Key Skills

For each role or responsibility identified as part of the problem or solution, determine the required skills. These can be technical skills, soft skills, or a mix, depending on the problem. You don't need to do a full in-depth analysis—this is the high-level information needed to fully explain your solution, and how skills and skills data are part of the solution. To identify the required skills, you can reference job descriptions, industry standards, and performance benchmarks. You can also ask internal stakeholders, who may have firsthand knowledge of the skills gaps contributing to the problem.

4. Map the Solution Proposal

Once you've identified the problem to solve, the stakeholders, and the skills related to the problem, the final step is to propose a solution. Because most organizations don't have the skills data they need to easily make workforce decisions, the solution will likely involve some aspect of data collection and analysis before it can be implemented. Here is a way to structure the elements in a solution proposal that requires skills data to execute:

1. Data sourcing or collection strategy
2. Analysis
3. System or process implementation
4. Ongoing support needed for the solution

First, you have to identify what data is needed to power the solution. For example, if you've identified a need for your software developers to begin incorporating AI into their development practices to accelerate their velocity, you will need to know what AI skills currently exist on your software development team. Is this data already available somewhere? If so, where and how can you access it? If not, how could you collect that data?

> **Skills Tip**
>
> This is an example of how skills strategies can get stuck. If you make skills-data collection too complicated, you will likely stall in delivering a solution. Ask yourself, what is the least amount of data, at what level of validity, needed to make a decision at a particular risk level? For example, would you trust inferred or self-reported skills-level data to make learning recommendations? Would you trust it to make promotion decisions, or would you need multiple data points of higher validity? We'll dig deep on this in chapter 6, where we discuss the "three V's" of skills data.

Once you've collected the data, what analysis do you need to do to create the path forward? This is the second step in mapping your solution proposal, and a critical stage for validating it. Maybe you already suspect what the data will tell you, but prepare to be surprised, and to adjust your proposed solution. For example, if you have identified the business problem as increasing customer satisfaction scores in your call center, you may assume that the skills to target are human skills. However, you may find through your analysis that the issue is actually product knowledge or lack of familiarity with internal processes. Be prepared to support whatever skills gaps you find during the analysis phase.

> **Skills Tip**
>
> One pitfall in the analysis phase is having too little data to accurately diagnose a complex problem. Several years ago, I was working with a product team that had identified a list of features to sunset on its platform. The team had run an analysis of the least-used features and prioritized them for sunset. As I reviewed the list, one stood out to me as odd. I asked the team members what data they had used, and I asked them to cross-reference usage data with sales win-loss data and discuss it with the sales engineering team. It turns out that the feature they had flagged to sunset was a differentiator for us in the market, and although customers were rarely using it, it was one of the top reasons our product was selected over competitors'. By not understanding the full complexity of the situation, the product team had

considered only one point of view and one dataset. When drawing conclusions in your analysis, consider all the different aspects of the problem.

The third step, your proposal for implementing a new process or system, is when you really dig into the solution. What is the needed solution? And if there is a skills gap, what are the options to close that gap? Not surprisingly, you can get bogged down here if "the juice isn't worth the squeeze." Solutions need to make sense from a time and investment perspective to appeal to your stakeholders. This is also where data can play a key part in measuring impact.

There are lots of examples of skills strategies; here are a few:
- You've identified a skills gap in your sales team's ability to effectively communicate to customers how your product brings them value. You've done an analysis of the sales team's presentations and have identified product knowledge as an area where they are less confident and inconsistent in their presentations.
    - *Proposal:* Recommend product training.
- Your product development team has a 20-plus-year tenure on average; many members lack knowledge about newer technologies and systems. You've identified some key skills related to innovation initiatives, and the team rates very low in those skills.
    - *Proposal:* Upskill the team with innovation-intensive sessions, and create talent acquisition profiles for hiring new members to the team that highlight missing skills.
- Your company's employee retention rates are very low in a key area of your business. Your data analysis has identified a gap of leadership and management skills in the relatively young leaders on that team, resulting in a high turnover rate that is affecting the business.
    - *Proposal:* Recommend intensive leadership development training and a coaching program for new managers.

Some of these proposals might be implemented with lightweight changes to processes and better data analysis, while others might require investments in supporting resources, processes, or technologies. Mapping your recommended solution's costs to the anticipated benefits to the business is critical to make sure you can sell the benefits of your proposal to the organization.

Finally, you need to map the ongoing support costs and describe what your solution will need to be maintained. Are ongoing skills validations needed? Do you need to invest in platforms or technologies to make your processes more efficient or easier to manage? Think about not just a one-time solution, but a way to ensure that the problem you are solving will not reoccur.

Now that you have defined your objectives, identified your stakeholders and participants, determined the required and key skills, and mapped your proposed solution, it's time to create your pitch to generate buy-in for your solution.

Generating Buy-In From Stakeholders

Who? What? When? Where? How? Why? Not necessarily in that order, but those are the questions your stakeholders will have about getting started with skills. Think of generating buy-in as an exercise in storytelling, but the story that you tell will vary depending on the needs of your different stakeholder audiences. The audiences to consider include executive stakeholders, talent and human resources, learning and development, line of business leaders and managers, and employees.

Executive Stakeholders

These are the C-level executives who ultimately will fund your endeavor. They care about the underlying the reason for the investment, including the risk of not investing. They will want to understand the overall benefits to the business and the cost. They will also want to know the timeline and resources needed, both for short-term initiatives and the long-term investment plan. Paint the vision of the future for this audience, but also be very specific about how you will get started, and how you will measure success along the way. They will want to know the impact on business metrics specifically—will these initiatives help make more money? Save money? And how?

Skills Tip

I recommend one trick for communicating with executive stakeholders: Deliver the punch line first, and then support it with details. Along with a well-crafted presentation of a business case and plan, executives will want the executive summary of your proposal and will ask detailed questions (which you should have prepared for in your supporting slides or documents) about anything that is unclear in the summary or to dig in to your execution plan. Because many skills strategies are initiated by the C-suite, they will have a vested interest in supporting a successful start to the journey, as well as in understanding the timeline and process to reach your long-term goals. So, remember to speak their language when presenting and understand what's most important to your executive stakeholders.

Talent and Human Resources (HR)

In some organizations, the ownership of a skills strategy resides within talent and HR. Maybe that's where you are and what led you to this book! Whether you're part of talent and HR or not, however, generating buy-in with this group is critical to long-term, if not short-term, success.

The talent and HR group is concerned with supporting the people within the organization, so its interest will be people-related. How will your proposal help employees be successful in their roles? How will the data you are collecting help them make better decisions about investing in the workforce? They are also the audience that will most likely have questions about risks. Be prepared to answer questions about the data you're collecting, including the intended use cases and how the data collection adheres to data privacy and security requirements such as regulations around personally identifiable information, which vary globally. HR and talent will be key stakeholders that will be deeply interested in how the skills data you're collecting and analyzing can be trusted (we'll explore this topic more deeply in the following chapters).

HR and talent may ask questions about the scope of decisions that can be improved with skills data, beyond your first use case. As it will have a systems approach and think about how to scale point solutions, it's essential that talent and HR fully embraces the long-term vision of evolving to a skills-based organization. These stakeholders will also likely own any platforms or technologies related to skills, so they will need to be deeply invested in planning and monitoring progress of your skills journey proposal and engaged with IT to support any technology investments.

Learning and Development (L&D)

Besides talent and HR, learning and development teams are the other area of the business most likely to own an organization's skills strategy. In some organizations, these two groups fall under the same leadership; in others, L&D is a separate function. Some companies are now creating skills-specific teams and roles, which typically fall under talent and HR or L&D. Regardless of the structure, skills strategies are becoming a key collaboration point between HR and L&D, and creating bridges across the focus areas of the two functions.

While many of the needs that talent and HR focus on are shared by L&D, there are some unique differences. One of the concerns unique to L&D is how an organization's skills strategy may inform investments in learning. If an organization understands what skills its workforce has and what skills it needs, L&D is responsible for closing that skills gap. L&D can also use skill validation and measurement strategies to show the impact of learning initiatives on workforce skills, helping to finally answer the critical question: "What is the return on investment of learning?"

L&D areas of focus also fall into the web of skills data, mapping skills to content, job roles, and people through skills assessment and validation. Because L&D typically owns skills assessment activities, they are the keepers of the ongoing skills-data collection that helps organizations have insight into how skills in the workforce change over time.

Similar to talent and HR, L&D will often have questions about more systems-level approaches that can extend from your starting point use case. L&D will be interested in technology investments as well, and seek to understand how any proposed solution fits into the existing technology ecosystem. If L&D owns the company's learning management system or learning platforms, it may already have access to some skills technology or platform functionality that can support your solution proposal.

Line of Business Leaders and Managers

In any organization, as go its leaders, so goes the business. This makes leaders and frontline managers the connective tissue between your skills strategy and the steps needed to evolve to being skills-focused. If you don't sell the value to your middle management, generating buy-in from employees will be next to impossible. Why? Because almost every problem an organization faces needs to be solved by your people managers, directors, and vice presidents. They are the liaisons with the C-suite and your individual contributors; they are the peer group working together to make change happen.

To generate leadership buy-in, you need to both get them excited about the impact to the business, and make the benefits clear to them personally. The work you do at the leadership level to make change can make or break your initiative, and it's this audience that can be your eyes and ears for obstacles and impact.

Strategies to win their support are as varied as the leaders themselves, so for each leader, start with what business problem you can solve for them with your first proposed solution. Yes, you'll need to paint the picture of what the full evolution looks like and its benefits, but starting with the immediate need will help overcome any skepticism of the long-term vision.

Focus on areas where you can make their jobs easier through your solution. Ask yourself:
- Will you provide deeper insights into their teams?
- Can you offer more guidance for their team members on professional development?
- Will your solution give more clarity around career path opportunities or job readiness for new hires?
- Will your solution provide deeper data to support coaching conversations with their team members?

> **Skills Tip**
> Ensure that your solution doesn't require managers to take on more work in order to make the solution work! Many plans for change include a heavy lift for managers to make the change possible. Any skills solution should ultimately benefit all stakeholders, so think through the value to managers before you bring your proposed solution to them.

Getting managers on board with skills can be the keystone of organizational adoption because they are the catalysts for change. Be prepared for robust conversations and questions that get into the specifics on implementation and rollout. Think deeply about timing and the impact on managers and their teams—if your first area of goal is sales, don't roll it out at the end of the fiscal year, for example. Your focus for generating buy-in from leadership is to create champions who can explain the value as well as you do—so you must prepare in order to prepare them to be your allies and advocates.

Employees

What do employees need to know about your journey to becoming a skills-based organization?

The best way to secure employee buy-in is to frame your solution in terms of the value to them. Employees will likely be the most affected by your data strategy because you'll be capturing data about their skills and using it in new ways to help them in their career. Without framing the benefits of your skills-based solution in terms of "What's in it for me?," you run the risk of your skills solution being perceived as something that is being done to them, not with them or for them.

There are several benefits of skills-based organizations for employees; the trick is to meet your workforce where it is, and clearly communicate your short- and long-term intentions. Some common things that employees value are:

- More personalized or guided learning and development recommendations
- Visibility into potential career paths and opportunities

- Improving performance in their current role
- More relevant coaching conversations
- Leveling the playing field for internal mobility

Skills Tip

In some organizations, employees don't trust their companies to use data to support them. There have been instances in which skills data has been used for performance evaluations or even layoff decisions, leading employees to resist sharing any skills data or participating in data collection efforts. Beware how your company uses skills data and the cultural implications. No one will want to participate in sharing information when it could be used against them.

Think about how your proposed solution meets the immediate needs of employees, and start to build your story of the long-term vision of change to the organization becoming skills-based. Your aspirational goals, well communicated to employees, can help drive momentum and change. Gauge the sentiment of employee groups as you are communicating to get ahead of any detractors or resistance, and address questions clearly and transparently to build trust in the process.

Skills Tip

Who owns skills data? One of the pitfalls of creating a top-down system of data collection (inferring skills and manager ratings) is that employees may feel like they aren't aware of, or don't have a say in, what information is being gathered about them. Any system of collecting data that doesn't include employees in the process, or that doesn't center employees as owners of their skills data, is at high risk of failing. While inferring skills has been a trend to gather a lot of data quickly, beware the message that you are sending to employees by not including them in the process.

Overcoming Resistance

Each of the stakeholder groups outlined may have different areas of concern in moving forward with a skills-based strategy. Here are a few of the most common points of resistance, and strategies for overcoming them.

Trust in Skills Data

Objection: Is the skills data you're collecting accurate?

This is probably the hardest objection to answer succinctly, because of the complexities of skills data and what it means to different people and different organizations. We're going to do a deep dive into how to answer this question confidently from a data perspective in the upcoming chapters on skills data, but there's another way of thinking about this objection: What is causing hesitancy in the person raising the objection? There is a very good chance that they are more worried about the impact of making a bad decision based on skills data rather than the skills data being untrustworthy.

Here are some specific ways to answer:

- Skills data isn't (and shouldn't be) the only data used to make decisions.
- Would skills data enable better decisions than the data you're using to make those decisions today?
- Do you have buy-in and participation across the organization on validating skills data?

Often, when objections are raised about the validity of skills data, it's because the perception is that skills data will replace current mechanisms for making decisions or recommendations. The truth is that skills data should be seen as augmenting, not replacing, data currently used to make people-related decisions. By focusing on the additive value of skills data, and comparing the new process to existing decision-making processes, it becomes clear that having more data to make decisions is almost always better.

Trust in Use of Data to Make Decisions

Objection: What will this data be used for?

Whether or not you get this objection likely depends on your organizational culture, and you will most likely receive this question from employees and people managers. As mentioned previously in this chapter, when data has been weaponized by an organization, employees will remain suspicious of how data about them is being used. One example: I was on-site with a large insurance company, discussing the rollout of its skills strategy to its employees. One of the L&D leaders said, "I think it will be difficult to get people to rate their own skills, or to participate in this initiative at all." I asked why, and she mentioned that a year prior, the company had asked for each employee and manager to rate their skills, and the data was then used in making decisions related to a large layoff. When I heard that, we started to pivot the discussion to how to be transparent about how data would be used, but I was honest with them that this was a cultural trust issue that likely would not be solved only with clear communication about intended data use.

Your organization's specific culture of trust will dictate how much resistance you see to the collection of skills data. Here are some ways to overcome this objection, which may not happen overnight:

- Tell them what you're going to do, and then do what you said and show them you did it. Sometimes the only way to build trust is by demonstrating you're trustworthy. In these cases, overcommunicating and showing your work will help build trust over time.
- Start with small pilots and focus groups to build trust as you go.
- Bring resisters into the process to help convert them to promoters. By including folks who are hesitant in your initial groups, you'll identify their concerns so you can address them. You'll also (if you do it well!) ideally generate buy-in from early participants, who can act as evangelists across the organization.

Trust is something that is earned, so objections related to data usage and trust can be addressed only by building that trust over time.

Time, Expense, and Workload

Objection: This initiative will take too long, cost too much, or increase the workload of the team.

If an objection is raised about any of these aspects, it's because the person objecting has not bought in to the value of your solution. You should respond by providing as much data as you can about the potential impact and value to offset concerns about time and investment.

Before responding to this objection, determine which stakeholder group is objecting. Is it your C-level executives? If so, you need to emphasize and reinforce the business case. With this group, it is helpful to have an executive champion who is responsible for bringing the rest of the executive team along. If the initiative has support from the CEO, often that will drive the necessary buy-in from the group.

If the initiative is coming from talent and HR, or L&D, it's important to ensure that you also have buy-in from the line of business leaders. The focus of this group will be the anticipated return on investment, so lean in to that focus when responding to this objection.

If your resistance is coming from HR or L&D, make sure that you have not only sold the business context, but also created realistic timelines and distribution of responsibilities. Often, this is a prioritization and focus exercise because introducing new work to these teams may mean that other work is sidelined unless additional headcount is added.

If the objection is being raised by people managers, it's likely related to timing or workload. Ensure that you're aware of any other initiatives affecting the targeted teams and confirm that your proposal won't conflict. Also be very clear about the work required from managers and their teams to set appropriate expectations. In some cases, managers and leaders may not have the power to push back (especially if you have C-level buy-in), but you need to make your proposal as easy for them as possible. Selling the value to this group is important; focus on the value to the business, the value to their teams, and the value to them personally.

Skills Tip

For leaders, supporting or resisting organizational changes is sometimes a strategic career move. Leaders who aspire to continue their growth will want to support initiatives that align with the needs of the business and have a high likelihood of success because these can be career-defining moves. Similarly, if an initiative doesn't have strong support, leaders are less likely to want to be associated with it. Ensure that your proposal gains traction and attracts advocates by focusing on value and marketing your successes along the way. Everyone wants to be on the winning team!

Finally, if resistance is coming from employees, it's most likely because of workload. Data collection strategies such as inferring skills seek to remove the burden on employees to provide skills data, but the trade-off is that employees may not feel like the data inferred accurately represents their skill sets. This is another audience that is best served by starting small and building value—rather than one big heavy lift period, spread work out over time to minimally affect employees' workload.

Agreement on What Skills Are Important

Objection: Are you focused on the right skills?

I might be biased, but I think this is one of the easier objections to handle because consensus building and data can override opinions. When considering what skills to focus on for your proposal, there are different ways to prioritize (which we'll discuss in detail in upcoming chapters). But truly, this objection is questioning whether the skills you're focused on are the skills that will address the problem you've identified to solve. The best way to handle it is to map the problem and solution to skills, which can be done by:

- Looking at skills ontologies or mapping systems and identifying which skills are related to which job roles, jobs to be done, or tasks
- Surveying your internal experts and stakeholders for the problem to solve and building your skills priorities based on their feedback

If there are differing opinions on root cause or even skills to address, you can see if a solution is having an impact by starting small. If not, you can pivot. Responding to this objection may just be a matter of clarifying the stage gates for measuring impact, with planned steps to pivot if necessary.

Agreement on the Definition of a Skill

Objection: How are you defining skills? Do you need to create a whole ontology of skills to get started?

Briefly, the answer to these objections are "flexibly" and "no." To get started with skills, you don't need a defined ontology, nor do you need a very specific definition of skills. My recommendation to overcome this objection is to have a plan for which base ontology you will use (there are several crafted by different companies and associations, and any of them is a reasonably good base), and then be sure that skills data can be captured at multiple levels of specificity and that skills ontologies should evolve over time to stay relevant. In the time it would take you to define a static ontology, it would likely already be outdated. The most important thing is to get started and mold your base ontology over time to be specific for your organization.

> **Skills Tip**
> All of these potential objections have one thing in common: They benefit from having a "land and expand" strategy to start. If you start small, focus on solving a specific problem, and show the benefits and impact, you can earn trust to do more and expand the scope and investment in your journey to becoming skills-based.

Determining Risk and the Risk Comfort of Your Organization

When it comes to people decisions, there are several factors to consider in determining risk:

- Is this an HR risk or a business risk? (The two are differentiated here by risk associated with human capital management areas or a company's financial results; they may not be mutually exclusive.)
- Is this a legal risk or a reputational risk?
- Is this a decision that can be reversed or changed?

There are many different HR risk assessment models; chances are your HR team already uses a model to conduct risk assessments. Using skills data for decision making creates an additional opportunity to use that model, the results of which may determine whether you need to invest more in skills-data quality, or which internal use cases would be best to begin your skills journey. But one simple way of determining risk comfort is to plot the decision on a risk-trust matrix (Table 4-1).

Table 4-1. Risk-Trust Matrix for Skills Data

High Risk, Low Trust Can you trust this data to make this decision?	High Risk, High Trust Can you ensure that data quality remains high?
Low Risk, Low Trust What data is "good enough" for these use cases?	Low Risk, High Trust Are you overinvesting in data quality?

For example, if you have a high-risk decision and you have new, highly trusted skills data to help inform that decision, you may want to prioritize that use case for your skills-based journey to reduce the risk. However, if you have only low-validity skills data, you might choose to delay using skills data to inform a high-risk decision until you have a strategy to collect higher-validity data.

What are some examples of high- and low-risk decisions that could be informed by skills data?

- High-risk decisions might include:
    - **Compliance**—legal risks and penalties resulting from noncompliance
    - **Recruiting and hiring**—failure to find and hire top talent
    - **Retention**—failure to retain top talent and key skills
    - **Compensation**—introduction or perpetuation of inequitable compensation
    - **Employee relations**—poor culture or employee engagement

- Low-risk decisions may include:
    - Learning activity recommendations
    - Career pathing recommendations
    - Coach or mentor matching

Organizational comfort with risk varies considerably depending on the culture and the leaders of the organization, as well as the location of the business. Regional differences exist around handling personally identifiable information, and data privacy and security standards may fall under different legal requirements based on the country or countries where the business operates. Because there are a range of approaches to skills data (to be discussed more in the following chapters), it is important to identify your organization's risk tolerance and data policies up front.

To prepare for these questions in advance, make sure your HR, legal, and data teams are part of your readiness assessment, as well as your strategy planning team. Getting the right people involved early can help avoid stumbling blocks as you consider the first steps on your skills journey.

Conclusion

Once you've identified the business problem to solve—along with the proposed solution and how it could contribute to a long-term vision—and successfully generated buy-in across your organization, you'd think the hard part would be over! But implementing the blueprint for a skills-based organization is a complex data problem, and as you embark on the process, it's important to have a perspective on how you'll tackle it for your organization. Your skills data strategy is the keystone for success in your skills journey. Let's dig in on skills data in the following chapters.

Creating a Skills-Focused Development Strategy in a Small-to-Medium-Sized Organization

Contributed by Matt Hayward, Global Learning Manager, Medical Protection Society

An L&D strategy focused on skills development has traditionally been the realm of larger organizations. Developing the foundations to focus on skills development, such as identifying skills and creating a comprehensive skills taxonomy, can require resources that smaller organizations would not be able to prioritize above more-pressing challenges. However, with advancements in technology, it's time for smaller organizations to rethink this because it is arguably more important for smaller organizations to underpin their learning and talent strategies with a skills focus.

I argue that smaller organizations require a focus on skills because of the depth and breadth of skills that individuals need to acquire. Larger organizations have the luxury of specialization areas because of their scale, and with that a focus on technical skills.

However, individuals in smaller organizations need to technically perform in their primary function, but also rely on nontechnical skills—such as influencing, negotiation, and stakeholder management—to be effective in executing that function. If smaller organizations want individuals to be more effective in their roles, they need to look at all the skills required to be effective in that role, not just the technical skills.

I'll give an example: A system tester in an IT department at a large organization may be responsible for creating and running test scripts with the team leader or manager responsible for the project liaison. However, in a smaller organization with limited resources to support change, a system tester may also be part of project meetings and the point of contact for testing within the project; therefore, they will require a broader skill set, such as effective communication, stakeholder management, and influencing.

If smaller organizations do not recognize this nuance and identify these skills, then they won't be able to set individuals up to be truly effective in their roles.

Using AI to Develop Skills Taxonomies

A skills development strategy starts by identifying the skills needed within an organization, both present and future, to achieve the organizational strategy. Only a few years ago, identifying all the skills and applying a criterion to then indicate how the skill would be demonstrated at different levels would have taken a substantial amount of time and resources to develop. But with generative AI tools such as ChatGPT, this can now be done in a matter of weeks and with reduced resources. I know; I have done it! In three weeks, I was able to map more than 130 skills relevant to my organization and create criteria across five levels. A number of these skills were then ratified with the relevant departments to ensure that they were representative, and barring a few tweaks, the skills we did ratify were largely on point for what they would expect to see.

Developing a skills taxonomy for an organization is not as time consuming or resource heavy as it once was, allowing smaller organizations to find an equilibrium with larger organizations and gain some of the competitive advantages that having well-skilled employees brings to larger organizations.

But it doesn't stop there; a well-defined skills taxonomy and clear criteria aid in the facilitation of richer and deeper development discussions.

Supporting Better Development Discussions and Planning

In smaller organizations today, we expect a lot from leaders. They must run their departments, deliver on strategic objectives, oversee budgeting and financial processes, and support and nurture their teams. But let's be honest; when all is said and done, the operation will always be a priority. Asking them to analyze everyone on their team, the skills required, and then how those employees are performing against those skills will play second fiddle to delivering for the organization, so we need to help them. Identifying the skills required in a role, and having clear criteria for expected skills levels, helps the leader frame the development conversation and gives them a road map. Also, it gives individuals clear expectations and allows them to hold their leader accountable for how they'll support them in achieving that level.

Leaders have expressed to me that having these tools in place will also allow them to have trickier development discussions around personal effectiveness skills, which can be overlooked for fear of upsetting someone. If the criteria are spelled out clearly in the skills framework, the discussion can be around the evidence and demonstration. Individual and strategic development plans can then be built to address any skills gaps in the organization, ensuring the correct targeting of resources and budget.

Developing Skills With Fewer Resources

The final piece of the puzzle is how you provide development for all the skills that you have identified when you have limited resources. Naturally, if you identify skills that you want individuals in your business to have or develop, other leaders will be asking how that will be supported. Smaller organizations won't have the deep pockets that larger organizations have.

After my analysis of the skills and the criteria that exist where I work, a common theme became apparent. As individuals level up through a particular skill, development becomes more about experiences and scope of work than it does about principles, models, knowledge, and theory. We have applied five levels to our framework, and level 5 talks more about application of a skill at the organizational strategic level, whereas levels 1 and 2 focus more on acquiring the base knowledge and principles regarding a skill and starting to apply it. Using cost-effective tools such as LinkedIn Learning alongside coaching and mentoring can aid in the development of base knowledge and principles. Then, levels 3, 4, and 5 focus on experiences and scope of work, while still being supported by coaching and mentoring.

In the end, organizations do not need to spin up large L&D functions to support their skills strategy; there are plenty of cost-effective solutions out there and within the organization to develop skills effectively.

PART 2
Planning and Strategizing for Skills

When I began thinking about writing a book on skills, this is the core of what I wanted to write. In fact, if you read only this part of the book and find value, I would be OK with that. While becoming a skills-based organization is complex, and so many organizations get stuck sorting through the multitude of skills-data-related decisions, my hope is these chapters can help guide you through the various decision-making layers of skills and skills data and help you anticipate the potential obstacles to using skills data effectively.

CHAPTER 5
Defining Skills Data

In this chapter, we'll cover:
- Dissecting what a skill is and the differences among skills, competencies, and other terms
- Determining ways to group skills to make them meaningful in different organizational contexts
- Considering proficiency levels in skill assessment

So, what are these skills that everyone is talking about? To begin a skills journey, you have to have a common language. It may seem like semantics, but understanding what skills are will make the complex conversations further down the line much easier.

What Is a Skill?

It seems like defining what a skill is should be simple, but it's probably one of the hardest and most foundational parts of your data strategy. Every organization on a skills journey has resolved what a skill means for its team, and unfortunately, each has landed on a slightly different definition. If your organization has already worked through this process, this section may be a review or validation of decisions it has already made. If your organization hasn't yet defined what a skill is, this section will help focus and streamline the process.

So, what is a skill?

> A skill is a thing you can do. Or, more formally, a skill is the use of one's knowledge to perform or execute a task.

A skill has both elements of understanding and the ability to do things, which can be at different levels. This knowing-doing gap explains why knowledge assessments are insufficient to measure a skill and why skills are more meaningful to correlate to work performance. It means that skill assessment and validation need to focus on behavioral evidence in combination with knowledge.

This critical implication can help guide organizations to focus on defining the skills that are meaningful to them.

> A skill is the use of one's knowledge to perform or execute a task that can be measured.

The ability to measure a behavior is essential to being able to measure a skill. If it is difficult to determine how to measure a particular skill, maybe it's not really a skill, but an attribute, or a cluster of behaviors. Think about customer service as an example. Can you measure customer service? Maybe at a high level, but it would be hard to do without breaking it down into measurable behavioral elements, such as oral communication or problem solving. Skills categories or groupings such as customer service, leadership, or project management more likely align to many different skills that can be measured and then aggregated to tell a story about a person's competencies in their job role. (We'll touch on skills categories and competencies later in the chapter.)

Some organizations have included attributes or characteristics in their definition of skills. For example, "creativity" is a relatively common skill in organizational ontologies. But how would you measure creativity? One organization I worked with had a skill of "lifelong learning." When challenged with how to measure these types of proposed skills, the real decisions are:

- How can you collect evidence of the skill?
- How do you want to report the evidence of the skill?

Take leadership as another example. I would argue that leadership is a category or cluster of skills that can be measured. Collecting evidence of these individual skills (including conflict resolution, storytelling, and coaching) is easier and more useful for targeting skills development. But your organization may also want to understand someone's holistic skills level for leadership, which would necessitate aggregating the different types of skills evidence into a singular measure of "leadership." You lose the detailed nuance, but you can tell a simpler story across a large population by looking at leadership as a sum of its parts rather than each part on its own. So, is leadership a skill? That will vary across organizations. Emerging technology can help create connections to smooth out some of the challenging gray areas of determining what a skill is.

Different Kinds of Skills

There are different types of skills, just as there are different kinds of things you can do (and measure). While different organizations may give these types of skills different names, for simplicity's sake, I'll talk about three types of skills that are present simultaneously when we work:

- **Job skills** are the skills you need to do a specific type of work. For example, demand generation marketing, quality assurance review, and building a road map for a product are all job skills. Different jobs and job roles will have different types of required skills, and in some cases, the same skills may be required for different types of jobs or work. Many job skills are uncovered by asking employees more deeply about the work they do every day.
- **Technical skills** are the skills needed to use the technology, machinery, equipment, and so on associated with work that needs to be done. Many technical skills are job specific, and sometimes they are company specific. If you are applying for a sales job, the company may want to understand your skills related to Salesforce; if you are applying for an HVAC job, your experience with different types of heating or cooling systems may be important. Technical skills can be identified by asking about the software, hardware, or other tools an employee uses to do their work.
- **Human skills**—also known as "soft skills," "power skills," "noncognitive skills," "social-emotional skills," and "core

skills"—refer to the skills that all humans have to some extent, and that are used no matter what type of work you are doing. Human skills include written communication, problem solving, conflict resolution, and so forth. They are typically a set list of skills that have been identified through different models. As a data point, human skills might be the skills that you measure for all employees.

Unpacking the Complexity of Competencies

Depending on whom you ask (whether it's a psychometrician, an educator, a data scientist, or an organization development consultant), you'll likely get a different answer about what a competency is. It only adds to the confusion in defining *skill* when we struggle to define *competency*.

For the purposes of this book, let's go with a workplace-friendly definition: A competency is a set of skills, knowledge, and personal attributes that an employee needs to perform a job or task. In other words, if your job is customer service representative, then the competency of customer service would be made up of all the skills you need to perform as a customer service representative, all the things you need to know to be a customer service representative, and the attributes or personality traits that are important to the job, such as empathy and curiosity.

This definition can help answer the question of how to bundle skills to share meaningful metrics. A competency of "people manager" or "leadership" could be a way for you to differentiate between a single skill and a bundle of skills, even outside a specific job role. Thinking about competencies as a way to aggregate skills provides a framework for sense-making within your organization, one that's as important in telling a story as understanding what a skill is. It also provides context to employees to answer the question: What skills do I need to be successful in my role?

Competencies are usually developed through education and training, so they can be closely tied with job-training programs or onboarding programs for new hires. Competencies are often targeted in upskilling or reskilling initiatives in organizations and can be tied to metrics such as job readiness.

Is Knowledge an Indicator of Skill?

Knowledge is a theoretical understanding of something, such as facts, information, and principles. It can be acquired through education or experience (which is why knowledge is sometimes a prerequisite to a skill).

Having knowledge of something is different from being skilled in it. I know a lot about football, but I would never say I'm a skilled football player. Similarly, someone could learn a lot about the principles of baking, but that doesn't mean that their cupcakes will be delicious. Most golfers know the rules of golf and even the principles of a good swing, but the skill of golf is something that requires extensive practice for most players.

For some skills, knowledge is a must. It would be difficult to be a software developer without understanding how coding languages work. Learning the principles of negotiation means that you can begin to practice them and improve your negotiating. Going back to baking, some knowledge of cooking and baking is a must to understand recipe instructions (In the infamous words of Moira Rose from *Schitt's Creek*, "Fold it in, David!", referring to a recipe direction that neither understood, which instructed them to "fold in the cheese.").

Can knowledge indicate skill? Assessing knowledge alone will create an incomplete picture of someone's skills and capabilities, but knowledge can be a signal, if not proof, of skill.

How Is a Behavior Related to a Skill?

A *behavior* is something you do, but a skill is something you can do repeatedly, in different contexts.

When I worked for a company with a large library of video-based courses, the most popular video was how to build a pivot table in Excel. I myself used that video to help me build pivot tables, at least a few times a year. The truth is, I never really learned how to build a pivot table and would use the video to help me every time. On those occasions, my behavior was to build a pivot table, but I never had that skill (and still don't, to be honest).

Behaviors are observable, and in that way, they can be used as evidence of a skill, but with caution—just because someone demonstrates a behavior doesn't necessarily mean they possess a related skill.

Personality Traits

Many organizations leverage personality assessments to better understand how their employees' or teams' personalities affect workplace interactions and success. While disagreements abound on how legitimate personality assessments are, we know that personality traits affect us at work, and it is meaningful to understand how they influence our work and careers.

Is a personality trait a skill? I would have answered no before doing a deep dive into the literature, but there is a wide body of research that categorizes personality traits as a subset of social-emotional skills (Laible et al. 2020).

Social-emotional skills are human skills that relate to relationships and emotions. Examples of social-emotional skills that are also considered personality traits include:

- **Self-awareness**—recognizing your emotions and how they affect your behavior
- **Self-management**—taking control of your thoughts, emotions, and actions
- **Social awareness**—putting yourself in others' shoes and acting with empathy
- **Integrity**—adhering to moral and ethical standards
- **Perseverance**—exhibiting follow-through
- **Confidence**—believing in your abilities

Personality traits have been linked to job performance, employment, and wage growth. Recent research suggests that employers increasingly value social-emotional skills over cognitive abilities because social skills facilitate better teamwork, reduce coordination costs, and contribute to the overall performance of firms (Laible et al. 2020).

So, is a personality trait a skill? Yes and no. Yes, personality traits are skills that may affect work performance, and could provide valuable insights into job performance and team dynamics. But personality traits are not as easily learnable or trainable as other human skills, and even less so than job skills or technical skills. Personality assessments are less reliable than behavioral or performance assessments and should be considered with caution as a stand-alone metric in making people decisions. When it comes to building your skills strategy to create a skills-based organization, human skills related to behaviors will be more valuable than personality traits for gathering reliable skills data for decision making.

Mindsets

Mindsets and skills are two distinct but related aspects of personal and professional development. To repeat, a *skill* is an individual's use of knowledge to perform or execute a task that can be demonstrated through actions and outcomes and acquired through education, training, practice, and experience. In contrast, a *mindset* is an individual's attitudes, beliefs, and perspectives; it influences how that person approaches challenges, learning opportunities, and setbacks, and it can influence various aspects of their life, including their career, relationships, and overall well-being.

A popular example is a growth mindset, which is characterized by a willingness to learn, embrace challenges, and persist through setbacks. A growth mindset is highly valuable in learning, and it's a critical skill employees need to adapt to the rapidly changing needs of the modern workforce.

While skills are often the focus at the beginning of a person's career, their mindset can become increasingly important as they progress. Some say that mindsets are more important than skills, and that employers are more interested in attitude than skill, but any organization that is embarking on its skills journey has made the decision that skills are a critical part of the conversation. A positive mindset only goes so far when an organization needs skills and experience to stay competitive in the market. A good attitude plus skill is the best of both worlds—demonstrating what you can do and how you do it.

Data Relationships in Building a Skills Strategy

How do these all relate to skills? As you are identifying your skills-data structure, as well as the types of data to collect to build your skills database, think about them in this way:

- **Skills**—baseline data for skills
- **Tasks**—description of the work to be done
- **Job, technical, and human skills**—different skills data categories
- **Competencies**—skills data plus job context
- **Knowledge**—what someone knows (can be a prerequisite to a skill or behavior)
- **Behaviors**—what someone does (can be evidence of a skill if the behavior can be repeated)
- **Personality traits and mindsets**—give context to skills and how they may be applied or show up at work

As you begin to identify sources of these different types of data, you can build relationships among them, specifically related to jobs and roles. For different use cases, different data points may be important.

For example, if you're looking to fill a software engineering role, you may rely more heavily on technical skills and competency data to screen qualified candidates. If you're hiring for an engineering director, you may focus more on human skills. If you are looking to build a team that works well together, you may consider the technical skills required for different roles on the team, as well as human skills and personality traits to select complementary or diverse team members.

Understanding the different types of data related to skills can help you identify what types of data you have, and what data you need to empower more informed decisions.

Another important aspect of skills is that they are rarely applied in isolation. While you may document or assess them separately, job skills, technical skills, and human skills are typically used together in context.

Let's take a sales scenario: trying to close a SaaS deal. A sales representative needs to understand the process for contracting (a job skill), how to use Salesforce to document their deal parameters (a technical skill), how to negotiate with the customer on final deal terms (a human skill), and perseverance (a personality trait) in getting the deal to close as quickly as possible. Yes, all these skills are observable and measurable separately, but as we go about our daily work, we leverage them in combination to do our jobs successfully and hit achievement milestones.

It's also true that if you have one skill, you likely possess related skills. As we assess skills, we can make some assumptions or connections. For example, if I am a user experience designer and have user experience design skills, it is highly likely that I have prototyping skills, technical skills using Figma, or user research skills. As we dig into skills ontologies and skills inference, we'll see that AI and machine learning can help us better understand the connection and relationship among skills, in terms of both how skills are combined to be successful at work and how they give insight into someone's potential range of skill adjacencies based on what we know about their skills.

Grouping Skills

Many organizations want to add context to skills to make them meaningful in different situations. There are two main ways that organizations group skills: by job role or function and by skill category.

Grouping Skills by Job Role or Function

Your organization may be most driven by how skills relate to work, so it may want to organize its skills data around job roles. This process looks something like this:

- Identify the job roles within a team or department. For each role, identify the skills required to be successful.
- Assess employees against those skills.
- Build development or hiring plans to close skills gaps.
- Repeat this process at some regular cadence.

This is a very pragmatic approach to setting baseline skills data, and with buy-in and available data sources, organizations can move relatively quickly to arrange skills data in this way. It's also a skills-based strategy that allows you to start small (you can limit your scope to specific, critical roles) or use inference models to get a lot of data quickly.

The biggest challenge with this approach is the speed of change in an organization, specifically around job roles needed and the skills required for those roles. In a market with more and more project-based work, two people with the same job may be working on very different types of work and need different skills. Organizations may hire people for desirable skills and then deploy them on different projects where their skills can be best utilized, often on teams that need diverse skill sets to be represented. Some workforce professionals have begun to imagine a future without job roles, in which skill combinations are assessed and assigned to the work that needs to be done. This may seem radical, but this model allows for more flexibility in adapting to the rapidly changing needs of the market and the dynamic nature of work. For organizations that build a skills strategy around job roles, a move to this type of model would require a full reimagining, and because building a skills-data strategy is a complex, long-term investment, some companies are opting to move away from job roles as the focus of their skills-data organization.

Another major challenge is the potential for bias. If you have a static list of skills needed for a particular role, it's easy to assume that someone in a role can be successful only if they have those skills. Often, it's actually a diversity of skills that make teams successful, and a cookie-cutter approach to what good looks like will limit your insight into potential high-performing employees. Take the SaaS sales rep example—some sales representatives are highly skilled in relationship building and negotiation, and they hit their targets based on the strength of the relationships they have with their customers. Other sales reps are focused on following the process, with high attention to detail in following the steps to get their deals closed. Both sales reps may be highly successful in closing their deals, but their skills profiles would look very different. And just like sales reps with different mixes of skills, different customers have different personalities, cultures, and needs—and therefore might respond better to one type of rep over another. There is rarely a one-size-fits-all list of skills for a particular job role, so focusing on skills related to jobs could become an oversimplified, and biased, approach if not designed to identify the critical skills for success with allowances for variations in what good looks like.

Grouping Skills by Skills Category

Another approach companies are taking to organize their skills data is by skills category. This approach demands that organizations define the skills data they care about, and then cluster those skills into related groups. For example, social-emotional skills might be a category of skills that an organization defines for the entire organization, but job skills or technical skills might be defined by department or function, such as leadership, marketing demand generation, and project management.

This approach has multiple advantages. First, the nature of work is changing rapidly, and most jobs are no longer static. In a model that groups skills by jobs, an organization runs the risk of constantly having to reorganize its skills grouping architecture as jobs change. This is an extra level of complexity—with a job-centered model, you also have to constantly evaluate and update the jobs and roles within your organization, then evaluate if the skills related to those jobs have changed, and then update your skills groupings accordingly. This extra layer might be minimal in organizations with jobs that don't change regularly, but for more dynamic organizations, this is more work. By grouping skills by category, you can evaluate which skills are needed in a particular category separately from evaluating which skills are required for certain roles.

A second advantage is the ability to evaluate skills evolution for categories without depending on job architecture. For example, if you are able to evaluate emerging skills for AI, those skills might be relevant across your entire organization but applied differently based on a role. This works for human skills as well, which are skills everyone possesses independent of their job in an organization.

A third advantage is the ability to easily show skill adjacencies and cluster skills that are related to one another. Grouping skills by category means you can quickly see what adjacent or related skills someone might (or should!) have once you establish a skill in that grouping. If a user experience designer has prototyping skills, they likely have or should have user research skills, and this is something that can be assessed and flagged for development if needed.

There are some cons in moving forward with grouping skills based on skills category. For one, in this model, you don't see the relationship between skills and the jobs or work that needs to be done, so you will still need to map skills to jobs. Luckily, this is something that AI and inference models can increasingly tackle (at least to establish a first pass that you can refine). But, know that the relationship between skills and work is an important one for many of the use cases for skills data, so this mapping will still need to be done.

The other main con for grouping skills by category is that you need to define the skills categories. This could be a fairly easy lift for some organizations, depending on their comfort level with data architecture, but for others, this can be a time-consuming effort.

> **Skills Tip**
>
> To move past this step quickly, it can be helpful to break skills initially into job skills, technical skills, and human skills, and then define categories or groups within those three buckets.

Proficiency Levels and Skills

Many organizations start by thinking about what skills are, and then jump to assessing and measuring skills without considering proficiency levels. Proficiency relates to how well you can do something; in relation to skills, it refers to how proficient you are in that skill.

Proficiency levels are the solution to providing a deeper level of insights into skills. There is no standard for measuring skill proficiency, so each organization needs to determine the proficiency levels it would like to measure against, and the definitions of those levels.

While most organizations I've worked with select a 3-, 4-, or 5-level scale, I've seen everything from a binary scale (you have the skill or you don't) to a 100-level scale. The challenge in selecting a scale is balancing two divergent problems: If you have too few levels, it's difficult to show skills growth or development as a person learns and practices a skill; however, if you have too many levels, it becomes difficult to determine the difference between levels. For example, in the case of a 100-level scale, what is the meaningful difference between a level 67 and a level 74?

I'll share an example of a five-level system that I think works well as a rubric for organizations that are looking for a starting point for their own skills-leveling decisions:

- Level 1. Beginning
- Level 2. Developing
- Level 3. Proficient
- Level 4. Advanced
- Level 5. Expert

Level 1. Beginning

The individual demonstrates limited awareness and understanding of the skill. Their actions may be inconsistent, and they often require significant guidance.

Characteristics:
- Shows minimal understanding or capability
- Frequently makes errors or struggles to apply the skill
- Requires constant supervision or assistance
- Lacks confidence and is unable to perform without direct support

Example: Can describe the skill in basic terms but cannot apply it independently.

Level 2. Developing

The individual demonstrates a growing awareness and some application of the skill. Their performance may still be inconsistent, but they are beginning to show improvement.

Characteristics:
- Demonstrates some understanding but with noticeable gaps
- Applies the skill with moderate success in simple situations
- Still requires support and feedback but shows signs of improvement
- May lack confidence in applying the skill independently

Example: Can perform the skill with guidance in familiar situations but struggles with more complex applications.

Level 3. Proficient

The individual consistently demonstrates competence in the skill in familiar and routine contexts. They can perform the skill without supervision, but they may still require occasional guidance.

Characteristics:
- Shows solid understanding and application in familiar situations
- Rarely makes significant errors and can self-correct when needed
- Can work independently but may seek help in complex situations
- Demonstrates confidence and reliability in most tasks

Example: Consistently applies the skill in day-to-day tasks and can adapt to common challenges with minimal support.

Level 4. Advanced

The individual demonstrates a high level of competence and can apply the skill in complex or unfamiliar situations with minimal support. Their actions show depth and efficiency in performance.

Characteristics:
- Demonstrates deep understanding and applies the skill effectively in a wide range of contexts
- Consistently produces high-quality results with minimal errors
- Solves complex problems independently and efficiently
- Confidently adapts the skill to new or challenging situations

Example: Can teach others the skill and apply it in unfamiliar or challenging contexts with ease.

Level 5. Expert
The individual demonstrates mastery and innovation in the skill, consistently excelling beyond standard expectations. They are able to guide, mentor, and set best practices in the skill area.

Characteristics:
- Demonstrates an exceptional understanding and skill application
- Innovates or improves existing methods and techniques
- Routinely mentors others and leads complex problem-solving efforts
- Expertly adapts to any situation and consistently produces superior results

Example: Serves as an authority on the skill, offering new insights and guiding others to proficiency.

Skills-Proficiency-Scale Mapping

Once you have selected your organization's proficiency scale for skills, the fun is not over! Because different assessments and skills validation tools use different scales, and most organizations use different internal assessments with their own scales, you'll need to be able to map any skills assessment scale to your proficiency scale. For example, if you choose to move forward with a five-level scale, and you have a skills assessment that uses an eight-point scale, you'll have to map the results from that assessment to your five levels.

One model that works with many assessments that use a "percent correct" to report their results is to set achievement percentages that match your levels. For example, if you are assessing negotiation skills, you may be able to map your "percent correct" on the assessment as a signal of proficiency level.

> **Skills Tip**
> A single data point or assessment is likely not enough data to make a highly confident claim on skills proficiency. To increase your confidence level, you should aggregate multiple data points that indicate proficiency and analyze for agreement among those data points.

Skills Tip

The difficulty level of an assessment factors into what the results of an assessment can indicate. If an assessment is designed to assess someone's expertise, then the following model could work to signal to the highest proficiency level. However, if an assessment is designed only to test reasonable proficiency to apply a skill and not to assess for expertise, then a high score in that assessment would not correlate to advanced or expert levels, but only to the maximum proficiency level that the assessment is designed to measure.

Skills, Proficiency, Prediction, and Potential

The trifecta of skills-based decisions includes knowing what someone can do at a certain level of capability, as well as their potential for future growth (Figure 5-1).

Figure 5-1. Degree of Difficulty to Measure Related to Level of Prediction

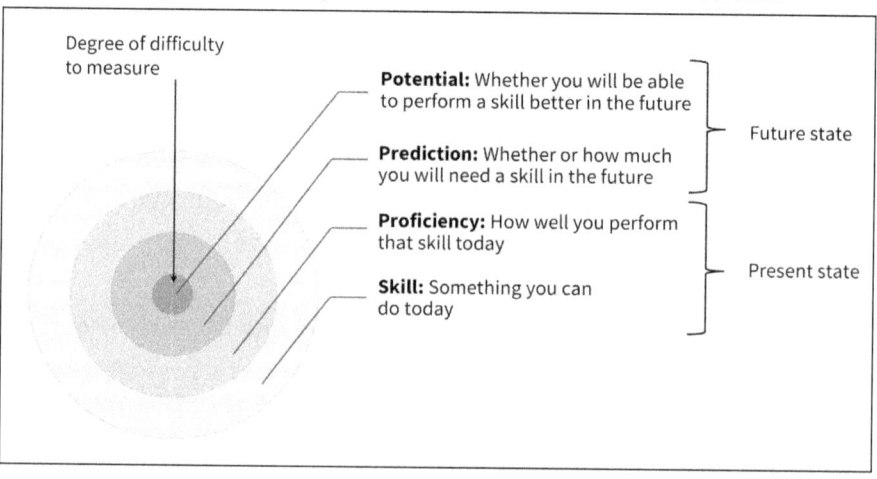

Embarking on a skills journey requires you to view skills data from multiple windows. Instead of looking back on job history or educational credentials, these windows are forward-looking and predictive. The types of questions that skills data is best suited to answer are questions that represent the current state or predict the future-state. For example, an employee could ask what skills they should develop to perform better in their current role or to prepare for the next step in their career. In either case, skills data is being used to answer predictive questions and make deeper recommendations on development to prepare for the future.

When you add in layers of proficiency data, you are adding complexity to the current- and future-state lens. Not only do you need to understand someone's proficiency today, you also must predict what proficiency will be required of them in the future, given their current role and potential future role.

That leads us to predicting potential. Skills initiatives are founded on predictions, and humans are, in this predictive lens, evaluated on potential—to build a skill or be successful in a role. Can we really evaluate human potential in a skills initiative?

A better way to answer that question is to step back and acknowledge we are evaluating potential daily, whether there is data to support our intuition or not. Skills data can help us refine our current assessment of potential. It can do that in several ways. Skills data provides an objective, measurable framework for assessing an individual's abilities and competencies, reducing the reliance on subjective judgments. By analyzing data from sources such as certifications, project outcomes, work performance, and training completions, organizations can gain a clear and precise understanding of an employee's current expertise. This data-driven approach ensures more accurate talent identification and development, enabling businesses to make informed decisions about role placements and career advancement.

Skills data plays a crucial role not only in identifying gaps in an employee's skills, but also in understanding the relationship of skills adjacencies. When organizations have access to detailed insights into an employee's skills profile, they can develop personalized learning and development plans that focus on closing gaps or assessing and developing related skills. Potential can be assessed by analyzing which skills an employee already has and how closely related, or far apart, missing skills are from their current skill set. For example, the skills overlap between a financial analyst and a data security engineer is quite high, so we could predict that success in one role would have a high correlation to success in the other. The skills overlap between a content marketer and a software engineer is very low, so the potential for a software engineer to be a successful marketer is low.

In addition to evaluating current capabilities, skills data can be a powerful tool for predicting future success by looking at human skill and behavioral data signals. By tracking patterns in skills acquisition, continuous learning, and demonstrated growth, organizations can identify high-potential employees who are likely to excel in leadership roles or other strategic positions. Patterns of behavior in developing skills, as well as showing investment in human skills that relate to agility and adaptability, are all signals that can help predict future performance, even under conditions of uncertainty or rapid change.

But using skills data in assessing potential has its limitations. First, skills data is an incomplete picture of human potential. No one can really predict the future, and skills data is still a reflection of what someone has already done rather than what they can do in the future. It's also more difficult to assess some of the most predictive human skills, such as creativity, adaptability, and motivation. Because these skills are more difficult to assess than job skills or technical skills, you may inadvertently underestimate individuals with significant untapped potential. Similarly, if an organization is primarily measuring job skills or technical skills, it might not have data at all on the skills most likely to indicate potential.

Outdated or stagnant data can also be a problem in assessing potential. Skills data can become outdated quickly, especially in industries with rapidly evolving technologies or methods. If organizations rely on static skills profiles or data that is not continuously updated, they risk basing decisions on irrelevant or incomplete information. This limits the ability to accurately assess potential in a dynamic environment.

Another potential limitation to assessing potential is how the skills data is collected. The way skills data is collected and interpreted can introduce bias. For example, self-reported skills can lead to inflated assessments, while differences in how managers rate employees can create inconsistencies.

Finally, a lot of skills data lacks the context in which skills are demonstrated. An individual may have completed a certification or training program, but the data doesn't always indicate whether they can apply those skills effectively in real-world situations. Without contextual information, it's difficult to assess how well skills translate to potential.

Because using skills data to assess human potential offers significant opportunities and has its limitations, to fully assess human potential, organizations should complement skills data with other insights—such as behavioral assessments, peer feedback, and real-world performance evaluations—to form a more holistic view of an individual's capabilities and future potential.

Conclusion

One of the most difficult aspects of conversations about skills-based organizations and the journeys that organizations are embarking on to become more skills-based is ensuring that everyone has a common understanding of what a skill is. While it's important to understand what a skill means in your organization, it's also important to keep an eye on industry standards. Skills ontologies are helping with greater standardization, but consistency within an organization is key to creating data systems that stakeholders can trust.

The Half-Life of Skills

Contributed by Matthew J. Daniel, Senior Principal, Talent Strategy, Guild Education

What if I told you that the half-life of skills isn't some new idea or research driven by cloud computing or AI? It's a rather old idea that hasn't been updated in more than 50 years. Worse yet, the whole concept, as seen in nonstop L&D marketing, is really a misquote that's taken on a life of its own.

Let's start with some history.

In May 1969, before many of us were born, a professor at the Philadelphia College of Textiles and Science wrote a paper for the

Association for Talent Development's journal in which he analyzed how quickly the courses in five different engineering programs at five different universities were changing. From that, he estimated that the obsolescence (or half-life) of knowledge, not skills, tied to a role for just five different engineering jobs was decreasing.

Fast-forward to a congressional hearing in May 1983, during which an economist, seeming to quote from this journal article, testified to the committee that "technology half-life is no longer a comfortable five years—perhaps two years in some technologies. What does such sweeping change imply for the nation's educational and training institutions?" When the chair of the committee summed up the testimony, he erred in recounting the words used, and instead said, "The speed of changing technology constantly reduces the half-life of the skills of the work force." Thus was born the modern-day hysteria around decreasing the half-life of skills. It showed up in a few pieces throughout the 1990s and 2000s, but when a 2016 Deloitte infographic on the half-life of skills emerged, this data point became prolific.

What had been a relatively simple research project using course names to point out that there was a half-life to required knowledge for a few jobs became a narrative about how the half-life of all skills was suddenly dropping. This misquote of the research has become the basis of numerous podcasts, think pieces, LinkedIn ads, books, and more over the past nine years.

The problem with the focus on the half-life of skills isn't that some skills aren't more perishable than others, nor that we shouldn't have a conversation about it—some skills are indeed more durable, and we need to talk about the implications (Shah 2024). It's fairly intuitive, when we think about upskilling in a tight economy, to focus on skills that will endure.

The problem, rather, is the inherent belief that half-lives of all skills are actively shortening right now, and that this is a relatively recent phenomenon that should drive a change in our approach. It's not, and it shouldn't.

This belief in a perpetual and shortening skills cycle of development and attrition has also contributed to the current "skills technology" movement, in which tens of thousands of skills must be captured in our systems because they're changing so quickly. While data from America Succeeds shows us that many skills are evolving, an analysis of 80 million job postings from 2020 to 2021 reveals that seven out of 10 most-requested skills for jobs are in fact durable skills that show up year after year (America Succeeds 2021). Many of these durable skills are soft skills that are foundational for the workforce. America Succeeds' research shows that the top 5 durable skills were requested in job postings 4.7 times more often than the top five hard skills.

The contrast between the real business needs of our internal customers around developing these durable skills and the noise from learning suppliers on the ability to generate and scale content creates a natural tension. But at a moment when pressure is mounting to solve business problems (such as retention, internal mobility, and gaps in recruiting talent), we must invest in next-generation skilling that truly works for learners and the business. Balancing durable and perishable skills shouldn't be predicated on a false notion that skills expire like yesterday's milk.

There was a time when employees weren't hurriedly pushed through dozens of e-learning modules a year—or, if they had a perceived skills deficit, they weren't encouraged to just go watch a TED Talk or a video. When we needed to develop critical durable skills such as communication, collaboration, and critical thinking, we would send employees to a one-to-two-day training event or workshop, or a robust development program, so they could be immersed in a topic and have the chance to practice with instructors and other learners.

The most important reason to talk about skill durability is that the belief that a skill is durable has historically translated into willingness to invest a significant amount of time in developing that skill, because the return on investment was high. Updating our beliefs about the half-life of skills (and occupations) is a required step toward making the right strategic workforce investments in the early stages of a massive AI-driven transformation. To illustrate the necessity of investment in durable and transferable skills, consider these data points:

- Employees in the lowest wage quintile (earning less than $30,800 a year) are 10 times more likely to need to change occupations by 2030 than the highest earners (McKinsey 2023).
- Soft-skill-intensive jobs will account for two-thirds of occupations by 2030 and grow at 2.5 times the rate of jobs in other occupations (Deloitte 2017).
- Forty percent of employers think that Gen Z is unprepared for the workforce, with gaps in communication and other durable skills being a primary driver (Intelligent.com 2023).

To state it succinctly, the opposite of "throwaway training" on perishable skills isn't to double down on investing in degrees and credentials for everyone. It's having a strategy that works for you and your workforce.

Yes, some of these skills are exactly the kind we expect college graduates to have when they enter the workforce, but forcing folks into degree programs isn't the solution. Instead, the market needs development that leads to mastery of durable skills through practice, feedback, and application—and that development must be available to frontline and early-career employees at scale to build the resilient workforce needed for the future of work.

When that professor wrote his paper on knowledge obsolescence 56 years ago, his premise was right—a strong workforce reskilling strategy and infrastructure are needed in American society. And yes, technologies were and are constantly evolving.

However, a bedrock of durable skills will help any organization weather the coming storm—their half-life is not falling. The 2020s are not a time for microdosing and microskills; it's time to double down on the durable skills that the future of work will be built upon.

CHAPTER 6
Planning for Skills-Data Collection and Analysis

In this chapter, we'll cover:
- Building confidence and trust in skills data
- Collecting skills data continuously
- Analyzing skills data to inform decision making

Once you have defined skills for your organization, you're ready to get started, right? Well . . . there's a little more defining to do. One of the worst things you can do on your skills journey is take for granted that people will trust the data to make decisions. This chapter helps you prepare to answer questions about your skills data and build trust.

Building Confidence in Skills Data

One of the aspects of skills data that sometimes gets lost in building a skills-data strategy is whether people in your organization will believe the data is valuable in helping them make better decisions. For many organizations (and depending on the organizational culture), this is a perception problem fueled by questions such as:
- How do I know that people actually have the skills this data says they do?
- Do I believe the data sources?
- Will using this data enable me to make better decisions?

Level of confidence in skills data is an evaluation of how well the available data reflects a person's, team's, or organization's actual abilities, based on factors such as the credibility of the sources, the objectivity of the measures, and the consistency of the evidence. Ultimately, if you are responsible for collecting and analyzing skills data to help your organization make business decisions or employees make better career decisions, you should be transparent about your confidence in the data, to help the decision maker know how confident they should be in using the data to guide decision making. Several factors go into determining a level of confidence for skills data including the source credibility, the objective or subjective nature of the measures, consistency across sources, the recency of the data, the context of the data collection, the frequency of the skill's use, the level of transparency, and the breadth and depth of evidence. (We'll cover these in more detail later in this chapter.)

Building Trust in Skills Data: The Three V's

In early 2020, while I was working in product at a learning platform company, I developed a deck to explain how our skills-data engine worked, what it could do, and what its limitations were. One of the areas that I struggled with was how to explain data that could be used to show evidence of a skill. It was clear that things like learning activity, project work, job descriptions, self- or peer ratings, and even the content of meeting descriptions, emails, or text messages could all be used as evidence that someone had a skill, but none of these data points were definitive proof. My hypothesis was that these data points were all "skills signals" that could be aggregated to show either agreement to build confidence that someone had a skill or disagreement to demand more evidence to prove that skill.

Further, I knew that some data points had more validity than others; direct skills assessments, for example, were more valid than skills ratings, which were more valid than skills inference. With more data points, I believed, a variety of skills signals could build a higher level of confidence in the data and allow organizations to trust the skills data they were collecting to make better-informed people decisions.

To be honest, when I proposed this idea of skill signals, it wasn't well received by my colleagues. "No one will know what a skills signal is," was the general consensus. But I knew directionally, I was right—that variety, validity, and volume were the three parameters (or V's) that were important to consider in an aggregate view of skills data to build trust, and that any one data point was just a signal, not definitive proof, of skills.

In the last five years, significant progress has been made in organizations' understanding of the benefits and limitations of skills data. Some organizations have leaned into inference, some have started with self-reporting, and others have begun to use higher-validity assessments or labs to collect more meaningful signals.

Let's dive into the three V's of skills signals, and how to build a skills dataset you can trust. Each section also includes details about how to assess your level of confidence for each data point, providing a transparent way to communicate trustworthiness.

Validity (and Reliability)

If you had to focus on only one aspect of the skills data you're collecting, validity is the most important to consider. Why? Because if you're going to build trust and confidence, you have to be able to stand behind the data that you are collecting. If you want to make good decisions based on skills data, that data has to be trusted and as accurate as possible. Validity of skills data has the single biggest influence on trust in your data, and therefore should be at the forefront of your data strategy. Without data you can trust, decisions based on that data will also not be trusted. One piece of high-quality, highly valid skills data is better than 1,000 pieces of data with low validity. If you have the bandwidth to collect only a little bit of data, then make it good data. Everything else can follow.

So, what is *validity*? It is how accurately a methodology measures what it is supposed to measure. *Reliability* is its close counterpart—how consistently a methodology measures what it's supposed to measure. These two concepts, validity and reliability, work hand in hand to build trust. When measuring skills, they are the keystones for highly trusted skills data.

For skills signals, it's important to understand the validity of any particular data point. How can you assess the validity of a skills signal? There are several elements that determine how valid a data point is: application, potential for bias, methodology, and recency of data.

Application of a Skill

Skills demonstrated in real-world situations (such as actual project work) or under challenging or high-stakes conditions tend to carry more weight than those shown in controlled, artificial, or low-pressure environments (such as classroom simulations). This is why competency data becomes meaningful for adding job role context. Evaluating a skill in context ensures that the individual can transfer theoretical knowledge into practical situations. It goes beyond simply knowing how to do something and focuses on when and why to use the skill. For example, someone may know the steps of conflict resolution, but assessing their ability to mediate a disagreement in the workplace confirms true competency. Contextual evaluation provides a more accurate picture of capability, ensuring that the skill has practical, actionable value in relevant environments.

Assessment Methods

There are several assessment methods you can use to demonstrate the application of a skill:

- **Scenario-based assessment.** Present individuals with realistic scenarios so they must demonstrate the skill in action. These scenarios should reflect the complexity and unpredictability of real-world situations. For instance, a customer service professional could be asked to handle a simulated client complaint.
- **Observation.** In workplace or learning environments, observe how the individual applies the skill during their normal activities. This could include shadowing them in tasks that demonstrate the critical skill or gathering feedback from peers and supervisors.
- **Performance review.** Review specific instances in which the individual has demonstrated the skill in relevant contexts. Look for evidence that they can adapt the skill to various situations.

Level of Confidence Factors

Consider these factors when determining your level of confidence in the skills data.

Source Credibility

The level of confidence in skills data depends strongly on the credibility of its source. Data from highly reputable sources—such as industry-recognized certifications, formal education, or validated testing—tends to inspire greater confidence. In contrast, self-reported skills or informal peer assessments may require additional corroboration to be trusted.

In evaluating source credibility, consider using a scale from low to high confidence and rating your data sources along that scale. Here's an example:

- **High confidence:** Certifications from accredited institutions, validated assessments, and formal degrees
- **Moderate confidence:** Manager reviews, peer feedback, and project outcomes
- **Low confidence:** Self-reported skill levels without external verification

Context of the Data Collection

As noted previously, the context in which you collected the skills data can affect confidence. Skills demonstrated in real-world situations or challenging or high-stakes conditions tend to carry more weight than those shown in controlled, artificial, or low-pressure environments.

The challenges for organizations in collecting data in context are how systems are currently operating, and whether high-stakes conditions happen on a regular-enough cadence for skills to be assessed. While those types of conditions might elicit data with the highest level of confidence, it may not be realistic to collect data under those conditions in a consistent way. In these cases, simulations or labs for validation might be a reasonable and preferred alternative.

Here's an example of how to rate data sources along a scale of high to low confidence:

- **High confidence:** Skills demonstrated in real-world, high-pressure projects
- **Moderate confidence:** Skills demonstrated in simulations or low-pressure environments

- **Low confidence:** Skills assessed in situations not directly tied to job performance or real applications

Frequency of the Skill's Use

Confidence in skills data can also be tied to how frequently the skill is used or demonstrated. Skills that are regularly applied and shown in various contexts give higher confidence in their validity. In contrast, skills that are reported but not often used or demonstrated may generate lower confidence. In some contexts, skills aren't frequently used but are critical to someone's job performance—think firefighters, military units, and rescue teams. In these cases, application of skills in training scenarios may serve as an adequate substitute for real-life application of skills.

Here's an example of how to rate data sources along a scale of high to low confidence:

- **High confidence:** Frequently demonstrated and applied skills
- **Moderate confidence:** Occasionally used skills
- **Low confidence:** Infrequently or never demonstrated skills

Potential for Bias Is Minimized

Reducing bias in skills assessment ensures fairness and accuracy. Biases, whether conscious or unconscious, can skew results and lead to misleading conclusions about an individual's capabilities. This is especially important in professional settings because assessments may affect career progression or educational opportunities. Objective data, such as test scores, certification completion, and performance metrics, tends to provide higher confidence because it is measurable and standardized. Subjective data, such as peer reviews and self-assessments, can be useful but may require more corroborating evidence to ensure accuracy.

When you minimize bias, the evaluation process becomes more reliable and equitable, ensuring that all individuals are assessed solely on their performance, not on external factors such as gender, race, and personal relationships. This fosters trust in the assessment process and leads to more legitimate outcomes.

Assessment Methods

There are several assessment methods you can use to minimize bias:
- **Standardized evaluation criteria.** Use clear, objective, and standardized rubrics that outline the specific behaviors and outcomes expected for each skill level. Ensure that the criteria are applied consistently across all assessments.
- **Blind reviews.** Where possible, anonymize the data during the evaluation process. This could include removing identifying information when reviewing written assessments or video-recording skills demonstrations for later review without knowing the person's identity.
- **Diverse assessors.** Engage multiple assessors from different backgrounds to evaluate the same skill. Collect feedback from peers, supervisors, and external reviewers to minimize individual biases.
- **Bias training.** Ensure that assessors are trained to recognize and avoid bias during the evaluation process.

Level of Confidence Factor

Consider this factor when determining your level of confidence in the skills data.

Objective Versus Subjective Measures

Confidence in skills data also hinges on whether the data is based on objective or subjective measures. In evaluating the level of confidence based on objectivity versus subjectivity, identify the level of confidence based on the type of measurement:
- **Objective data (higher level of confidence):** Skills demonstrated through measurable outcomes (such as test results, completed certifications, and hands-on labs)
- **Subjective data (lower level of confidence):** Skills reported through feedback or self-assessment, which may be affected by bias or over- or underestimation

Transparent Methodology

Transparency in the assessment methodology builds trust and accountability in the evaluation process. When individuals understand how they are being assessed, they are more likely to engage meaningfully and prepare appropriately. For those using the data—such as managers, HR professionals, and executive stakeholders—transparent methods ensure that decisions are based on clear, understandable criteria. It prevents misunderstandings or misinterpretation of results and allows for informed decision making. Transparency also provides a basis for improving or challenging the methodology if necessary, ensuring that the process evolves to remain fair and effective.

Assessment Methods

There are several assessment methods that you can use to promote transparency:

- **Pre-assessment communication.** Provide individuals with clear documentation that outlines how they will be assessed, the criteria being used, and the specific components of the assessment. Make sure they know what to expect.
- **Feedback loop.** After the assessment, provide detailed feedback to individuals and stakeholders, explaining how the evaluation was conducted and why certain scores or conclusions were reached. Offer opportunities for individuals to ask questions and clarify the process.
- **Documentation of methods.** Make the assessment methodology available to all stakeholders. This could include making evaluation rubrics, benchmarks, and scoring systems accessible, along with guidelines for how the data will be used in decision making.
- **Openness to review.** Allow for the assessment methodology to be reviewed and challenged if necessary, and be open to improvements or changes suggested by individuals or data users. The more open you are to feedback from your users and stakeholders, the more data will be trusted.

Level of Confidence Factor

Consider this factor when determining your level of confidence in the skills data.

Level of Transparency

The level of confidence increases when the methodology for determining skill levels is transparent and consistent. Rubrics are an example of a transparent methodology for determining skills, especially when shared with employees so there is a common understanding of expectations. When methodologies are not shared or understood, which is often the case in inference, confidence in the data is diminished.

Here's an example of how to rate data sources along a scale of high to low confidence:
- **High confidence:** The methodology is transparent and consistent, such as a rubric
- **Moderate confidence:** Methodology is explained and consistent, but not well understood
- **Low confidence:** Methodology is not transparent, and results seem arbitrary or inconsistent

Recency of the Data Collected

The relevance of a skill can change over time, and individuals may improve or lose proficiency. Therefore, using recent data ensures that assessments reflect the current abilities of the individual, not outdated information. This is particularly crucial in fast-evolving fields because skills may need frequent updates to remain valid. For example, in technology or medical fields, relying on old data might overlook important recent developments, new technologies, or new competencies the individual has acquired.

Assessment Methods

You can use several assessment methods to increase relevance:
- **Regular reassessment.** Set specific timeframes for re-evaluating skills, particularly in fields that evolve rapidly. For instance, an

annual or biannual assessment may be necessary for technology-related skills, while less frequent reviews might suffice for skills that don't change as quickly.
- **Skill logs.** Encourage individuals to maintain a log of when they have demonstrated or used the skill recently, especially in professional contexts. This self-reporting can be corroborated with observations or feedback. Even better, leverage data tracking in your technology ecosystem or AI analysis to record when an employee is interacting with others in relation to a skill. This analysis can review email or chat interactions (in Microsoft Teams or Slack, for example) and be a signal that someone is leveraging a skill.
- **Check for updates in skill requirements.** Regularly review if the skill being assessed has changed because of new industry standards, technology, or best practices. Adjust the assessment criteria accordingly to ensure that it measures current competencies. This requires leaders and managers to be stakeholders in skills requirements, taking care not to generalize that all employees need the same skills to be successful.
- **Review of recent performance.** Ensure that any assessments of performance are tied to recent tasks or projects, using the most up-to-date examples to judge proficiency.

Level of Confidence Factor

Consider this factor when determining your level of confidence in the skills data.

Recency of the Data

Skills data that is recent and regularly updated tends to inspire higher confidence than older or outdated information. In fast-changing industries, skills can quickly become obsolete, and relying on outdated data reduces confidence in the current applicability of a skill. Recency matters with both technical skills, which evolve rapidly, and human skills, where continuous practice improves capabilities over time.

In making skills-informed decisions, recent data should be weighted more heavily than older data, not averaged out, as skills develop and fade over time dependent on investment in growth and application of those skills. Here's an example of how to rate data sources along a scale of high to low confidence:

- **High confidence:** Data from the past six to 12 months, regularly refreshed
- **Moderate confidence:** Data collected more than a year ago but still relevant
- **Low confidence:** Data more than a few years old, especially in rapidly evolving fields

Skills Tip

The phrase "garbage in, garbage out" is often used in reference to making poor decisions based on bad data; skills data is especially beholden to that sentiment because the decisions affect people's lives. Data quality should not be taken lightly, and decisions have ripple effects far beyond an organization's bottom line. Here are some tips to get started:

- Start with the least amount of data that you can trust.
- Find a high-validity data source that can be the first you collect. Run sample scenarios for decision making based on that data versus current decision-making practices. Review whether decisions would be different from current methodologies:
    - If decisions align with current methodologies, does using this skills data help you make faster decisions?
    - If decisions don't align with current methodologies, does using this skills data help you reduce biases? Potentially make better decisions? Identify hidden talent or skills?
- Add skills data to the mix of current decision-making practices. Does its inclusion lead to better outcomes?

Volume

The volume of skills signals can significantly increase trust in skills validation by providing a larger pool of evidence that confirms a person's abilities. When someone presents multiple skills signals, especially skills signals collected over time, it enhances the overall credibility of their expertise. An abundance of evidence helps diminish doubts that might arise from a single or limited number of skills signals. However, there are some considerations for tackling the right volume of skills data. How much is too much, in that it causes confusion around which data point is the most important? How much is too little to determine whether the needed skills exist within an organization?

Here are a few ways the volume of skills signals can increase trust:

- **Reinforcement of expertise.** The more skills signals provided, the more opportunities there are to demonstrate competence in different areas. This repetition of skills across various signals reinforces the idea that people's abilities are genuine and consistent over time, making it harder for doubts to persist about the data's trustworthiness.
- **Consistency over time.** A large number of skills signals over time shows that the employee has maintained or grown their skill set. This is particularly important for industries with rapidly changing technology or standards. When someone provides numerous skills signals that span years, it shows dedication, continuous improvement, and adaptability.
- **Mitigation of outliers.** With a large number of skills signals, any single outlier—such as a mediocre project or a less-than-stellar peer rating—has less impact on the overall validation. The sheer volume of other positive signals dilutes any anomalies, ensuring that the overall assessment remains strong and trustworthy.

Level of Confidence Factor: Breadth and Depth of Evidence

The more data points that support a particular skill, the higher the confidence in that data. For instance, an employee who has demonstrated a skill in several projects, earned multiple certifications, and received positive feedback from peers is likely to inspire greater confidence than someone with just one piece of evidence for that skill.

The right volume of skills to build confidence is a conversation that needs to start from the very beginning of your skills strategy planning. You must decide: How much data is enough to build confidence that someone has a skill at a particular proficiency level? To determine the level of confidence, the following parameters apply:

- **High confidence:** Numerous data points from diverse sources supporting the skill
- **Moderate confidence:** A few data points, but from credible sources
- **Low confidence:** Limited evidence or data supporting the skill

Variety

The final V in building trust in skills data is variety. Different types of data sources build confidence when they are in agreement and ensure that different facets of skills are considered. Variety of skills data is potentially the hardest to tackle for skills-based organizations because it requires them to identify the different data sources that relate to skills and aggregate them. It also requires a strategy for how to handle disagreement among different data sources, as well as rules about which data sources are weighted more heavily when there is disagreement.

If you are able to tackle the volume aspect of trust with skills data, it is not a surprise that a higher volume of skills-signal data very likely means that validation comes from a variety of sources, including self-ratings, peer reviews, manager evaluations, and real work-project outcomes. A diversity of sources adds legitimacy and trust because it's unlikely that multiple independent sources would incorrectly validate the same skills. Agreement of skill across diverse sources creates credibility and trust in the skills data; disagreement requires organizations to identify which sources of skills data have the highest validity (going back to our first V).

Even if you have started with one type of skills-data source—the one that is good enough to get started with and build trust with your organization for lower-risk decisions—eventually variety will become important because trust will be challenged for higher-risk decision making. Relying on a single skills signal, such as a degree or certification, can be limiting and may not fully reflect someone's capabilities in real-world scenarios. However, when multiple types of skills signals are considered—such as formal education, professional certifications, work experience, project portfolios, peer reviews, and endorsements from trusted peers or managers—they collectively form a more comprehensive and nuanced picture of the individual's expertise.

Here's why diverse skills signals build trust:

- **Create a comprehensive view of skills.** Different skills signals highlight various aspects of a person's abilities. For instance, formal education shows foundational knowledge, while practical experience demonstrates applied skills. Together, they paint a fuller picture of someone's qualifications.
- **Cross-verification.** Multiple signals act as cross-checks, verifying the validity of each claim. For example, someone may list a certification, but if they also have a portfolio showcasing real-world applications of that skill, it strengthens the claim, increasing confidence in the individual's ability.
- **Reduced bias and misrepresentation.** No single skills signal is infallible. By considering different types of evidence, the risk of bias or misrepresentation is lowered. This is particularly important in areas that rely on subjective assessments or varying standards.
- **Adaptability and continuous learning.** Diverse skills signals also reflect a person's ability to learn and adapt. Continuous professional development—demonstrated through a mix of certifications, self-directed learning, and evolving projects—suggests that the individual stays up to date with industry and job role changes, showing that they are able to maintain or grow skill proficiency even as skills requirements evolve.
- **Context-specific skill validation.** Different skills require different validation methods. For technical roles, work samples and certifications may be more relevant, whereas leadership or creative roles might benefit more from peer endorsements or

project outcomes. Having varied signals means that the validation process can be tailored to different kinds of skills.

By blending different types of skills signals, you can create a more accurate and trustworthy representation of someone's expertise. This diversity increases the reliability of the overall skill assessment and reduces the likelihood of overvaluing or undervaluing an employee's skill.

Level of Confidence Factor: Consistency Across Sources

The level of confidence increases when skills data is consistent across multiple sources. For example, if an employee's self-assessed skills are backed up by peer feedback, manager reviews, and performance metrics, confidence in the accuracy of that skill level is higher. When multiple independent sources verify the same skill, it reduces the risk of bias or misreporting. Patterns of consistency across multiple data points also help offset anomalies that may inevitably occur.

- **High confidence:** Consistent validation from multiple sources (such as self-reporting, peer feedback, and certification)
- **Moderate confidence:** Data validated from one or two sources
- **Low confidence:** Conflicting or uncorroborated data from different sources

Measuring Your Organization's Level of Confidence

To build trust in skills data, you need confidence in validity, volume, and variety. The level of confidence in skills data represents the strength and reliability of the evidence supporting an individual's claimed skills. High confidence means the data is well supported, credible, and up-to-date, while low confidence suggests the need for further verification or additional evidence before that data should be trusted for high-risk decisions. Along these parameters, you can assess your level of confidence as a calculation to be shared within your organization related to any skill measurement. As companies begin to aggregate skills data to assess skills, a confidence rating is key to establishing transparency and trust.

Figure 6-1 is a sample analysis of what you can use in your organization to determine your own level of confidence in your skill data:
- In organization 1, the high validity and low volume but moderate variety would give you moderately high confidence in the data.
- In organization 2, there's a lot of data but low validity and variety, which would give you a moderately low level of confidence.
- In organization 3, validity is moderate, as is volume with a higher degree of variety. You could rate this with a moderately high level of confidence as well.

Figure 6-1. High, Medium, and Low Confidence Levels

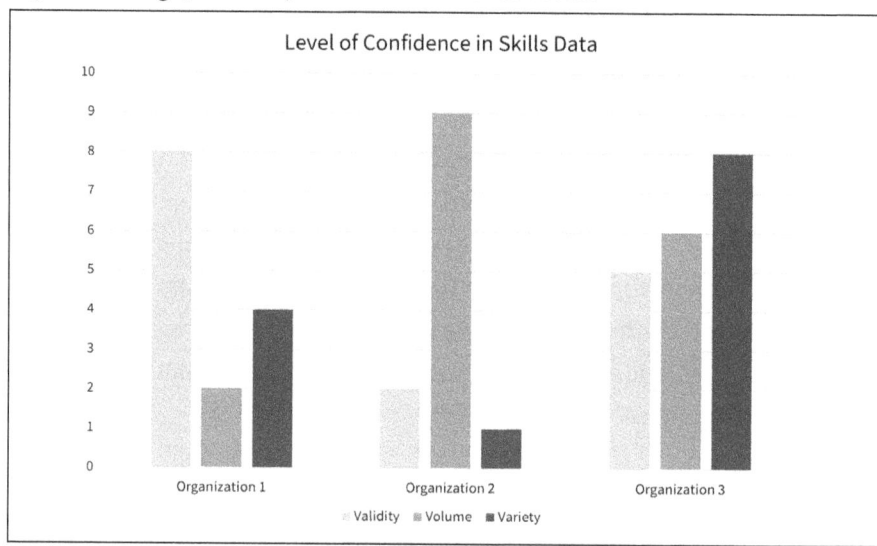

Collecting Skills Data Continuously

You've built a skills-data strategy that considers the three V's (validity, volume, and variety) and what data your organization will need to trust to make more-informed people decisions. Now, where can you find that data? What sources already exist in your organization, and what sources do you need to start collecting?

Sources of skills data within an organization typically come from both formal and informal systems that capture data that reflect employees' competencies, performance, and development. And because skills are constantly changing based on learning and experience, these sources can help you set a baseline from which you can measure change. This allows you to see the impact of learning, training, and job experience on an individual employee's skills. From an organizational impact perspective, you can see the overall impact of learning and development solutions, as well as shifts in skills due to hiring and attrition. It's not enough to do a one-time data collection effort to fuel your skills-based organization; it's absolutely essential that you develop a plan for continuously collecting and evaluating skills data to provide an accurate snapshot of skills at any point in time to make informed people decisions.

Examples of key sources and some strategies for collecting skills data on an ongoing basis include:

- **Employee profiles and resumes.** Many internal HR or talent systems store detailed profiles where employees list their qualifications, past experiences, certifications, and educational backgrounds. These may include applications, resumes, CVs, LinkedIn profiles, and other information collected when an employee was interviewed as part of the hiring process.
- **Performance reviews.** Regular assessments conducted by managers or peers provide insights into employees' strengths, areas for development, and demonstrated skills through their work performance. Performance reviews may not currently be skills-related for your organization, so you may need to infer skills from the information shared. Building skills-data collection requirements into regular performance reviews ensures that updates are gathered systematically. During these reviews, managers can assess and record the skills that employees have developed or demonstrated since the last review period, providing a structured opportunity to capture new data. Employees can also rate their own skills to share in conversation with managers about their performance.
- **Employee self-ratings.** While self-ratings may not be the highest-validity data you collect, it is a low-effort way to collect skills data at a frequent cadence. Self-ratings in combination with

other data sources provide a mechanism to keep data fresh through variety and volume. Encouraging employees to perform self-assessments at regular intervals, outside the process of performance reviews, allows them to provide insights into their skills growth, new expertise, and areas of improvement. You can conduct these assessments through surveys or dedicated software platforms, which can be aligned with organizational skills frameworks. You can also employ periodic surveys or pulse checks to ask employees to update their skills or reflect on new areas of expertise they have gained. These quick surveys can be tied to specific periods, such as after training or major project completion, ensuring continuous and timely skills data updates.

- **Training and certifications.** Records of completed internal or external training programs, along with certifications earned, reflect employees' ongoing skills development and specialized expertise. Internal certifications may be tracked through a learning platform; for external certifications, records may be stored in other HR or talent platforms. Many certifications are job or role specific, so some investigation may be needed to see where this data is stored.

- **Project contributions.** Data from project management systems or records of individual and team contributions to specific projects can reveal practical applications of skills, as well as collaboration and leadership abilities. Project-based work can also consider the person's role on the team and what skills are required for that project role. Integrating project management tools with skills-tracking systems can automatically log the skills involved in various tasks, providing a dynamic and real-time view of employee capabilities. Other enterprise collaboration tools that are used for specific domain areas (such as Teams, Jira, and Salesforce) may provide valuable insights into daily work that can support other data points, such as peer, manager, and self-ratings. Using this strategy will likely require the assistance of AI

to review and infer skills through an employee's interactions in a specific software application.
- **360-degree feedback.** Feedback from colleagues, managers, and direct reports can offer a well-rounded perspective on soft skills such as communication, teamwork, and problem solving. In many organizations, this feedback is collected once or twice a year in more formal feedback cycles and aggregated in HR or performance management systems. For a skills-based organization, continual peer reviews and 360-degree feedback offer another avenue for collecting skills data. Colleagues, direct reports, and managers can provide regular feedback on soft skills (such as communication, teamwork, and leadership) and technical skills demonstrated in day-to-day work and more closely aligned to ongoing projects or internal delivery milestones. For teams that conduct retrospectives, skills feedback could be included in the debrief or review as a project concludes. This practice of collecting feedback in the flow of work or aligned to work completion milestones is a way to integrate skills into everyday work reviews.
- **Coaching and mentoring feedback.** Coaching and mentoring programs offer opportunities for collecting skills data through regular feedback sessions. Coaches and mentors can provide insights into the skills development of employees, particularly in areas such as leadership, decision making, and critical thinking. This data, in combination with peer, manager, and self-ratings, can have a direct link to development efforts that are supported by mentors or coaches.
- **Learning platforms.** Learning platforms track employees' participation in courses, workshops, and e-learning programs, highlighting the continuous learning paths of employees related to specific skills. Some platforms can track social learning as well as employee contributions to knowledge bases, or user-generated content. These types of skills-data points may indicate skills as well as skill proficiency level because employees are often

assessed during learning experiences. Regularly monitoring completion rates and skills improvements through these systems provides real-time data on employees' learning progress, giving organizations insights into how skills are evolving for an individual employee and across the workforce.

- **Skills assessments and tests.** Internal assessments or external skills tests can provide objective data on specific technical or professional abilities relevant to an employee's role, especially when implemented periodically to allow for regular and consistent measurement of skills over time. These assessments can take many forms, such as on-the-job assessments, skills validation labs and simulations, and written assessments. Different skills may require different types of assessment and you should consider whether an assessment is testing for knowledge or application of skill. These assessments can be prompted by the organization, initiated by an individual, or tied to work milestones or team cadences.
- **Employee development plans.** Employee development plans can provide ongoing updates on skills data as employees pursue their goals. By tracking progress against these plans, organizations can collect data on how employees are building new skills and competencies aligned with career growth objectives. For organizations that have goals to improve retention through internal mobility, this strategy can set up internal job marketplaces up for success.
- **Work samples and portfolios.** Portfolios or documentation of work completed, such as reports, designs, and presentations, serve as concrete examples of an employee's skills in real-world situations. Other work interactions, such as emails, team collaboration software, and company intranets, may also have valuable data to demonstrate work effort related to a skill. If these types of systems will be monitored for skills signals, employees should be aware that this is a strategy for skills-data collection.

By aggregating varied sources of skills data, organizations can form a comprehensive and accurate view of the skills present within their workforces. And when organizations bake continuous data collection into these sources, it enables them to collect a steady flow of relevant and up-to-date skills data. To power your skills-based organization with up-to-date data, developing a plan for continuous data collection is an integral part of ensuring that data doesn't become stale and can continuously be trusted, and that you can demonstrate the impact of skills development efforts on employee and workforce skills.

Analyzing Skills Data to Inform Decision Making

While understanding the complexity of skills data is important, the real benefit of understanding the details of skills data sources and structure is being confidently able to answer the question: "Can I trust the data to make this decision?"

Up to now, this chapter has focused on being able to better understand the data and the factors that can build confidence in how accurately the data represents the skills that someone possesses. Let's dig into the variety of decisions that skills data can be used to make.

Key Skills Questions

Depending on your organization's starting point with skills, you will have different questions that you want to analyze your skills data to answer. In analyzing skills data to help answer these questions, you may find that skills data alone is not enough. Combining skills data with other business data and performance metrics, however, can be a powerful way to glean deeper insights into critical business needs.

Your first step is to determine which questions you want the skills data to answer. Use the following examples, separated by decision maker, to start thinking about how skills data can be put to work in your company.

Business executives and HR professionals may want to ask:
- What skills do I have in my organization today?
- What skills do I need in my organization today?

- What is the skills gap between what I have and what I need in my organization?
- What does the nonlinear professional progression for my roles really look like?
- Where can I fill stretch assignments with highly skilled people in my organization?
- What types of skills are leaving my company?
- What skills make some of my top performers top performers?
- What skills are people highly interested in developing in my organization?
- What are some emerging skills in the market and my company?
- What skills will my organization need in the future to stay competitive?
- What skills are most critical to my organization's success?

Talent and recruitment professionals may want to know:
- Who in my organization is a fit for a critical role I need to fill?
- Who within my organization is qualified for open roles?
- How do internal candidates compare with external candidates' skills?
- Which candidates best match a job's requirements?
- What skills are in highest demand for candidates?
- What skills are in most demand in the market?
- What skill adjacencies would make a candidate a good fit for future growth in the organization?
- What skills should I look for in every candidate for every role?
- What skills are most aligned for success in the organization's culture?

People managers may want to understand:
- What are the key strengths of each team member?
- What skills gaps exist within the team, and who needs further development?
- Which employees are best suited for upcoming projects based on their skill sets?

- Who on the team is ready for leadership roles or promotions based on demonstrated skills?
- Which team members are consistently learning and acquiring new skills?
- What certifications or qualifications does the team currently possess?
- How well do the team's collective skills align with current and future business needs?
- Who are the top performers in specific skill areas, such as technical, creative, or soft skills?
- Which team members are best positioned to mentor or coach others based on their skills?
- Which training programs or learning opportunities would most benefit individual employees or the entire team?
- What impact have recent training initiatives had on improving the team's skills?
- Are there any critical skills missing from the team that could hinder performance on key objectives?
- How adaptable is the team to new technologies or industry trends based on members' skills data?
- Which employees are underutilized in their current roles due to untapped skills?
- What is the current skill level distribution across the team, and where are the outliers?
- Which projects or tasks could be reassigned to better align with employee skills and interests?

The L&D function may want to know:
- What are the most common skills gaps across the company?
- Which skills are most critical for future business success, and how proficient are employees in these areas?
- Which departments or teams have the greatest need for upskilling or reskilling?
- What percentage of employees actively participate in learning and development programs?

- Which training programs have the most measurable impact on skills improvement?
- How do employees' skill levels align with the organization's strategic goals?
- Which employees have demonstrated significant growth through training and learning initiatives?
- What certifications or qualifications are most in demand across the company?
- Which roles or departments require more investment in leadership development?
- How many employees have completed key training programs, and how has that affected their performance?
- What are the top skills that employees request or need based on industry trends?
- Which employees are ready for internal mobility based on their current skill sets?
- What is the overall proficiency level in critical technical or soft skills across the workforce?
- Are employees able to keep pace with new technologies or industry demands through available training?
- Which learning resources or courses should be prioritized based on company-wide skills needs?
- Which learning methods (such as workshops, e-learning, or on-the-job training) are most effective in boosting skills acquisition?
- How well do employees in different regions or business units compare in terms of skill proficiency?
- What percentage of employees are engaged in continuous learning, and how does that affect business outcomes?
- Which areas of the workforce show the greatest potential for future leadership or high-level roles?
- Are there specific roles or teams that have an issue with skills redundancy or shortage?

- How is the company's skills profile evolving in comparison with competitors or industry benchmarks?
- Which employees show the greatest aptitude for cross-functional roles based on their skills data?
- How can skills data inform succession planning and talent development pipelines?
- Which skills will be critical for the company in the next three to five years, and how can L&D programs prepare employees for these needs?

Employees may want to understand:
- What are my strongest skills, and how do they compare with my peers'?
- What skills gaps do I have that could hinder my career progression?
- Which new skills should I focus on developing to align with future career opportunities?
- Which skills have I demonstrated the most in my recent projects or tasks?
- How well do my current skills align with the organization's goals or my team's needs?
- What training programs or learning opportunities should I pursue to close my skills gaps?
- How do my technical skills compare with my soft skills, and where can I improve?
- Am I ready for a promotion or leadership role based on my skills data?
- What skills do I need to develop to move into a new role or department?
- What areas of continuous learning have the most potential to enhance my career prospects?
- How can I leverage my current skills for internal mobility or cross-functional roles?
- What feedback have I received about my skills from managers, peers, or formal assessments?

- How can I use my skills data to negotiate for a raise, promotion, or new opportunity?
- Which mentorship or coaching opportunities could help me develop my weaker skills?
- How does my skills profile match the requirements for my desired career path?
- What additional qualifications or learning could help me transition into a leadership position?
- How can I use my skills data to build a more tailored personal development plan?
- What areas of expertise should I highlight in my performance reviews?

When kicking off any new skills initiative, it is important to understand what questions you want to be able to answer, and for whom, to ensure that you are collecting the right data. As your organization becomes a more mature skills-based organization, the ability to ask different questions for different audiences on demand will put pressure on its overall skills analytics capabilities. Skills analytics is a subset of data analytics that leverages skills data to answer skills-related questions. Whether you tackle skills analytics as part of your overall data strategy or partner with a supplier to support you, the first key to success in powering skills analytics is having trustworthy data.

Conclusion

I can't overstate the importance of building trust with your skills data strategy. This single issue can derail an otherwise on-track skills initiative or cause organizational change efforts to hit major roadblocks. Being intentional and thoughtful about the data you're collecting can help you anticipate questions and build confidence in your stakeholders that your skills data is trustworthy in informing people decisions in your organization.

Verifying Skills in the Workforce

Contributed by Dani Johnson, Co-Founder and Principal Analyst, RedThread Research

In recent years, many organizations have made tremendous progress toward infusing a skills mindset into their businesses. Whereas just a few years ago leaders were only beginning to grasp the benefits of thinking in terms of skills, now many of them are firmly on the skills path. At RedThread Research, my research firm, we speak with many people leaders—and we're increasingly hearing about organizations that have identified employees' skills and begun tying those skills to roles and business strategies.

However, as the initial tasks of collecting skills data and identifying employees' skills become more commonplace, leaders are also starting discussions about the validity of their skills data. Learning leader Mitchel MacNair, director of talent development and learning at Crown Castle, said in a research interview: "Once you've identified skills, the very next thing that happens in your evolution of thinking is, 'OK, let's start verifying skills.'"

Mitchel's sentiment is not unique. Leaders focusing on skills understand that the level of decisions that can be made based on skills data depends on the validity and nuance of that data. From this understanding, we're seeing a dramatic rise in leaders' interest in and efforts surrounding skills verification.

What Does Skills Verification Mean?

Interestingly, we've noticed that different people make different assumptions about what verification and related terms mean. For example, *verification* and *assessment* are used interchangeably by some leaders, but not by all. Detailed proficiency levels are an integral part of verification for some organizations, but not others.

At RedThread, we define *skills verification* like this:

> Confirming that someone has a skill, and often the extent to which they have it

In other words, skills verification is the act of ensuring that employees are proficient in the skills they're reported to have. This confirmation of skills allows for higher-level, more consequential, or more nuanced decisions.

Verification can happen in two ways:
- **Verifying that someone has a skill.** This is a yes or no judgment.
- **Verifying to what extent an employee has a skill.** Here, an employee's skill proficiency is rated, often using a multilevel proficiency scale.

Some of the verification methods I'll cover next are more often used to verify that someone has a skill. Others are used more to verify the extent to which someone has a skill.

Seven Methods for Verifying Skills

There is no one-size-fits-all approach to verifying skills. Different verification methods may better suit a given situation or a given organization's needs and available resources. Here are seven methods that organizations can use to verify skills, ranging from simple to more complex.

- **Self-assessment.** Employees rate their own skills, often through tools such as performance reviews or learning platforms. While this is the simplest method, it may not be the most reliable because it relies on personal judgment.
- **Performance feedback or informal observation.** Managers or peers provide feedback on an employee's performance, which includes their skills. This is the most widely used method because it can integrate into existing performance review processes.
- **Formal observation.** A trained observer watches an employee perform a task or skill and rates them against a rubric. This more rigorous approach is often used in high-stakes environments, such as healthcare and other safety-critical industries.
- **Formal assessment.** This method tests an employee's skills against set criteria to judge their skills proficiency. Assessments

can be stand-alone or part of other formal development opportunities, such as courses, certification programs, degree programs, and apprenticeships.
- **Comparison to external benchmarks.** Skills are measured against industry standards or regulatory requirements. This method is useful for ensuring compliance or aligning internal skill sets with market trends.
- **Inference from HR data.** AI can predict a person's skills based on data including job history, development activities, and performance reviews. This approach is becoming more widespread as technology evolves.
- **Inference from work data.** This method is like inference from HR data, but the data is drawn directly from work systems. For example, data about completed tasks or project roles can help infer a person's skills. This method often requires deeper technical integrations.

While these methods are listed individually, organizations often use more than one—sometimes together. For example, self-assessment is often paired with inference from HR data or work data, providing more confidence in and nuance to someone's overall skills picture.

Choosing the Right Verification Method

Verifying skills can involve some significant costs and trade-offs. For example, some methods (such as self-assessment) are relatively low budget but impose a heavy lift on employees because they must spend time and effort assessing themselves. Other methods, such as inference from work data, can cost quite a bit (especially if you're working with an external firm) but are less burdensome on individual employees. The leaders we've talked with recommend considering these costs and trade-offs when choosing verification methods.

Fortunately, not all skills need to be verified with the same level of rigor. For instance, an organization may prioritize verifying customer-facing, safety-critical, or revenue-related skills more thoroughly than others—using, for example, formal assessments, observations, or a combination of methods to boost confidence in the data. However, for less critical skills, self-assessments or informal feedback may be sufficient.

Case Study: Ericsson's Approach to Skills Verification

Every year, Swedish global communications and technology company Telefonaktiebolaget LM Ericsson (Ericsson) identifies seven to eight skills—called "global critical skills"—that are directly derived from and intended to drive the business strategy.

Because they're business-critical, the global critical skills are verified more thoroughly and thoughtfully than other skills. As Peter Sheppard, head of the global L&D ecosystem at Ericsson, says, "The more important the use case, the more we think about which approach to use. If we need to verify a global critical skill, then we think carefully about the verification method we're going to use."

For example, while other skills may be verified using self-assessment or inference, global critical skills are also verified through formal assessments, credentialing, and work projects. This additional rigor gives Ericsson confidence in the skills it has deemed critical to future success.

The Future of Skills Verification

As organizations continue to invest in skills-based approaches, the importance of verifying skills will only grow. While the methods outlined here provide a strong foundation, new technologies will likely shape the future of skills verification. The key is to remain flexible and adapt these methods to fit the needs of the business, ensuring that skills data remains accurate, reliable, and useful.

A Performance-Based Methodology for Building, Applying, and Verifying Technical Skills

Contributed by Sarah Mullens, Senior Growth Product Manager, Skillable, and Maria Chrastka, Senior Product Manager, Microsoft

A *technical skill* can be defined as "an ability to effectively and readily perform a series of tasks from beginning to end from past experience or training." While traditional learning models focus on knowledge transfer, skilling leverages multiple learning modalities that allow learners to practice specific tasks within a technology or set of technologies. Interactive, scenario-based lab experiences are an essential element of these paths. These labs, among other assessments, can also be used to verify the skills a learner has built through training or work experience. When learners complete these tasks, they not only gain confidence in their job readiness but also provide performance-based evidence of their skills.

Skills have transitioned from being a background element to a forefront focus in learning," says Maria Chrastka, senior product manager at Microsoft. "While skills have always been part of content development, they were typically discussed by academics or HR during training design. Now, skills have become a hot topic among tech learners and professionals outside L&D. We are seeing a clear shift from role-based assembly of skills to in-demand skills being shared across different roles."

When talking about technical skills, we believe in these three principles—credibility, authenticity and relevance.

To drive credibility of verified skills, completion of clearly defined assessments validates a learner's knowledge of the skill. This performance-based approach, measured through a series of multi-modality assessments including interactive labs, ensures that the market can trust these skills.

Authenticity arises from the focus on the breadth and depth of each skill through detailed analysis and clearly defined tasks. If a learner has a skill on their profile, hiring managers know that learner has completed a set of tasks within the relevant technology.

"What we're really trying to solve is the problem of trust," Chrastka explains. "Everybody's talking about skills. People's profiles have countless numbers of skills, but there's a clear lack of trust. We know people embellish their profiles and achievements. To really democratize learning, to break down the barriers to opportunity, we must get to the point where skills are verified and trustworthy, so they provide the right level of context and proof. Authenticity is critical."

Authenticity also requires clarity on the level of specificity of particular skill. "If a skill is a container, what size is the container? Some people think a skill is a single task, like a particular Excel function," she continues. "Someone else might think it's something like 'data analysis' or an entire domain." Skills data is most useful when skills represent a midsize container that's specific enough to be clear on the tasks, but not so granular that someone has hundreds and hundreds of skills for a particular role.

When building the skill taxonomy, relevance of skills is a driving factor. "We're looking at the market data of roles and skills in-demand. We want to help our customers stay ahead and teach them skills that are needed," Chrastka says. "As a product manager, I'm asking questions like 'What audience are we trying to serve? What skills do people and organizations need to realize their investments in cloud technologies and products? How do we make it easier to learn new products or new features?' All of this is grounded in market trends and data."

As organizations transition to being skills-first, data from skills assessments becomes the connective tissue between learning, talent, and true job readiness. "As we shift to prioritizing skills as the foundation for content creation, significant and intentional change management is required. This applies to both content development and the evaluation of training ROI," she says. "Instead of focusing on 'time spent' in training, we can now emphasize 'skills acquired.' With new advancements emerging monthly, especially in technology, learners are increasingly valuing agility and thinking in terms of skills. Skills have become the new currency."

Through partnership with Skillable, the leading interactive labs platform, we are building and delivering scenario-based experiences for skill development, practice, and validation. "When it comes to technical skills in particular, we're seeing a dramatic shift toward interactive, performance-based learning," says Chris McCarthy, CEO of Skillable. "The ability to validate an individual's skills with high-fidelity evidence is foundational to building trust in the skills-based organization concept, as well as an employee's ability to do the required job. We're unlocking the power and promise of a skills-based organization with performance-based learning and assessment."

Focusing on a solution to the problem of trust in skills data generates great possibilities. "If we have evidence-based skills on profiles, talent pools can flow more freely. If there's a particular project or problem organizations are trying to solve, they could look for people with the right skills for that problem in particular," Chrastka explains. "Credentials hold significant value and will remain important because they provide peace of mind. However, we are also exploring new methods to verify specific tasks within the workflow. For instance, what can I demonstrate in 10 minutes between meetings? These are the kinds of questions we're asking."

We are co-innovating a new model for skill validation. One that's modular, builds over time, and fits more easily into a learner's workday. With a focus on AI specifically, the goal is to build a verified skill signal that carries enough rigor to be trusted, but feels lighter weight than the other credentialing options to serve a broader audience. "In a skills-first world, crafting careers will become more fluid," Chrastka says. "It can be scary and overwhelming, yet at the same time liberating. Skills are breaking down barriers for people and opening up new opportunities."

CHAPTER 7
Preparing the Skills Infrastructure

In this chapter, we'll cover:
- Distinguishing between skills ontologies and taxonomies
- Ensuring proper governance over skills data
- Building your skills-data associations
- Navigating the skills technology landscape

Do you need an ontology or a taxonomy to get started with skills? I'm frequently asked this question. And, although an ontology and a taxonomy are important concepts in the data infrastructure for a skills-based organization, they don't need to be your starting point.

Many organizations have gone down the path of becoming skills-based and have assumed that they need to have the full system in place before they can get started. Many invested in platforms that use ontologies, and one of the steps to get the platform working is to figure out your *ontology*—or the list of skills that your organization cares about measuring. Then, many of them got bogged down in figuring out the ontology, which does nothing to show the value of skills in helping the organization make better decisions. Agreeing on an ontology (which will change immediately once it's in use, by the way) is often an arduous process of getting different areas of the business to work on decision making in a way that they haven't worked together before. Starting with an ontology means you're taking your organization down a path of intensive change management and new collaborations before you've proved the value of skills data.

So, don't start with a skills ontology for your whole organization.

A better place to start is with a smaller list of skills you care about, whether a short list of skills across your whole organization or skills for a particular department or job function. Build a proof of concept around those skills, showing the business value and generating the buy-in you need to turn the investment in an organization-wide ontology. Along the way, you'll learn what works and what doesn't to inform the broader ontology strategy, providing leaders across your business with examples of what good looks like, along with impact data to justify the investment.

Eventually, yes, you will need an ontology. Understanding the terminology will help you set your organization up for success, communicate the purpose of an ontology across your organization, and be better educated about your organization's requirements before deciding on a skills-data architecture or engaging with skills platform suppliers. Let's dig into skills ontologies.

What Are Skills Ontologies and Taxonomies?

Contributed by Paul Turner, Product Executive and Big Data Strategist

One of the first lessons—and problems—I encountered in my skills journey is understanding and accepting that not everyone speaks the same language when it comes to skills. People use different terms to mean the same thing, and sometimes the same term to mean different things. This isn't unique to skills, but it makes rolling out a skills initiative more complicated.

Organizations usually think top-down first: If we just make up a list of skills, then the employees will use those terms. Unfortunately, what I have seen is the need for someone to constantly maintain a skills list. It is an impossible task, trying to govern the consistency of the skills' meanings and managing stakeholders who don't see the connections between skills and the work that needs to be done.

Exacerbating this problem is differences in skills-data sources. I have yet to find a common skills list between two organizations, datasets, or skills platforms. Instead of imposing skills top-down, consider thinking bottom-up first.

Regardless of the approach, the biggest challenge in being a skills-based organization is trying to make sense of all your data. This is why it's critical to understand what a taxonomy and an ontology are.

An *ontology* is simply a bunch of things (concepts, terms, or, in our case, skills) with metadata and a defined relationship. It's that simple. And a *taxonomy* is an ontology in which the relationship is hierarchical. I like to remember that all taxonomies are ontologies, but not all ontologies are taxonomies.

Let's consider an example using the relationships within a family with two parents (mom and dad) and four children (two daughters and two sons). A taxonomy would place the parents at a higher order than the four children, with lines connecting each parent to each child.

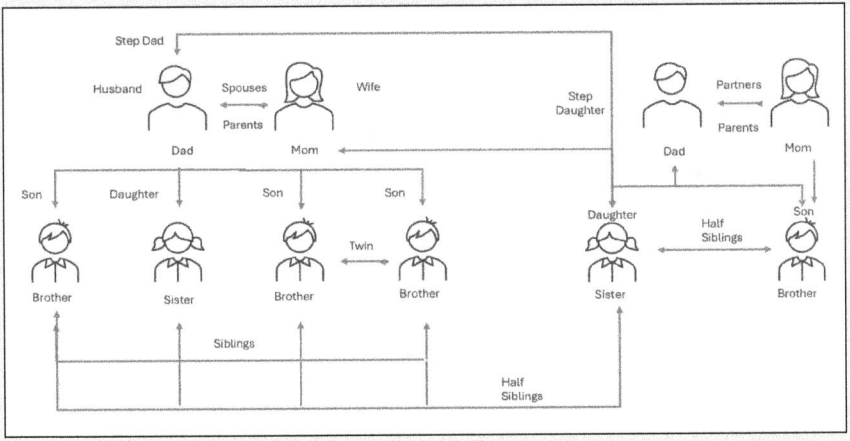

But in an ontology, we can imagine the same family and all the different types of relationships that exist. Consider it from the perspective of a son, who has relationships with his parents, defined as "mom" and "dad," and with his siblings, defined as "sister," "sister," and "brother."

In this dynamic world, we know that mom and dad mean something slightly different (because we have different expectations in mom's and dad's roles, versus the category of "parent" which focuses on similarities between the roles); they might even mean something slightly different within the family itself because many families define their own expectations of moms and dads. And there might be different things that influence how those relationships have come to be.

Now that we are starting to think about all the other relationships in the family, we also know that they are not the same for every member. The mom-daughter relationship can be different for each child, as well as the dad-daughter relationships.

In an ontology, these differences are shown by distance. The closer the two people, the stronger the relationship. This is really complex even within a single family, but it can get particularly difficult when you go beyond one family and add more to the map.

For example, there might be many reasons one of the children from the new family has a "mom" relationship with the other family; the reason is not important, just that it exists. We do not want to assume what the relationship is between people simply because of the label or name we give it.

Also, consider that mom could actually mean a lot of different people in different countries, religions, or even families. The label mom can be applied but it's really what mom means that is important.

All of this holds true for skills. We call a lot of different skills by the same name across different teams, organizations, and companies. This is why setting up your skills in an ontology is important. It helps connect your skills not by the name of the skill, but by the meaning of the term.

There are two great advantages to being able to connect skills terms this way:

- **Everyone can really use their own terminology.** We have all likely been through a standardization process at a company.

Trying to get everyone to use the same term, intuitively, is difficult. Embrace the fact, as part of your skills strategy, that there will be differences.
- **You identify and leverage new skills emerging in your organization even if they're not already part of your ontology.** New skills are simply added or split off from existing skills depending on how the terms and their meanings change over time.

Skills Tip

The use of a skills ontology provides the flexibility needed to evolve, just as the skills, tasks, and jobs in your company evolve. It allows for associations of skills, which helps identify skills groups or related skills, and it helps identify new or emerging skills. The most connected skills are often the most high-impact skills in your organization and should affect your investments in skills validation and development.

Skills Inference

As organizations strive to collect more skills data to drive their decisions, skills inference is increasingly part of organizations' strategies to get a lot of data quickly, often to build a baseline of skills data. *Skills inference* refers to the ability to identify someone's skills based on what you know about them from data sources that can be used as skills signals. The idea of inferring skills is appealing, but there are real differences in how inference could work. Understanding different inference models will help you assess which one may be right for your organization, and provide transparency on where data is coming from.

Skills inference models aim to infer or identify an individual's skills based on available data, such as their educational background, work experience, or even their behavior and interactions in digital environments. These models use algorithms and data analysis techniques to deduce skills that an individual has and help organizations understand the capabilities within their workforce. They are often used in conjunction with natural language processing, deep learning, and other AI methodologies to analyze large datasets, which may include resumes, job descriptions, and other workplace assets that can attribute evidence of skills.

Let's explore the various types of skill inference models, how they can be used, and the challenges with skill inference.

Types of Skills Inference Models

Skills inference models may loosely be categorized into several types of approaches. Each uses various techniques and data sources to reach the desired outcome.

- **Rule-based models** rely on predefined rules and patterns to make inferences of competencies from structured data, such as resumes and job descriptions. For instance, if "Python" appears in a resume, then the rule-based model will infer Python programming skills for that individual. Although simple and rather easy to implement, these models are not very flexible and miss the subtlety of language and context.
- **Machine-learning models** learn from data algorithms to make assumptions. Some are trained on labeled datasets in which skills are tagged to blocks of text. Decision trees, random forests, and support vector machines are common algorithms developed around them. Machine-learning models are able to cope with more complex data patterns than rule-based models, but require volumes of labeled data to train on.
- **Deep learning models**, especially those based on neural networks, can grasp patterns and relationships in data that are even more complex. Recurrent neural networks and transformers (such as BERT and ChatGPT) have been used to infer skills from text in resumes, social media profiles including LinkedIn, and internal communication. These models really shine when it comes to handling unstructured data and can understand context

very well, although they require substantial computational resources and large datasets to be effectively trained.
- **Hybrid models** combine the strengths of both the rule-based and machine-learning approaches. For example, a hybrid model might make an initial identification of possible indications of skills using a rule-based system, and then apply a machine-learning model to refine those inferences with context. This will provide even greater accuracy and reliability, particularly if the situation is complex or ambiguous.

Challenges in Skills Inference Modeling

While inference can help you gather a lot of skills data quickly and continuously, skills inference models have several limitations that you and your organization should consider before implementing skills inference as a means of skills validation.

The effectiveness of skills inference depends on the quality and amount of data on which the inference is based. In many sources used in inference, data is incomplete, inconsistent, biased, or otherwise problematic. In addition, data privacy and security considerations can further limit the availability of valuable sources of data. And because skills are constantly changing, inference models need to constantly learn and change as well. The need to retrain and adapt a model to correctly infer skills means that inference models are not static and must be constantly evaluated for accuracy.

Skills inference models also lack transparency. Most inference models don't cite the data source from which a skill was inferred, making the data difficult to defend or rely on for high-risk people decisions. If that data is biased, the model can reinforce that bias in the inferences it makes. Limited transparency makes minimizing bias difficult.

Last, context is important to infer skills correctly. Is reference to Java a programming language, a geographical location, or coffee? Inference needs to be sophisticated enough to understand the context of a skill to accurately interpret or identify it.

Despite these limitations, the rate of innovation in AI and machine learning means that inference is likely to get better, and therefore more trustworthy, over time. Some trends that are signaling inference improvement include:

- Integration with knowledge graphs (which demonstrate the relative connectedness and relationships of different data types or data points), which will improve the amount and quality of data from which inferences are made
- Improvements to natural language processing, which will in turn improve understanding skills context
- Standardization of AI ethics to help reduce bias
- Advances in explainable AI to bring more transparency to how inferences are made
- Real-time skills inferences so data can be updated continuously, giving a current skills view on demand

Is Skills Inference Right for You?

With the current limitations on skills inference, you may be tempted to avoid it as part of your skills-data strategy. It can generate a lot of data quickly, but, as discussed in the previous chapter, that data won't have high validity because of its inability to minimize bias and its lack of transparency. It could be a bad idea to jump to inference at the beginning of your journey instead of focusing on less plentiful but more valid data.

The case for inference really depends on your business use. Are you trying to understand skills patterns across your organization quickly, or are you trying to identify the most qualified person for a role? If the former, inference can get you the data you need, fast; if the latter, you may not get the requisite data to make a promotion or hiring decision.

Also, if you introduce inference early and focus on improving data quality over time, you may be able to generate support from key stakeholders, who you need to buy in to the long-term vision of skills. Carefully consider the needs of your organization, the willingness to increase trust in data over time as quality improves, and the complexity of mixing higher-validity data in key areas with inferred data to give a more general view of skills. Knowing that inference will eventually be a part of every skills-based organization's journey, time the introduction of it into your organization for when it works best for your needs.

Skills-Data Governance and Integrations Across Enterprise Systems

As your organization begins its skills journey and focuses on the problems that skills data can help solve, it can be easy to overlook skills-data governance and enterprise system integration, and their importance to the success of the organizational transformation. Governing how the organization collects, maintains, and uses skills data builds ongoing trust and ensures consistency, accuracy, and relevance for critical people decisions. In addition, integrating skills data across enterprise systems—including human resources information systems, learning management systems (LMSs) and performance management platforms—creates a unified, data-driven approach to your skills strategy, from deciding on your "single source of truth" to creating the directional rules for how skills data is shared across systems.

Skills-data governance refers to the set of policies, standards, and processes that regulates skills data within an organization. Effective governance ensures that skills data is accurate, up-to-date, and standardized across the organization and builds trust through transparent rules. An effective governance policy defines clear ownership of skills data, establishes protocols for updating and validating it, and ensures compliance with data privacy regulations. By thinking through skills-data governance, you can ensure that your skills-data strategy meets the short- and long-term needs of the company.

Elements of a skills-data governance framework should include:

- **Data ownership and accountability.** Who owns the data in your organization (HR, managers, or employees)? Who is responsible for data management and maintenance? Who are the stakeholders and reviewers of skill data policies?

- **Data collection standards.** What skills data will be collected? How will skills be defined and categorized? From what sources will skill data be collected?
- **Data quality management.** Outline the details of processes to ensure accuracy and consistency of skills data; a description of how skills will be validated; and processes for maintaining data quality, including updating or correcting skills data as needed, and defining how often skills will be reviewed and updated.
- **Data privacy and security.** Ensure compliance with employee data privacy regulations (for example, the General Data Protection Regulation or GDPR), policies for who can view or access skills data, and measures for securing skills data.
- **Data usage policies.** Determine how skills data will be used within the organization, such as for talent development, succession planning, or project assignments; alignment with business objectives and employee consent; and rules for sharing skills data internally and externally.
- **Data classification and ontology.** Agree on the definition of the ontology being used and data classifications to organize skills data, details for how the ontology can be adapted over time, and definitions of terminology related to skills to create consistency in the organization.
- **Employee involvement and consent.** Outline protocols for employee consent regarding the collection, validation, use, and sharing of their skills data.
- **Change management and communication.** Determine the process for updating the skills-data governance framework as needs evolve and communication plans to inform stakeholders about changes to data policies and procedures.
- **Ethical considerations.** Outline policies to avoid discriminatory practices or bias based on skills-data insights.

Skills-data governance may not be the sexiest part of your skills-based journey, but it will be the foundation of its success and should be factored in to decision making as you embark on your journey. Like many aspects of the evolution to becoming a skills-based organization, it doesn't all have to be done at once, nor does it have to be done to get started with skills. Knowing the elements you should develop over time will help you know which questions you need to ask as you continue in your skills-data journey.

Alongside skills-data governance, integration across your enterprise systems enables seamless sharing of skills data across the organization's various platforms, breaking down silos for using skills data for various use cases. By connecting skills data into your enterprise technology ecosystem, you can use it to inform decision making across the entire employee life cycle: hiring and onboarding, learning and development, performance reviews, and succession planning. Integration ensures that all relevant systems reflect the most current and comprehensive skills data, providing real-time insights that drive personalized learning, optimized project assignments, and better talent matching. This interconnectedness also supports advanced analytics, enabling you to anticipate future skills needs, track trends in workforce development, and align talent strategies with business goals.

One important aspect of skills-data integrations is identifying your organization's skills-data "source of truth." As you develop your skills-data strategy, you begin to aggregate, save, and share skills data in your ecosystem. It is critical to understand where skills data is coming from, how you aggregate skills signals into a synthesized assessment of skill and proficiency, and then what systems receive that synthesized skills data. It's often easiest to visualize this as a map to provide transparency for data privacy and security questions. Figure 7-1 is a simplified example of how you could visualize the data flow from skills-data integrations in an enterprise ecosystem.

Figure 7-1. Data Flow From Integrations

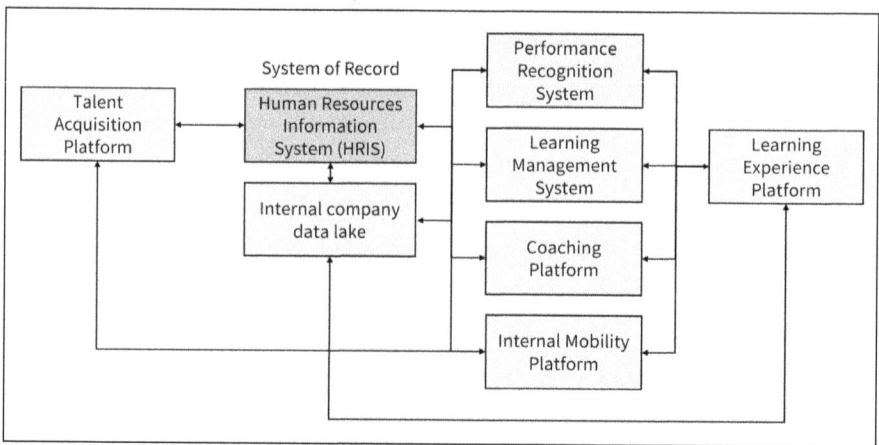

Note that some platforms in the ecosystem provide the data into your skills-data hub, others receive it, and some do both, with data flowing bidirectionally. Understanding how data is flowing in integrations is an important part of data governance; the transparency of these integrations is another way to build trust across all levels of your organization.

Skills-Data Associations

To power your skills-based organization, there are some common skills associations that are prerequisites to common skills use cases, such as recommending people for learning experiences, jobs, or projects. As you build your skills-data sets, you will also need to build your skills-data associations. These are the most common:

- Mapping skills to people
- Mapping skills to content
- Mapping skills to jobs, roles, and work that needs to be done

These three areas of skills association build the foundation for skills-based decisions across hiring, learning and development, people management, workforce management, and succession planning, as well as connect skills data to the other critical datasets that power a skills-based organization.

Mapping Skills to People

Mapping skills data to people allows organizations to gain a clear understanding of the current capabilities within their workforce. When skills are mapped to individuals, organizations can identify gaps, optimize work assignments, and ensure that employees are placed in roles that best use their talents. It can also facilitate personalized development plans and foster continuous learning.

Depending on your internal systems and data architecture, the keys to mapping skills data to people are to first have a place where skills data can be stored; then to ensure that skills can be associated with a person, such as with a skills profile; and finally to collect skills-data signals, ideally with proficiency levels, for that person.

Once skills data has been collected and associated with a person, you have the first building block to understand what skills someone has, which is the first piece of the puzzle in understanding what skills they need, either today or in the future. Skills gaps can then be addressed, and opportunities identified.

Mapping Skills to Content

Mapping skills to content is crucial for creating targeted learning and development programs that address the specific needs of employee skills gaps. Without a clear understanding of the skills that each piece of learning content addresses, organizations may offer generic or misaligned training. Skill-to-content mapping ensures that learning materials, courses, and training modules are relevant to the skills that employees need to develop or refine, promoting effective upskilling and reducing skills gaps.

You should tag all learning content and experiences with the relevant skills so learning activity can be mapped to those skills. Learning platforms and content libraries can be structured around skills tags; you can determine your own focused set of skills tags for your organization or use an ontology to represent a broader set of skills when your organization is ready.

Mapping skills to content makes it easier for employees to access the right training materials at the right time, enhancing their learning experience and boosting their skills and competencies in areas that align with both personal and organizational goals.

Mapping Skills to Jobs, Roles, and Work

Mapping skills to jobs, roles, and work defines the competencies required for success in each position within the organization. This creates a standardized framework for recruitment, employee evaluation, and career development. When you map skills to roles, you can ensure that employees are equipped to perform the tasks needed to drive business success. This can also support succession planning by identifying employees who are close to meeting the required skills for higher-level positions.

Mapping skills to jobs or roles requires defining what skills align with work, including technical skills, job skills, and human skills. Not only should you identify skills needed for jobs, but you should also document the proficiency level needed to effectively do the job. You should write and update job descriptions to reflect the skills required.

Once you define skills-based roles and write job descriptions, you can use them for a variety of purposes in combination with employees' skills data, including skills-based hiring, internal mobility, project staffing, professional development or learning plans for employees, workforce planning, and succession planning, to name a few.

The Rise of Task Intelligence

If the goal of a skills-based organization is to have deeper insight into the skills it has and the skills it needs, the organization needs to go beyond assessing the skills in its workforce. To truly understand the work that's done in the organization, it's necessary to define organizational work tasks. This has led to the use of the term *task intelligence*, which describes the tasks required for the organization's work (Figure 7-2).

Tasks and skills are inherently interconnected. A *task* is a specific unit of work that requires execution, while a *skill* is a capability or competency that enables the completion of that task. Each task demands a unique combination of skills, ranging from human skills to technical skills.

Figure 7-2. Task Intelligence

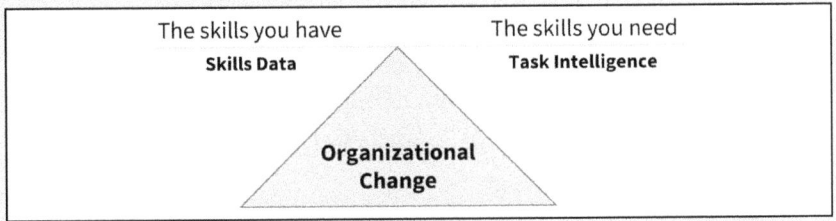

For example, conducting a financial analysis requires data interpretation, financial modeling, and critical thinking skills. Similarly, designing a marketing campaign necessitates creativity, strategic planning, and digital marketing proficiency skills. The effectiveness with which a task is performed depends on the alignment between the skills an individual possesses and the skills the task demands.

By mapping tasks to skills, an organization can build a skills-based workforce that is better equipped to adapt to evolving job roles and technological advancements. It allows the business to focus on skill development that is directly relevant to operational success.

In addition, by clearly defining tasks, organizations can gain several other advantages:

- **Increased clarity and efficiency.** Well-defined tasks help employees understand expectations, thus reducing ambiguity and enabling focused execution.
- **Improved talent alignment.** By defining tasks, organizations can better match employees with the right skills to the right work, which improves performance and engagement.
- **Enhanced learning and development.** A clear task framework allows organizations to design targeted training programs and ensure skill development aligns with business needs.

- **Optimized workforce planning.** Understanding tasks helps in workforce planning, which allows companies to identify skills gaps and make informed hiring or upskilling decisions.
- **Greater agility and innovation.** Organizations with a strong task framework can quickly reallocate resources and adjust work processes in response to market changes.

Despite these benefits, defining tasks within an organization also comes with several challenges:

- **Task complexity and overlap.** Some tasks are multifaceted and overlap across roles, which makes it difficult to define them with precision.
- **Rapidly changing job functions.** The modern workplace evolves quickly, and rigid task definitions may become obsolete and require continuous updates.
- **Subjectivity in task assessment.** Different teams or individuals may perceive tasks differently, which leads to inconsistencies in definitions and execution.
- **Resistance to change.** Employees and managers may resist a structured task framework, particularly if it alters established workflows or requires new skills.
- **Balancing standardization and flexibility.** While defining tasks brings structure, excessive rigidity can stifle creativity and adaptability, so it's essential to maintain a balance.

Task intelligence—an organization's capability to analyze, execute, and optimize tasks by leveraging relevant skills—is one of the critical foundations of a skills-based organization. By clearly defining tasks and linking them to essential skills, organizations can enhance clarity, improve talent alignment, and drive continuous learning. This involves recognizing patterns, improving efficiencies, and adapting to changing requirements to enhance outcomes. When an organization cultivates task intelligence among its workforce, it enables employees to navigate complex workflows, automate repetitive processes (especially in the age of AI), and make informed decisions, thus enhancing productivity, innovation, and agility in responding to market dynamics.

AI can be very helpful when developing your organization's task intelligence. There are several vendors on the market that can input your existing job architecture and job descriptions and analyze the tasks associated for each role. While you should still have humans validate the output, you can leverage these tools to associate the tasks with skills once you've defined them. In many cases, you can also get critical insights about which tasks are most likely to be affected by AI and automation.

With skills data mapped to people, content, and jobs, your organization has the foundation to make decisions based on skills data. While data mapping can be done manually to get started, AI and machine learning will not only support initial mapping efforts but also maintain relevant mapping over time. When larger-scale data-mapping efforts are required for your organization, it may be time to consider what existing tools and platforms are available in the market. The next section will review the types of technologies and platforms available to support organization-wide systems in a skills-based organization.

The Skills Technology Landscape: Understanding What You Need

Because skills affect so many areas of an organization, it's no surprise that the technology and supplier landscape has been awash with skills. You may hear firms describing themselves as upskilling, reskilling, or skills development platforms, or framing their capabilities as skills management, skills intelligence, skills analytics, skills assessment, skills validation, and more. As you begin your journey to tackling the skills-based-organization blueprint, a deeper understanding of what technologies exist and what they can do will help you make better investment recommendations for your organization.

Skills Tip
It isn't necessary to buy a technology before you can get started with skills! It's better to navigate your strategy, do pilot testing, and prepare your skills-data strategy before engaging with a supplier. While skills tech companies have developed ways to scale your skills strategy, many solutions are complicated to implement and slow to have real impact if you haven't worked through your data strategy first.

When you're ready to invest, integrating the right technology solutions can help you effectively manage, track, and develop workforce capabilities. From learning management systems to AI-powered skills analytics and talent marketplaces, these solutions can enable organizations to build and sustain a skills-driven framework that meets the evolving demands of the modern workforce. What I'll share next will by necessity be a snapshot of the supplier landscape prior to publication; it cannot reflect the constantly evolving market.

Skills Tip
If you are about to embark on researching technology suppliers for skills, do your homework! These firms' capabilities and areas of focus are constantly shifting, and the right partner for you should depend on your specific requirements.

With all these disclaimers, here are the categories of technology companies that support skills-based organizations.

Products That Help You Collect Skills Data
The first step in building a skills-based organization is understanding the skills within your workforce. Several products focus on collecting skills data, through skill assessments, skill validation, and automated inference of skills.

- **Inference of skills.** These tools leverage AI to infer employees' skills based on their work history, projects, performance

reviews, and learning patterns. They use machine learning and predictive analytics to match employee skill sets with industry standards and job market trends. This automatic inference helps organizations capture a complete picture of their workforces' current skills and identify gaps or future skills needs.
- **Skills-to-jobs databases.** Some products are less technology than data, helping to maintain extensive databases that match skills with job roles. These databases help organizations understand which skills are needed for specific roles, allowing for better workforce planning and alignment of learning initiatives with organizational goals.

Products That Help You Assess and Validate Skills

Skill assessment is a critical part of understanding an employee's current competencies and identifying areas for development. Several technology solutions offer tools for assessing and validating skills through different approaches.
- **Skill assessments.** Platforms provide rating scales to evaluate an employee's proficiency in specific skills, allowing managers and employees to rate competencies from beginner to expert levels. Certification programs also play a key role in verifying skills acquisition, with many platforms integrating certifications from industry-recognized bodies.
- **Skill validation.** Ensuring that employees have the skills they claim to possess is essential. Labs, portfolio reviews, and video analysis tools allow for the validation of hard and soft skills. For creative roles, portfolio review tools allow employees to showcase past work, while video analysis tools evaluate soft skills such as communication and leadership during interviews or assessments.

Products That Help You Manage Skills-Data Infrastructure

As skills data accumulates, organizations need robust skills-data infrastructure to store, organize, and manage this information. Several suppliers focus on managing the infrastructure that allows companies to maintain up-to-date skills inventories.

- **Skills inventory platforms.** Suppliers in this category offer centralized platforms where organizations can store and track employee skills, certifications, experiences, and competencies. These platforms act as a single source of truth for skills data, making it easier to manage learning and development initiatives, match employees with roles, and make informed workforce decisions.
- **Skills ontology management.** Suppliers also offer tools for managing a skills ontology that categorizes skills in ways that align with business needs and industry standards. These ontologies ensure consistency across the organization when evaluating and developing skills.

Products That Help You Analyze Skills Data

Analytics plays a key role in driving data-driven decision making within skills-based organizations. Several firms offer products that provide insights into workforce skills, enabling organizations to plan for the future and address skills gaps proactively.

- **Skills analytics platforms.** These products help organizations analyze the skills data they have collected. They provide insights into employee skills utilization, track how learning and development programs affect skills acquisition, and identify skills gaps that need to be filled to meet future business demands.
- **Predictive analytics.** Platforms using AI-powered predictive analytics can forecast the future skills needs of the organization, enabling proactive workforce planning. These tools analyze data trends to help organizations predict which skills will be in high demand and plan development programs accordingly.

Products That Focus on Building Skills

Skills development is a continuous process, and organizations need tools to help their employees learn, practice, and improve. Several products focus on building skills through personalized learning, coaching, and hands-on practice.

- **LMSs and learning platforms.** Companies such as LinkedIn Learning, Udemy, and Coursera offer extensive libraries of courses and learning paths to help employees develop new skills. Many of these platforms can be integrated with organizational LMSs to provide tailored learning opportunities based on individual skill assessments.
- **Coaching platforms.** These platforms provide employees with access to professional coaching to help them develop leadership, communication, and other soft skills. These platforms facilitate one-on-one coaching, often supported by AI-driven assessments and development plans.
- **Practice labs.** These platforms offer practice environments where employees can apply what they've learned in real-world simulations, allowing employees to practice and validate skills.

Products That Help You Hire for Skills

As organizations shift toward skills-based hiring, technology plays a vital role in hiring based on skills rather than traditional credentials or job experience. Several products focus on helping businesses identify and hire candidates with the skills they need.

- **Skills-based hiring platforms.** These products assess candidates based on their skills and potential. They use AI and machine learning to analyze resumes, assessments, and interview data to match candidates with roles that align with their skill sets.
- **Pre-employment testing.** Some suppliers provide pre-employment tests that assess candidates' technical and soft skills. These tools ensure that candidates possess the necessary competencies before they move forward in the hiring process.

Products That Address Internal Mobility

Internal mobility—allowing employees to move between roles or departments based on their skills—has become a key focus for organizations looking to retain top talent. Several platforms facilitate internal mobility and career development.

- **Internal mobility platforms.** These products provide internal talent marketplaces that match employees to internal job opportunities, projects, or short-term gigs based on their skills and career goals. They encourage internal mobility, helping organizations retain talent while offering employees new growth opportunities.
- **Career development tools.** These tools guide employees in identifying the skills they need to advance within the organization. They use skills data to suggest learning opportunities or roles that align with an employee's career aspirations.

Products That Support Workforce Planning

Workforce planning in a skills-based organization requires a forward-looking approach that focuses on future skills needs and aligning talent with business strategy. Several tools support workforce planning by analyzing current and future skills gaps.

- **Workforce-planning platforms.** These platforms integrate skills data with business strategy to enable effective workforce planning. They provide insights into talent supply and demand, helping organizations anticipate hiring needs and plan for future skills shortages.
- **Succession-planning tools.** These products help organizations plan for leadership transitions by identifying potential successors and developing leadership skills within the existing workforce.

Products That Focus on Career Pathing

As employees take ownership of their career growth, organizations must provide the tools to support career pathing and development. Several suppliers offer solutions that allow employees to map their career trajectories based on their skills and interests.

- **Career-pathing tools.** These tools help employees visualize potential career paths within the organization. They offer personalized recommendations based on employees' current skills, their desired roles, and available learning opportunities, helping them take proactive steps toward career growth.

Skills Tip

Looking ahead, technology firms will increasingly focus on employee value—helping organizations recognize and reward employees not just for their skills, but for the overall value they bring to the business. Future-focused platforms will emphasize employee contribution, engagement, and growth potential.

These employee value platforms will integrate skills data with performance and engagement metrics to provide a holistic view of employee value. They will allow employees to own and tell the story of their skills, and enable organizations to recognize high-performing employees, offer personalized career development, and create reward systems that go beyond traditional compensation models.

The technology supplier landscape for skills-based organizations is diverse and rapidly changing, with specialized tools for collecting, validating, managing, analyzing, and building skills. Not only are new tools coming to the market, but specialized tools are being acquired by larger platforms, making this a landscape to watch closely. Because skill technologies are still relatively new, the best approach for organizations may be integrating these solutions. Through careful analysis of the best technology solutions to meet your needs, you can create a robust, data-driven approach to managing your workforce, ensuring that the employees in your organization have the skills they need to thrive in the future.

Conclusion

In every skills-based organization, skills data and the infrastructure that supports it become the foundation of people-related decisions. Without a solid foundation, discrepancies can emerge and distrust can fester. By thinking through a right-sized foundation for each step of your journey, you can build a strong foundation as you go, without the necessity for massive upfront investment in time or resources to get your journey off the ground. Incremental investment in skills infrastructure, from ontologies to governance systems to technologies, will ensure that your organization maps its skill investment relative to the value that's being created.

Bringing Data Analytics to the Table in Your Skills Journey

Contributed by Angela Le Mathon, Founder and Chief AI Officer, People Alkemie

Does your human resources, talent, or people leadership team have data and analytics sitting at the table?

Within most companies, data analytics is typically buried deeper in the organization, often under talent or operations. As a result, analytics focuses on solving issues specific to those areas rather than contributing to the broader HR agenda. But with data, the difference means having the chance to say, "How have we thought about this? How have we considered that? Hold on, there's a better way to approach this." It's an opportunity for companies to think about optimizing for data analytics from an HR perspective, which ends up upskilling the leadership team.

When I joined my current company, the CHRO made the intentional decision to have data analytics represented at the leadership table. The idea was to leverage data to drive strategic decisions, set priorities, and improve how HR operates. As part of the leadership team, I began observing the discussions and participating in initiatives.

One such initiative was experimenting with a talent marketplace. The organization had gone through significant transformations—teams and roles had changed and career ladders no longer existed in their previous form. Employees didn't know where to find opportunities, and there was a clear gap between demand and supply within the organization.

To address this, we decided to facilitate connections through a talent marketplace. After leadership chose to use Workday's Skills Cloud as the platform, I was brought in to assess its capabilities. Initially, there was enthusiasm about the data we could collect on skills, but I cautioned them that "The Skills Cloud won't provide the kind of insights you're envisioning."

As the organization didn't yet have a deep understanding of data analytics, there was skepticism. I suggested we move forward and learn together. When we launched the platform and reviewed the data, the limitations became clear. Employees were defining skills inconsistently, often using job titles or departmental terms instead of actual skills. There was no shared understanding of what a "skill" meant or how to develop one. Similarly, managers who created part-time projects or mentorships weren't framing them in terms of skill building.

This experiment revealed that our foundation—skills data—was flawed. We needed clean, structured data to make meaningful use of the marketplace.

A Different Approach

After consulting with various companies and networks, we decided to partner with TechWolf, a skills intelligence vendor specializing in producing high-quality skills data.

We piloted TechWolf's solution, leveraging our robust data infrastructure, which made us AI-ready. Within a few months, we gained insights into our data's quality, learned how operational skills data could work in a live environment, and tested an integration with Workday. We piloted the solution across three areas:

- **R&D.** This function was the most complex in terms of skills. They valued TechWolf's granular approach because it aligned with how they define roles and expertise.
- **Tech.** This rapidly evolving function appreciated the live, continuously updated nature of the solution.
- **HR.** This slower-changing function found the platform insightful for understanding skills and delivering HR services.

The pilot programs confirmed the platform's scalability and its ability to provide actionable skills data. We also discovered the importance of skill ontologies—relationships between skills that inform capabilities and development opportunities. This shift in understanding was pivotal: we weren't just identifying individual skills but creating a framework to link skills, capabilities, and career development.

From here, the focus became tying skills data to development plans. For example, if someone needs a particular capability, we can identify the associated skills and create a curriculum to build it. However, this raises a few questions, including:

- How long will it take to develop these skills?
- Should employees develop skills on the job, or is external learning required?
- If employees invest heavily in learning, what's the organization's obligation to provide opportunities in return?

We need to balance these factors carefully. While we now have the tools to infer, validate, and measure skills, the goal is to drive tangible outcomes. Skills data must deliver value, not just exist for its own sake.

One major goal for our skills journey is improving internal talent visibility. Currently, 70 percent of hiring is external because we lack insight into our internal workforce's skills. While we know what we're looking for when recruiting externally, we don't have the same clarity internally. Employees who may have valuable skills often remain overlooked because we lack the data to see their capabilities.

Inferred data gives us a baseline, and then we have to validate it to generate trust. Inference creates a list of skills based off your digital footprint at the company. And then as an employee or as the owner of a job role or requisition, you can validate and say, yes, I believe these are the skills the job requires. The hiring manager can also validate the skills, which helps gain alignment. This is a way to increase productivity—rather than starting with the blank slate of a job description, you can get 80 percent there through inference and then augment the additional 20 percent.

In the next few years, our goal is to create visibility for both internal and external talent. This involves building a robust talent pool and understanding how to act on the insights we gather. Ultimately, this journey is about transforming HR through better data and analytics.

What We've Learned

My biggest takeaway thus far in our skills journey is that it's very easy in change agendas to really get excited and seduced by the AI models and the technologies and to make the conversation about the platform. But when I step back and look at where we are today and the changes we're about to make, I think we might've missed a trick on having a conversation about the culture we're about to create.

Ultimately, we're creating a bunch of mechanisms for people to engage with a company in a very different way. They're going to define themselves in a different way. They're going to have different expectations for culture that's going to create, which you don't always have control over.

We did a few pilots and, in a controlled way, everything looked good. Now we're going to release our skills solution in the company, and it's going to grow and evolve. I don't know if we know what that looks like yet. I hope the talent pool becomes more visible. But then what behavior will it actually drive? And was that the true end goal? In doing this, are we going to see hiring managers start to pull from internal talent more than external? And if they are pulling internal talent more, are we preparing managers for more fluidity, more internal mobility?

This is going to be a fascinating experiment.

PART 3
Developing Your Blueprint

The magic happens after you've developed your plan to transform your organization to be skills-based and laid your skills-data foundation. Skills data can foster tangible improvements, and now you're ready to enjoy the fruits of your labor—to see the impact that skills data can have on specific challenges across your organization. Different from the earlier chapters in the book, the chapters in this part get specific about the use cases that are most affected by skills data and how you can take steps to make an impact.

CHAPTER 8
Transforming Hiring Practices

In this chapter, we'll cover:
- Moving away from credential-focused to skills-focused listings
- Using innovative techniques and tools for evaluating skills during the hiring process
- Integrating skills development into onboarding

Very little has changed for the last several decades (and maybe even longer) in how companies recruit and hire talent, with the exception of job notices moving from newspapers to online job sites. When I applied for my first job after college, I saw an ad in a newspaper, sent in my resume and cover letter, got a call for a phone screening, met with some people for in-person interviews, and was offered the job. That was 30 years ago and, besides the technology, not much has changed for every job I've had since then. My resume (and now my LinkedIn profile) has been the basis of my interviewing experience, and I know that I've received job offers based on my previous titles and employers, not for the skills I actually have. Have I always been the most qualified candidate for jobs I've been offered? Very likely not. Have I not received job offers where I was the most qualified candidate? Very likely.

Similarly, if you've worked at a prestigious company, you know that not every co-worker is a high performer. It reminds me of the old joke: What do they call the medical student who graduated last in their class?

A doctor.

Until recently, most organizations relied on two main types of data on job candidates: resumes and educational credentials. All other data in the interviewing process was limited, subjective, and easily biased. But with the introduction of skills data into the hiring process, recruiters and hiring managers have deeper, more reliable data on skills that can inform hiring decisions.

Traditional hiring practices are now being reimagined through the lens of skills-based hiring as part of the evolution organizations are undertaking to become skills-based. As businesses adapt to the demands of digital transformation, remote work, and a changing global workforce, the focus has shifted from assessing candidates based solely on their academic qualifications or past job titles to evaluating their actual skills and capabilities. Skills-based hiring emphasizes the importance of what candidates can do, rather than where they have been, allowing organizations to build more diverse, dynamic, and capable teams. This approach not only aligns with the needs of modern businesses but also offers a more equitable way to assess talent, leveling the playing field for individuals from various backgrounds.

Being a skills-based organization means prioritizing the identification, assessment, and development of skills throughout every stage of the talent life cycle—from recruitment and hiring to training and career advancement. By leveraging data-driven insights into candidates' specific competencies, organizations can make more-informed hiring decisions, ensuring a better match between job roles and the talents of incoming employees. This approach minimizes the risks associated with subjective hiring practices, such as unconscious bias or over-reliance on prestige-based credentials, which often overlook candidates' true potential. Instead, skills-based hiring fosters a more objective and transparent recruitment process, enhancing the quality and efficiency of hiring.

This chapter explores the principles and practices behind skills-based hiring in skills-based organizations, offering insights into how this approach can transform talent acquisition. It delves into the practical benefits of using skills data, such as automating candidate screening, creating targeted interview questions, and supporting long-term workforce planning. Additionally, it examines how skills-based hiring can improve diversity and inclusion, enhance the candidate experience, and better align recruitment strategies with broader business goals. By adopting a skills-based approach, organizations can not only attract top talent but also create a more adaptable and future-ready workforce.

The Evolution of Recruitment and Hiring Practices

Recruitment and hiring practices in most organizations follow familiar patterns that center on evaluating resumes and conducting interviews. Resumes or CVs serve as the primary gateway for job applicants, offering a self-reported summary of their education, job history, and skills. This initial step is often followed by interviews—either in person or virtual—to assess the candidate's fit for the organization. These interviews frequently focus on past experiences, perceived cultural fit, and general personality traits. In some organizations, the hiring process may include an additional portfolio review, presentation, or assessment, although these practices aren't consistent from company to company and may vary by role.

Challenges of Traditional Hiring Methods

Traditional recruitment methods present several challenges to finding the best candidates for a role. One of the most significant issues is bias. Unconscious biases—such as those related to gender, race, or educational background—can easily influence decisions when resumes are screened manually. This can lead to a range of undesirable outcomes, with one of the most risky being the creation of a homogeneous workforce that lacks the diversity needed for innovation and creativity.

Traditional recruitment processes can also be incredibly inefficient. Sifting through numerous resumes and conducting multiple interview rounds is time consuming for HR teams and hiring managers. Moreover, the emphasis on job titles and past experience can result in missed opportunities if candidates with potential skills for growth are overlooked in favor of those with more conventional backgrounds. If HR is screening candidates but knows little about the nuances of the role they're filling, the risk of missing highly qualified candidates is even greater.

Subjectivity is another challenge. Many interviewers rely on gut feelings or subjective impressions, making it difficult to maintain consistency in hiring standards. As a result, organizations risk hiring candidates based on personal rapport rather than concrete skills and abilities, leading to suboptimal hiring outcomes. Even when portfolio reviews or presentations are part of the interviewing process, evaluation of those additional elements is still largely subjective without clear evaluation rubrics.

The Emergence of Data-Driven Recruitment and Automation

In recent years, the recruitment landscape has evolved significantly, driven by technological advancements and a growing emphasis on data. The rise of applicant tracking systems, as well as recruitment tools powered by AI, has enabled HR teams to sift through vast pools of candidates with greater efficiency. These systems help automate the initial screening process, allowing organizations to identify promising candidates faster and reducing the time to hire.

Technology has made it possible to gather and analyze large amounts of data, ranging from candidate assessments to performance analytics. This shift has led to the emergence of data-driven recruitment, which uses objective insights rather than intuition alone to inform decisions. By leveraging data, organizations can build more reliable processes for evaluating candidates, assessing cultural fit, and predicting potential success in a role.

While there are benefits to using technology for screening candidates, there is also the risk of introducing unintended bias and screening for a standard profile instead of valuing diversity of experience in background and skills. Any new technology should be evaluated for its potential to reduce bias and introduce new biases.

Introducing Skills Data Into Recruitment

Among the various types of data now used in recruitment, skills data has become a point of interest. Unlike traditional resumes, which focus on job history and educational background, skills data provides a more precise understanding of what a candidate can actually do.

Incorporating skills data into recruitment practices offers a more targeted approach to hiring. By focusing on specific skills required for a role, organizations can better match candidates to jobs, reducing the likelihood of mismatches of candidates to open roles. This shift streamlines the hiring process and opens up opportunities for candidates who might have been overlooked by traditional methods. As a result, skills-based recruitment is helping companies move toward a more meritocratic and inclusive approach to talent acquisition.

Boosting and Broadening Candidate-Sourcing Efforts

Skills data can improve candidate recruitment by being more specific about the requirements of a job and mapping those requirements to a candidate's abilities. Instead of relying solely on previous job titles or degrees earned, organizations can focus on the skills that are directly relevant to the role. When recruiters pinpoint the exact capabilities they are looking for, candidate searches are more effective and precise. This approach can also create a more equitable hiring process and expand opportunities for underrepresented groups.

For example, instead of searching for candidates with a generic title like "software engineer," recruiters can focus on specific skills like Python programming, cloud computing, or machine learning. This enables organizations to find candidates who may come from nontraditional backgrounds but possess the skills required for success in the role.

Let's consider two companies to demonstrate the benefits of using skills data in recruitment. First, a multinational consumer goods company shifted its early career hiring practices to focus on candidates' potential rather than their backgrounds. By incorporating online games and AI-based assessments into the recruitment process, it was able to evaluate candidates based on cognitive ability and behavioral traits, leading to a significant increase in hiring diversity and a better overall fit for their roles.

Second, a multinational technology company embraced a skills-first approach in its hiring practices. By using data-driven assessments and focusing on specific technical skills, it has expanded its talent pipeline and hired candidates who may lack formal degrees but possess the right capabilities for the job. This shift has enabled it to address skills shortages in areas such as cybersecurity and cloud computing while promoting a culture of continuous learning among its employees.

Automated Candidate Matching Based on Skills

With the rise of AI-powered tools and machine-learning algorithms, it has become possible to automate candidate matching based on skills data. These tools can analyze both the skills requirements of a job and the skills profiles of candidates, creating a more efficient matching process. This automation speeds up the initial stages of recruitment by quickly identifying the most qualified candidates, enabling recruiters to spend their time on the most promising prospects.

Automated systems can parse skills data from various sources—including online portfolios, skills assessments, and social media profiles—to build a comprehensive picture of a candidate's competencies. This helps organizations move beyond surface-level qualifications seen in resumes and provides a more robust view of how qualified candidates may differ from one another in skill strengths and weaknesses.

Reducing Reliance on Resumes

We've already discussed how resumes can be inaccurate or an embellished representation of someone's skills, beyond the potential discrepancies in job history or educational qualifications. Because a resume is self-reported and largely unvalidated, it's unreliable. By instead focusing on skills data, organizations can shift away from the traditional reliance on resumes. Skills assessments and data-driven evaluations provide a more objective basis for understanding a candidate's abilities. This not only improves the accuracy of hiring decisions but also helps create a more level playing field for candidates from diverse backgrounds.

Skills-based assessments can include coding tests, project simulations, and real-world problem-solving exercises that demonstrate a candidate's practical capabilities. This ensures that hiring decisions are grounded in demonstrated skills rather than subjective impressions from interviews or resume reviews.

Take, for example, a multinational financial services company that implemented a skills-based hiring process to address underrepresentation in its IT department. By introducing skills assessments for coding and systems analysis, they reduced the emphasis on degree requirements and focused instead on practical competencies, allowing the hiring teams to focus on candidates who had the necessary skills, even if they didn't have traditional experience.

Expanding Talent Pools

One of the key advantages of using skills data in recruitment is the ability to expand talent pools. Many traditional methods exclude candidates who do not fit a narrow set of qualifications, such as specific degrees earned or colleges attended, or work experience at prestigious companies. Skills-based recruitment, however, allows organizations to consider a wider range of candidates who have the necessary abilities but may have followed nontraditional educational or career paths.

This approach is particularly valuable in today's competitive job market because the demand for specialized skills often outstrips supply. By focusing on skills, companies can access a more diverse talent pool, including self-taught professionals, career changers, and candidates from underrepresented groups. This helps address talent shortages and fosters a more inclusive workplace culture.

Consider the example of a global tech company that partnered with a recruitment company focused on a hire-train-deploy model. While the tech company focused its own team's recruitment efforts to a limited list of colleges and universities, the recruitment partner company took the list of skills requirements and screened from a broader range of smaller or less traditionally technology-focused schools. This partnership resulted in more qualified candidates from a broader range of experiences, uncovering hidden talent pools from which the technology company could find high quality candidates.

Addressing Unconscious Bias

Unconscious bias can subtly influence hiring decisions, leading recruiters to favor candidates who fit a certain profile or come from familiar backgrounds. Skills-based recruitment, however, centers the evaluation process on specific capabilities rather than personal identifiers. By relying on objective data about a candidate's skills, recruiters can minimize the impact of biases related to age, gender, ethnicity, or educational history.

For example, instead of evaluating a candidate based on the prestige of their alma mater, a skills-based approach assesses their proficiency in relevant technologies or problem-solving abilities. This shift not only enhances fairness but also broadens the pool of potential candidates, offering opportunities to those whose talents might otherwise be overlooked.

A leading technology firm implemented a blind skills-based shortlisting process to improve diversity within its software development team. By using skills assessments and data-driven algorithms and anonymizing the evaluation before mapping results to named candidates, the firm was able to screen candidates based solely on their coding abilities and problem-solving skills. As a result, it saw a 30 percent increase in candidates from nontraditional educational backgrounds reaching the interview stage.

This shift not only increased the number of women and minorities in the candidate pool but also led to better job performance and retention. The emphasis on skills allowed the company to identify high-potential candidates who might have been overlooked in a traditional resume-based process. This example underscores the potential of skills-based hiring to foster a more inclusive workplace.

Assessing Potential in Job Candidates

Assessing potential in a job candidate using skills data involves evaluating not only the candidate's current capabilities but also their ability to grow and adapt within the organization. Skills data provides a nuanced understanding of a candidate's strengths, learning agility, and readiness to take on new challenges, making it a valuable tool in identifying high-potential hires. Here are some key ways to assess a candidate's potential based on skills data.

Evaluating Core Capabilities and Transferable Skills

Skills data allows recruiters to see which fundamental skills a candidate has mastered, providing a foundation for assessing their potential. By focusing on core capabilities that are critical for success across roles (such as problem solving and communication) and on transferable skills (such as project management, leadership, and analytical thinking), organizations can determine whether the candidate has the foundational skills that could make them successful no matter how their role changes over time. This approach helps identify candidates who might not have extensive experience but possess the critical baseline abilities required for growth, as well as candidates who can transition across departments or take on more complex tasks as they progress within the organization.

Analyzing Learning Agility

A candidate's ability to acquire new skills quickly is a strong indicator of their potential for growth. Organizations can collect skills data about the candidate's history of learning new technologies or methodologies, as well as any additional certifications or training they have completed. For example, a candidate who has studied new programming languages or completed industry-relevant courses demonstrates a readiness to learn and adapt—qualities that are essential for long-term potential in fast-paced industries.

Measuring Growth Through Skills Assessments

Conducting skills assessments as part of the hiring process can provide a direct measure of a candidate's potential to perform in a new role. These assessments can simulate real-world scenarios or challenges that the candidate might face on the job, offering a glimpse into how they apply their skills in practice. A strong performance on such assessments, especially when combined with evidence of a candidate's ability to improve over time, signals that the individual is ready to tackle more complex responsibilities.

Mapping Skills to Future Needs

Using skills data, organizations can match a candidate's existing skills to the future needs of the company. This involves analyzing skills that are currently in demand alongside those that will be needed as the organization grows or as the industry evolves. Candidates who already demonstrate proficiency in emerging skills, such as data analysis or AI engineering, can be seen as having the potential to fill critical roles in the future.

Assessing Adaptability and Versatility

Skills data can provide insights into a candidate's versatility—how well they adapt to different roles or changing work environments. For example, if a candidate has shown proficiency in multiple related skills or has worked on varied projects, it suggests an ability to shift focus and learn quickly. This versatility is a key indicator of potential because it shows that the candidate will likely thrive in roles that evolve over time.

By focusing on these types of patterns in skills data, recruiters can gain a clearer picture of a candidate's potential beyond their past job titles or educational background. This approach enables organizations to make informed hiring decisions, ensuring that new team members not only fit the immediate needs of the role but also have the capacity to grow and contribute to the company's future success.

Improving the Interview Process

Skills data has revolutionized not only the initial stages of recruitment and hiring but also the interview process itself. By crafting data-driven interview questions, structuring interviews around skills assessments, and using data to evaluate performance, organizations can create a more consistent and fair interview experience.

Creating Skills-Centric Interview Questions

With access to detailed skills data, recruiters can design interview questions that directly align with the skills required for a role. Interviewers can probe specific skills, such as a candidate's proficiency in project management tools or their approach to problem solving in technical scenarios. This approach ensures that interview discussions are relevant and focused, providing a clearer picture of how a candidate's skills will translate to on-the-job success. This doesn't necessarily mean that the questions you ask candidates are dramatically different from what you ask them today. It really means that the answers you receive should be aligned with the skills required for success in the role and added to other data sources used in the candidate selection process.

You can use the following example questions to assess skills relevant to a variety of roles. As you can see, these are common interview questions that can be reimagined and evaluated through a skills lens:

- **Problem-solving skills:** "Can you walk me through a time when you encountered a complex problem at work? How did you approach it, and what was the outcome?"
- **Technical proficiency:** "Which software or tools are you most comfortable using for [specific task or industry]? Can you describe a project that required you to effectively apply these tools?"
- **Communication skills:** "Describe a time when you had to explain a technical concept to a nontechnical team member or client. How did you ensure they understood?"

- **Adaptability and learning:** "Tell me about a new skill or technology you recently learned. How did you go about learning it, and how have you applied it in your work?"
- **Project management:** "Can you describe a project you managed from start to finish? What methods did you use to keep it on track, and how did you ensure its successful completion?"
- **Collaboration skills:** "Give an example of a time when you had to work closely with a team to achieve a goal. What role did you play, and how did you ensure the team worked effectively together?"
- **Attention to detail:** "In your last role, how did you ensure the quality and accuracy of your work? Can you provide an example of a time when your attention to detail made a difference?"
- **Time management:** "Describe a situation in which you had multiple deadlines to meet. How did you prioritize your tasks, and what strategies did you use to manage your time effectively?"
- **Customer service:** "Tell me about a time when you had to handle a difficult client or customer. What steps did you take to resolve the situation, and what was the result?"
- **Analytical skills:** "Can you share a time when you analyzed data or information to make a decision? What was the process you used, and what impact did your decision have?"

These questions focus on a candidate's specific skills and how they apply them in real-world scenarios, as well as their approach to solving problems. They can be applied to a wide range of roles.

Structuring Interviews Around Skills Assessments

Incorporating skills assessments into the interview process allows for a more hands-on evaluation of a candidate's abilities. This could include practical exercises, such as coding challenges for software developers or case studies for business analysts. These assessments are not only more engaging for candidates but also provide tangible evidence of their skills in action, making it easier for interviewers to compare candidates based on their actual performance rather than their self-reported abilities.

Evaluating Interview Performance More Objectively

Skills data can also help standardize how interviewers assess performance. By scoring candidates against a predefined skills rubric, interviewers can minimize subjective judgments. This also allows organizations to ensure consistency across different interviewers. For example, if communication is a key competency for a role, candidates can be scored on specific criteria, such as clarity and effectiveness in presenting ideas (Table 8-1).

Table 8-1. Example Skills Rubric: Delivering Executive Presentations

Proficiency Level	Description	Behavioral Indicators
1 Emerging	Struggles to tailor messages to executive audiences; lacks confidence or clarity	• Overuses details or technical language inappropriate for executives • Presentation lacks clear purpose or structure • Reads slides or notes without engagement • Has difficulty answering high-level or strategic questions
2 Developing	Demonstrates growing ability to communicate with executives but needs support to be effective	• Begins to simplify complex ideas for business leaders • Requires coaching or rehearsal to deliver presentations • Shows effort in aligning message to executive priorities • May lack confidence or polish in delivery
3 Proficient	Presents confidently and clearly to executives, aligning content with business needs	• Tailors content to strategic goals and executive interests • Engages executives with focused, well-structured messaging • Anticipates key questions and provides concise, actionable answers • Uses visuals and storytelling effectively to enhance results
4 Advanced	Commands the room and consistently delivers high-impact presentations to executive audiences	• Synthesizes complex data into executive-ready insights • Influences decisions through persuasive and credible delivery • Facilitates executive discussion with poise and responsiveness • Adjusts on the fly to audience reactions and priorities
5 Expert	Seen as a role model for executive communication; trusted advisor and strategic voice	• Delivers visionary presentations that shape strategic direction • Regularly presents to C-suite or board-level audiences with influence • Coaches others on executive presentation skills • Builds alignment and buy-in for critical initiatives through compelling communication

This structured approach helps reduce discrepancies in evaluations and makes the final hiring decision more transparent. This is particularly important in large organizations that may involve multiple interviewers.

Enhancing the Candidate Experience

The integration of skills data into recruitment processes not only benefits employers but also enhances the experience for candidates. A more personalized and transparent approach to hiring makes job seekers feel valued and informed, while simplifying their path to applying for roles that match their strengths and reducing time wasted by applying for roles that aren't a good fit. Let's explore how skills data can transform the candidate journey, from tailored job recommendations to streamlined application processes and feedback mechanisms.

Personalizing Job Recommendations Based on Skills

One of the key advantages of using skills data is the ability to provide candidates with personalized job recommendations. By analyzing a candidate's skills profile—gleaned from their resume, online assessments, or professional portfolios—recruiters can suggest roles that align closely with the candidate's strengths and career goals.

This personalization saves candidates time and effort, guiding them toward opportunities that their skills are most relevant for. It also fosters a sense of engagement and enthusiasm because job seekers can immediately see how their unique abilities align with specific roles.

Transparent Communication of Skills Requirements in Job Postings

Skills-based job postings clarify what is truly needed for success in a role, offering candidates a transparent view of the essential competencies. This practice involves listing specific skills and proficiency levels required for the position, rather than using vague descriptors like "strong communication skills" or "relevant experience."

Such transparency helps candidates better understand whether they meet the qualifications before applying, leading to a more-informed and self-selecting pool of applicants. It also ensures that candidates are clear about what the job entails, setting realistic expectations from the outset.

Many current job descriptions include "years of experience" in a role as guidance for candidates. While time spent in a particular role might be a strong indicator of skills, it can also be misleading because it doesn't indicate parameters around success or responsibilities within a role. Plus, by listing time in a previous role as a qualifier, you exclude potentially strong candidates who have different but relevant experience.

From a candidate's perspective, skills-based job descriptions are the best way to provide the details of what is required and desired for a particular role so they can apply to the jobs that best fit their skills and not waste their time with those that don't.

Streamlining the Application Process

Skills data can also streamline the application process by automating parts of candidate evaluation. For instance, candidates can complete online skills assessments as part of their application, allowing recruiters to quickly screen for essential capabilities. This approach reduces the back-and-forth often associated with traditional hiring processes, making the application experience smoother and more efficient.

Automating these initial screenings helps candidates progress through the process more quickly, especially when they meet the required skill benchmarks. This creates a more positive experience because candidates do not feel like they are lost in a lengthy and opaque process.

There are multiple ways to conduct these initial screenings, from standardized behavioral assessments or questionnaires to open-ended prompts and video-based interviews. Exploring options to engage candidates around their skills during the application process provides more data to recruiters and hiring managers to make screening decisions, but it also allows candidates to engage more deeply with a potential employer than just sending over a resume to tell the story of their qualifications.

Feedback Mechanisms Based on Skills Assessments

Providing meaningful feedback is another way to enhance the candidate experience. Skills-based assessments generate specific insights into a candidate's strengths and areas for improvement, enabling recruiters to offer more constructive feedback. Even if a candidate is not selected, sharing insights from their skills assessments can help them understand how to better prepare for future opportunities.

For example, a candidate applying for a digital marketing role might receive feedback highlighting their strengths in search engine optimization (SEO) but suggesting improvement in social media analytics. This feedback empowers candidates to refine their skills, increasing their chances of success in future applications.

Aligning Recruitment With Business Goals

Effective recruitment is not just about filling immediate vacancies; it's also a strategic tool for aligning workforce capabilities with long-term business objectives. Skills data plays an important role in this alignment, enabling organizations to anticipate future needs, plan for talent development, and ensure that their workforces are ready to meet evolving challenges.

Consider a global logistics company that used skills data to future-proof its workforce as it shifted to digital operations. By analyzing the skills of current employees and identifying gaps in areas such as data analytics and software development, it crafted a targeted recruitment strategy. The company also used this data to design internal upskilling programs, ensuring that existing employees could transition into new roles.

Within two years, the company had successfully filled critical tech roles and retrained 25 percent of its workforce to adapt to the digital shift. This proactive approach not only supported the company's technological transformation but also improved employee engagement by offering growth opportunities.

Supporting Strategic Workforce Planning

Skills data provides a detailed understanding of the current capabilities within an organization, allowing leaders to identify gaps and develop strategies to address them. One of the key strategies to close skills gaps is hiring for missing skills, but hiring efforts must be aligned with broader business goals. As an example, if a company plans to expand its data analytics division, skills data can highlight the specific analytical skills that are missing, guiding targeted recruitment to fill those gaps. This strategic view of hiring ensures that recruitment supports the organization's growth plans and prepares it for future demands, rather than reacting to immediate hiring needs without a long-term vision.

Skills data can inform long-term talent acquisition strategies, helping companies build a talent pool that supports their strategic goals and ensures a robust pipeline of future leaders to support succession planning. By focusing on acquiring candidates with critical skills, organizations can ensure they have the right mix of expertise to navigate future needs and challenges.

Identifying Future Skills Gaps and Aligning Hiring Efforts

Because the business environment is constantly evolving, new skills are always emerging. Skills data allows companies to forecast future trends and identify the competencies that will become critical in the coming years. By proactively addressing skills gaps, organizations can position themselves to become or remain leaders in their industries.

For example, a manufacturing company transitioning to automation might use skills data to anticipate a need for more engineers with expertise in robotics and AI. By focusing recruitment efforts on these areas, it can build a talent pipeline that ensures smooth adoption of new technologies.

Conclusion

The integration of skills data into recruitment practices is reshaping how organizations attract and retain talent. By focusing on objective assessments, skills-based hiring creates a more inclusive and fair hiring process, enhances the candidate experience through personalized interactions, and supports long-term business strategies through strategic workforce planning.

Looking ahead, the role of AI and machine learning in analyzing skills data is poised to grow, offering even more sophisticated ways to match candidates to roles and predict their success. As organizations continue to refine their approaches, skills data will become an even more important tool in transforming talent acquisition and building a more adaptive, capable workforce.

The future of recruitment lies in its ability to adapt to the changing landscape of work, in which skills, rather than titles, are the currency of potential. Skills data is the key to finding hidden potential, driving recruitment practices that are as dynamic and diverse as the workforce organizations aim to build.

But adopting a skills-based culture goes beyond adjusting recruitment practices; it requires a mindset shift throughout the organization. A skills-based culture emphasizes the importance of continuous learning and development, encouraging employees to focus on building their capabilities rather than relying solely on their past experiences. This cultural shift can also inspire more inclusive internal mobility so employees are considered for new roles based on their skills rather than their tenure or existing position. Such a culture ensures that every team member has an opportunity to advance, creating a work environment that values potential and growth over static qualifications. In the next two chapters, we'll explore how organizational culture and talent management practices can be transformed in a skills-based organization.

The Evolution of Skills in a Tech-Driven World

Contributed by Rosellen Beck, Executive Leader of Global HR Technology and AI Strategist, GE Healthcare

Over the past few years, two competing views have stirred the waters of talent management:

- **Skills as the cornerstone of our future.** Skills are everything. As traditional career paths get tangled in today's fast-paced demands, the need to rethink work and chart a new course has become critical. Skills are the foundation of this new world.
- **Skills as expensive hype.** On the flip side, some folks argue that skills are a bit overhyped. They say skills are subjective, the return on investment is questionable, and the upkeep—well, let's just say it's a headache. Who needs more complexity, right?

Both sides have a point—at least, they did until now. Enter AI. It isn't just sitting on the sidelines; AI is shaking things up, connecting the dots between people and the skills they bring to the table. Suddenly, skills are the real MVPs—flexible, universal, and free from the usual baggage, such as cost and maintenance.

Think of skills as a new kind of currency, with AI as your savvy currency trader. Every employee is a bundle of potential, and AI is getting better at figuring out which skills are in demand and which ones are just waiting for their moment in the spotlight. Whether it's industry-specific know-how or a knack for navigating different geographies, AI keeps the value of these skills in sync with the market's ever-shifting currents—all without the traditional bureaucratic overhead.

For chief human resource officers (CHROs) and chief information officers (CIOs), this isn't just a game changer; it's an opportunity wrapped in a challenge. The challenge? Ditching the old-school methods of skills assessment and management. The opportunity? Harnessing AI to build, manage, and grow your talent base and supercharge your workforce, making sure that even skills that aren't a perfect match can still pack a punch and drive your business forward.

Let's paint a picture to bring this to life.

Take project managers and scrum masters, for instance. Traditionally, these roles are treated as apples and oranges, each with its own distinct skill set, despite scrum being an Agile project management framework. But what if AI suggests that someone with a project management background could be a rock star scrum master? At first, you might think, "Wait, what?" But hold on—are they really that different?

AI can dive deep into not just the surface-level skills but the full spectrum of factors—industry, department, seniority, location, budget, and, most important, the unique skills and experiences of the individual. It might turn out that the project manager's skills are just what's needed to round out a scrum team, especially if it's already swimming in scrum masters but missing some complementary abilities. AI can spot these connections—the ones that traditional hiring processes might miss—ensuring that your teams are as well rounded as they come.

Now, let's give a nod to our recruiter friends. They've been doing this matching dance manually for ages, combing through resumes and LinkedIn profiles like pros. But let's be real—it's a time-consuming grind, and there's only so much a human can process. AI picks up the slack, freeing recruiters to focus on the fun stuff—like making sure the skills align with your company's culture, rather than getting bogged down in the administrative weeds.

But what about this AI evolution from the job candidate's perspective? What about the people who aren't even looking for new gigs? Or the hidden gems who don't realize they're perfect for a role they've never considered? AI can guide individuals to roles that align with their unique strengths and career aspirations. In essence, AI becomes their career GPS, showing them where their skills—their personal currency—can make the biggest impact and how to boost their value over time.

Of course, as AI flips the script on skill matching, it's crucial to remember that your skills data—as either an employer or a job seeker—doesn't have to be flawless. From an employer's perspective, skills data does, however, need to be nurtured, validated, and aligned with its strategic goals. AI can help automate and standardize skills inferences.

As the market ebbs and flows, AI can ensure that skills and skills data remain sharp and relevant. Companies can then focus less on "babysitting" individual skill sets and more on making sure the right skills are in the right roles.

Returning to the project manager and scrum master example, AI isn't just playing matchmaker—it's evaluating the deeper competencies. It might find that the project manager is a whiz at facilitation and agile projects—key ingredients for scrum master success. Even if their job title doesn't scream scrum master, AI can alert you that they might have what it takes. It's like finding the secret sauce that turns a good team into a great one.

In short, AI and skills are teaming up to change the game. They're crafting an intelligent marketplace in which people's talents align seamlessly with business needs and budgets—without all the costly maintenance and management we used to dread. For CHROs and CIOs, this isn't just a nice-to-have; it's your ticket to optimizing workforce planning and ensuring that your organization is nimble, adaptable, and ready to conquer tomorrow's challenges. So get on board, because AI and skills are leaving with or without you!

CHAPTER 9
Fostering a Learning Culture

In this chapter, we'll cover:
- Collecting the data to show skills development and improvement through validation
- Connecting learning content with the unique needs and aspirations of each employee
- Designing upskilling and reskilling programs to future-proof the organization

By embracing skills, L&D as a function has an opportunity to be more important than ever before. It is true that for most L&D teams, this will mean a reimagining of their role and purpose within their organization. But L&D is uniquely positioned to support skills-based organizations in three important ways:
- Building needed skills within the workforce
- Validating skill data
- Demonstrating the impact of learning investments on skills and business metrics

Depending on your L&D function's current focus, introducing skills may mean taking on a dramatically different level of responsibility for the success of the organization. To build a skills-based organization, a skills-focused L&D team is essential to the long-term success of the system. To that end, this chapter focuses on the key opportunities for L&D to drive a skills evolution, both within the L&D function itself and across the business.

Learning Organization Personas

Before jumping into how L&D can be transformed (and transform the business) through skills data, having a snapshot of "L&D before skills" will help frame the difference that skills data can make. Let's be honest: In most organizations, L&D is not seen as a strategic driver of competitive advantage for the business. L&D organizations have generally taken on one of three roles, depending on the organization's culture:

- **Provider.** In some organizations, L&D is responsible for making sure content and learning experiences are available for employees, but it's not expected or asked to show the impact of the learning content or experiences on the organization. Organizations with a provider L&D culture typically see learning as a benefit, and employee awareness that learning is available is the primary goal. They typically look to employee engagement with learning as the primary success metric, and how they organize or invest in their learning programs greatly relies on what employees are asking for. Many organizations house L&D under HR, and tout the L&D-provided opportunities during employee recruitment and onboarding, but do little to connect learning to business impact outside employee engagement and retention metrics.

- **Planner.** In a planner L&D culture, the work is typically focused on compliance and tracking employee learning. These organizations are much more data driven but may not be strategically focused on how learning aligns to business metrics for success. They often look to completion rates and score tracking to evaluate the impact of learning investments. Learning in planner organizations is often focused on specific initiatives, a strategic priority of the business, or a particular issue in a team or department.

- **Promoter.** In a promoter L&D culture, organizations will often identify themselves as "learning organizations." They see learning as important to the overall success of the business, and they frame learning as one of their core values. Many organizations with promoter cultures share some characteristics with provider and planner cultures, with the main difference being that they hold continuous or lifelong learning as a core value. Promoter L&D organizations often market how their learning investments can help employees develop, and in some advanced cases, they tie learning investments to business impact metrics. Many executive teams have a chief learning officer who, in addition to the CEO, will regularly talk about how much they value learning. Metrics for promoter cultures range from usage, to engagement, to impact, and learning itself is often tracked, but ideally the impact of learning is discussed between managers and employees, typically in the context of performance reviews or conversations.

A skills-based organization can have a fourth role for L&D: performance-centered. These L&D teams are focused on three areas of performance: business, team, and individual. The focus of performance-centered learning organizations is on driving improvement in performance across the business, making these L&D teams data driven and impact-obsessed. They are huge supporters of continuous learning, but they want to see the results of their learning investments. Many of these teams experiment with different models and modalities of learning to see what works best in terms of business impact. They care about individual performance improvement, they analyze what makes teams high performing, and they know what key business metrics they are working to influence.

Performance-centered teams also view learning in the context of larger business goals, and they collaborate closely with HR, recruitment, and line of business leaders to ensure their work is aligned across the business. These teams speak the language of the business and are often seen as a strategic advantage to the organization—not just a cost center, but a necessary function in keeping the business competitive and high performing.

Performance-centered teams see themselves as part of the business, but also see the business as their customer. They are constantly striving to find ways to measure and communicate impact. Performance-centered learning organizations are the most prepared to adopt skills data because it helps tie learning and development to business needs.

Depending on how your L&D team currently functions, there may be different organizational challenges on your journey to becoming skills-based. Provider L&D teams will likely need to jump into data in a much more meaningful way, and taking on responsibility for assessing and validating skills may mean new responsibilities. Planner L&D teams are already data driven but need to shift their focus from learning metrics to skills and business metrics. Promoter L&D teams will need to shift their energy from learning to performance. Knowing where your organization is starting from can help you identify any gaps so you can evolve into a performance-centered culture that is most aligned with skills-based organizations.

These different roles for learning organizations play an important part in how skills may be received and how difficult the evolution to becoming skills-based may be from an L&D perspective. As you are embarking on a skills journey, understanding your organization's current attitude toward learning will affect the steps you may need to take to evolve the L&D function to best take advantage of skills data.

The Evolution of Learning and Development

Not every L&D team needs to be performance-centered to use skills to improve its outcomes, but all learning teams should take note: Skills are not an L&D movement; they are a business movement. L&D has the unique opportunity to take leadership in a skills evolution because of its unique responsibility of developing skills across the organization's workforce. For L&D organizations that have struggled to secure a seat at the executive table, skills present an opportunity: You can remain a function that focuses on content and programs, or you can evolve to be a team that builds the skills the organization needs. If an L&D team doesn't take this opportunity, it risks being left behind as AI innovation makes content development less and less burdensome. To stay relevant,

L&D must rise to the challenge of demonstrating the business value of learning through skills data.

Traditional Functions of L&D Teams

Regardless of the role of learning in an organization, L&D teams are typically responsible for a range of initiatives related to employee development, including:
- Onboarding
- Compliance training
- Systems or process training
- Leadership development
- Knowledge management
- Certification (as needed by the organization)
- Professional development

In some cases, L&D is housed under HR, and in others, it is a standalone function. In some organizations, L&D is centralized into one team that serves the business; in others, L&D is distributed throughout the lines of business and serves the needs of the team it is affiliated with (for example, sales, customer service, or engineering). Depending on the structure and reporting hierarchy, L&D may have its own budget and manage its own tech ecosystem, or it may be tied to a broader net of investments controlled and managed by the chief technology officer.

From the varying cultures and structures alone, it should be apparent that there is no one-size-fits-all approach to how L&D currently functions. Yet the practices covered by L&D are surprisingly consistent, maybe because of the historical view of learning as a cost center instead of as a driver of revenue.

What are the historical characteristics of traditional L&D programs? When most people think of L&D, they think of:
- Classroom training (or virtual synchronized instruction in a post-pandemic world)
- E-learning modules
- One-size-fits-all programs
- Top-down compliance

- Self-driven content libraries
- Assessment

These typical L&D characteristics and deliverables often struggle to gain traction with employees unless activities are required to be completed—and for good reason. First, traditional L&D programs lack personalization, providing the same content and experiences to every employee regardless of differences in skills, proficiency, job role, goals, or career path. This lack of personalization means that learning may be irrelevant or redundant, and in either case, seem like a waste of time.

A second challenge is limited feedback on training effectiveness. If an employee invests in participating in a learning activity, impact should be transparent to the employee, the employee's manager, and the organization. Without this transparency, it's impossible to understand the value of participating in learning activities.

A final challenge of traditional learning activities is the disconnect between the learning experience and where in the employee's work the learning (and new skills) can be applied. Most learning programs are relatively self-contained and don't extend to on-the-job application. Because of this, new skills can be learned in training, but if not practiced and applied at work, they can be forgotten.

A Shift From Learning to Skills Development

While organizations are discovering the value of skills to provide deeper insights into people-related decisions in the business, L&D will need to shift its mindset from learning to skills development regarding the value of L&D to the organization, as well as the measurable outcome that L&D can deliver. The relevance that L&D can struggle to provide in traditional models becomes clear with personalized learning based on skills-data insights. Skills assessments are a natural evolution of traditional assessments owned by L&D and can provide organizations with the critical data they need to power skills-based decisions.

The shift to being a skills-based organization means prioritizing the capabilities of its workforce. It's crucial to understand the distinction between learning and skills development, as well as the focus shift required for L&D. While these two concepts are interconnected, they represent different approaches to employee growth and performance. Traditionally, *learning* refers to the process of acquiring new knowledge, information, or techniques through education, training programs, or on-the-job experiences. On the other hand, *skills development* focuses on the practical application of that learning, ensuring that employees can effectively apply the knowledge they've acquired to improve performance in their roles, drive business results, and prepare for the next step in their careers.

The shift from learning to skills development is marked by a more focused, measurable approach that directly ties learning activities to the development of key skills. This shift enables organizations to not only provide training but also track the progression of skills over time, assess proficiency levels, and align skills growth with business needs. This results in a more strategic and effective way to develop employees, moving beyond the traditional learning model and fostering a workforce equipped to meet both current and future demands.

In skills-based organizations, understanding what skills an employee has and what skills they need provides the skills data to power more meaningful learning. Two types of skills-centered learning experiences support skills development and can be powered by skills-data insights:

- **Personalized learning** refers to a holistic approach to make learning more relevant to an employee, using whatever data is available to recommend content and experiences that meet the employee's learning needs. When skills data is available, personalized learning can be supercharged beyond recommendations related to role or career goals. Infusing skills data into personalized learning means that learning can be recommended based on skills gaps in an individual's current role, skills they want to focus on to achieve a personal development goal, or skills that they need to develop to be prepared for the next step in their career path.
- **Adaptive learning** refers to technology-driven learning systems that dynamically adjust content, pace, and difficulty based on

the learner's progress and performance in real time. It uses data analytics and algorithms to continuously modify the learning path to meet the learner's immediate needs, ensuring that they receive the right support at the right moment. As skills data is introduced into an adaptive learning system, it will be possible to adjust learning in real time to meet an individual's skill and proficiency needs. This is an advanced type of personalized learning, and while it may be helpful to the individual, it may make tracking what each employee is learning and the impact of that learning difficult, if not impossible. As L&D organizations become more data driven, learning what methodologies work best to build different skills means that some consistency in data is needed to show patterns between learning and outcomes. However, if your goal is to make learning hyper-relevant to the employee, and analyzing learning outcomes is less important, adaptive learning is becoming increasingly possible with AI.

Targeting Learning With Skills

Whether your organization experiments with personalized learning or adaptive learning, skills data allows you to create targeted learning initiatives to address skills gaps, build new skills, and help employees realize their career goals.

Skills data enables L&D to target learning solutions and investments by providing organizations with precise insights into individual and team competencies, focusing learning efforts where they will have the greatest impact. By addressing specific skills gaps, skills data helps identify areas where employees lack critical knowledge or proficiency. This information allows L&D teams to design tailored programs aimed at closing those gaps, rather than relying on generic training. For example, if an employee is skilled in most aspects of their role but lacks proficiency in data analysis, skills data will highlight this gap, prompting targeted training in that area to improve performance.

In addition to closing skills gaps, skills data is equally valuable in identifying and nurturing high-performing employees by offering learning opportunities that build on their existing strengths or expertise. Rather than focusing solely on weaknesses, skills data can highlight areas where employees excel, allowing them to deepen their expertise or take on more challenging projects. By leveraging these insights, organizations can provide advanced or specialized training, helping employees grow into leadership positions or become subject matter experts. This dual approach—addressing weaknesses and fostering strengths—maximizes the potential of each employee and aligns skills development with both individual career aspirations and business objectives.

Validating Skills Through Assessment

As L&D has primarily owned assessment within organizations, the shift to skills means rethinking assessments and what claims can be made based on them. Skills assessments (which often result in higher-validity skills signal data points) are evolving into skills validation, a rebranding of the more negative connotations of assessment. L&D is at the forefront of this move, and it can take on the responsibility of collecting the data to show skills development and improvement through validation.

Skills validation is the process of verifying and confirming that an individual possesses a particular skill or set of skills at a specific proficiency level. It is a step beyond self-reported skills or general claims of expertise, using objective measures to validate whether an individual can effectively apply their knowledge in real-world scenarios. Skills validation is crucial for building trust in the accuracy of employee skills data, particularly when this data is being used in higher-risk decisions, such as promotions or role assignments. While not every skill needs to be validated, and not every skill-informed decision is high risk, skills validation is important to consider for critical skills that inform key decisions.

Skills validation does not typically rely on a single skills signal, but an aggregate of signals that in combination meet an organization's threshold for validation. Here are example strategies that L&D can employ to collect data to validate skills:

- **Skills tests and quizzes.** These are standardized assessments designed to test specific knowledge areas or technical skills.

For example, coding tests for software developers, or quizzes on project management principles for project manager roles, can provide measurable proof of proficiency. Problem-based assessments, which ask employees how they would address a scenario or solve a problem, are particularly useful in focusing on skills rather than assessing for knowledge. These assessments provide immediate results, making them a popular method for skills validation in recruitment because specific skills may be a requirement for hiring.

- **Simulations.** Simulations replicate real-world tasks and challenges, allowing individuals to demonstrate their ability to apply skills in context. For example, business simulations might involve solving a company problem, while flight simulators for pilots test operational proficiency.
- **Case studies.** Case studies require individuals to analyze scenarios and develop solutions, showing their analytical and decision-making abilities. They may not need to be related to the employee's job role if the goal is to understand human capabilities rather than job or technical skills.
- **Portfolio reviews.** A portfolio review involves evaluating a collection of an individual's work (such as projects, designs, reports, or coding samples) to validate skills through tangible evidence. This method is commonly used in creative fields such as design, writing, or software development because the quality and impact of past work can effectively demonstrate expertise.
- **Certifications.** Certifications from recognized organizations provide a formal and credible way to validate skills. Many certifications are tied to a rigorous assessment process that includes testing, coursework, or practical assignments, and they demonstrate an individual's qualifications in specific areas, such as IT, project management, or data analysis. Credentials in medical, legal, and financial fields, for example, are also validated indicators of skill that require continuing education to

maintain. Organizations can use certifications and credentials to confidently trust proficiency for particular skills.

- **Performance reviews and managerial feedback.** Direct feedback from supervisors or peers, gathered through structured performance reviews or 360-degree assessments, can also serve as a method for validating human skills, such as leadership, communication, or teamwork. While subjective, when combined with objective measures, this feedback can give a fuller picture of an employee's skill proficiency.
- **Practical assignments or job trials.** Practical assignments or job trials involve placing an employee in a real-world situation that requires them to use the skill being validated. This could be a short-term project, a specific task, or a probationary period, but their performance is closely observed to ensure that they meet the necessary skill requirements. Often in these types of skills assessments, each employee partners with an evaluator, who observes the employee's skill. The goal is typically to determine not only skill proficiency, but also a promotion, a role change, or movement out of a probationary period.
- **Competency-based interviews.** While not the most common method of skill validation, competency-based interviews are an opportunity for L&D to deeply support skills validation by becoming an expert in conducting interviews. These interviews focus on asking candidates to describe how they've applied specific skills in past experiences. Interviewers look for examples of how skills were used to solve problems or achieve goals, offering insights into real-world application and validation of the candidate's abilities. Competency-based interviews are a relatively quick but human-powered way to collect skills proficiency data; to reduce the risk for bias, you should use clear rubrics to provide transparency in these interviews.

Skills validation provides both employees and employers with confidence in the skills data being used for people-related decisions. Each organization should evaluate the threshold for skills validation; that threshold may vary for different skills. L&D has the opportunity to own skills validation within an organization and provide clarity and transparency on how skills are assessed and validated. Because skills validation is not a one-time event, L&D can also own the continuous evaluation and data collection processes that will keep skills data up to date and relevant, confidently powering a skills-based organization.

Measuring L&D Impact and ROI

One of the greatest challenges organizations face in traditional L&D initiatives is measuring impact and return on investment (ROI) for the business. In many cases, L&D programs focus on delivering content without having a clear, measurable connection to the outcomes they seek to improve. The absence of direct ties between learning activities and business performance makes it difficult to demonstrate the value of L&D. Furthermore, traditional metrics such as course completion rates, learner satisfaction, or time spent in training do little to showcase the impact on productivity or organizational goals. As a result, L&D teams often struggle to justify their programs in terms of bottom-line results, which can lead to underinvestment in training initiatives or a lack of alignment with strategic business objectives.

Enabling More Accurate Measurement of Learning Outcomes

Skills data fundamentally changes the way organizations measure the effectiveness of their learning initiatives. Instead of relying on superficial metrics such as attendance or completion, skills data provides a direct link between learning and the actual acquisition and application of skills. By tracking employees' skills before, during, and after training, organizations gain a clearer view of how effective specific learning programs are at closing skills gaps. This enables L&D teams to shift the focus from mere participation to measurable outcomes such as development of new skills, increase in proficiency levels, and the practical application of skills in day-to-day work. With skills data, the value of learning initiatives becomes tangible, offering a more accurate reflection of how training affects employee capabilities and performance.

Skills Tip

Don't assume that improving skills and closing skills gaps is enough to show the impact of learning on an organization. Skills are not a business metric; skills data is simply an indicator of impact on key business drivers. Beware of thinking that skills are the goal—business performance is the goal, and focusing on skills is a way to more effectively address key needs that can help you achieve your business performance targets.

Linking Skills Acquisition to Performance Metrics and Business Goals

A major advantage of using skills data to measure L&D effectiveness is the ability to link skills acquisition directly to performance metrics and business goals. By mapping specific skills to key business objectives, organizations can ensure that learning initiatives align with strategic priorities. For example, if a company's goal is to increase its digital transformation capabilities, skills data can be used to track progress in key areas, such as data analysis, coding, or digital marketing. As employees develop these skills, their improved performance can be measured against relevant business outcomes, such as faster project delivery, higher customer satisfaction, or increased revenue from digital channels. This alignment enables L&D teams to not only demonstrate the value of skills development but also show how it contributes to larger organizational success.

Making the connection between skills development and business performance improvements can help L&D thread its work into business outcomes—something that has been elusive to most L&D teams in the past. To effectively communicate L&D's impact, L&D itself needs to build skills in executive communication, internal marketing, data analytics, and business metrics. For L&D to really own the impact of skills, it must speak the language of business metrics to show results and not limit its communication to learning or skills metrics.

Driving Learner Engagement and Motivation

A thriving learning culture is built on learner motivation and engagement, which in turn are driven by the psychological principle of personal relevance. When employees perceive learning as directly contributing to their professional growth or role-specific skills, they are more likely to engage deeply. For L&D teams, this means that the effectiveness of training programs hinges on their ability to connect content with the unique needs and aspirations of each learner.

Skills data makes this connection possible by identifying the specific skills that employees want or need to develop, making learning highly relevant. When L&D teams leverage skills data, they can offer learning paths that are customized to each role, or even to each person, and aligned with both employee growth and organizational goals. Skills data helps L&D create a learning culture in which development feels meaningful and directly beneficial.

Skills Assessments and Progress Tracking

While many skills initiatives are driven from the top down—with organizations identifying which skills are needed and providing skills development opportunities to employees to upskill or reskill—skills initiatives are not only valuable for the organization. L&D organizations supporting skills development must also consider the needs of employees and how skills-data transparency can empower bottom-up skills development. In fact, one of the most transformative aspects of skills data is that it empowers employees to own their development.

With access to skills assessments and progress tracking, employees can understand their current capabilities, identify areas for growth, and monitor their improvement over time. This transparency helps create a sense of ownership and responsibility, allowing employees to actively shape their learning paths in collaboration with their managers and L&D teams. For example, an employee might use skills assessments to pinpoint specific areas for development and work with their manager to select relevant training modules. This shift from passive participation to active engagement drives higher motivation and commitment to

learning, as employees see a clear link between their efforts and their career progression. For L&D teams to empower employees in this way, employees need to:
- Understand the skills they have.
- Understand the skills they need today.
- Understand the skills they need for the next step in their careers.
- See progress toward their skills development goals as they engage in learning and work experiences.

As L&D develops more skills-focused strategies, remember that learners (and learner motivation) are a critical component of skills development, and that empowering them with data and transparency can ensure that your organization is embracing skills development top down and bottom up.

Badges, Achievements, and Rewards

Many L&D teams leverage some kind of external motivation to drive engagement with learning. Gamification elements such as badges and rewards are effective tools for enhancing engagement in learning programs, but traditional learning metrics such as scores, number of completions, or time spent in learning can be disconnected from impact and business metrics. Skills data can provide a more meaningful foundation for gamification and rewards.

By tracking progress toward goals and achievement of milestones through skills data, L&D teams can create gamified learning experiences that celebrate achievements, like earning badges for mastering new competencies or advancing to higher skill levels. When implemented well, gamified elements can turn learning into a dynamic, game-like journey, encouraging healthy competition and fostering a sense of achievement among employees.

Skills data also allows L&D teams to recognize and reward progress by highlighting top learners or those who have shown significant improvement, helping maintain motivation and enthusiasm. This combination of real-time feedback, recognition, and rewards reinforces the value of continuous learning, making skills acquisition both engaging and enjoyable.

Extending a Learning Culture in Remote or Hybrid Work Environments

The shift to remote and hybrid work environments for many organizations has introduced new challenges for L&D teams, particularly in maintaining engagement and consistency in learning. Without the benefits of face-to-face training, informal mentorship, and in-person workshops, remote employees may struggle to access the resources and support they need to develop their skills or build the relationships with mentors and peers that support continuous skills growth and feedback. Additionally, the dispersion of the workforce complicates the measurement of learning outcomes because performance is more difficult to observe, making it difficult for L&D teams to track skills progression and the impact of training programs. These challenges require L&D professionals to rethink how they deliver and measure training to ensure that learning remains effective, even when conducted remotely.

Skills data enables a data-driven approach to learning in remote and hybrid environments. Digital learning platforms and tools that provide access to real-time skills data allow L&D teams to monitor each employee's progress, regardless of their location, ensuring that development stays on track. Data-driven platforms allow for remote coaching, online assessments, and virtual feedback sessions, creating an ecosystem for learning to thrive without in-person interactions. These solutions ensure that employees continue to receive the personalized support to develop the skills they need, even when working across different time zones or in dispersed teams.

Skills data is especially valuable in remote settings because it enables personalized learning experiences that can keep remote employees engaged. By using data to understand the skills that employees need most, L&D teams can deliver targeted training content that is directly relevant to their roles and career goals. Personalized learning paths guided by skills data ensure that remote workers focus on the right competencies, which helps them stay connected to their development goals. This relevance helps maintain engagement even when learning is conducted virtually, making remote training feel as meaningful as in-person sessions.

To deliver personalized learning experiences, L&D teams are increasingly leveraging virtual learning platforms, self-paced learning modules, and collaborative learning environments to address the needs of remote learners. Skills data supports these platforms by allowing L&D teams to track participation, engagement, and the effectiveness of each learning modality. Self-paced learning options enable employees to take courses at their own convenience, while virtual collaboration tools facilitate peer-to-peer learning and discussion groups. By integrating skills data into these environments, L&D teams can ensure that each employee's progress is visible, helping managers provide timely support and enabling a more cohesive, collaborative learning culture across remote teams.

Finally, transparency in skills data is critical for building a strong learning culture in remote teams. By making skills data accessible to employees, L&D teams empower individuals to take greater responsibility for their learning journey. This transparency allows remote workers to see their progress, understand where they need to improve, and identify the skills that are most relevant to their roles. When employees can track their development and see how their efforts contribute to team and organizational goals, they become more engaged and committed to continuous learning. This shared visibility fosters a culture in which skills development is valued and actively pursued, even in a remote setting.

Bridging Skills Gap With Continuous Reskilling and Upskilling Programs

In an ever-changing business landscape, future-proofing the workforce is a strategic priority for L&D teams, and skills data is at the heart of this effort. It's not typically effective to predict the future by looking at the past, but tracking the emergence of new and necessary skills can provide data that helps L&D teams identify the competencies that will be critical in the future. This data-driven insight powers strategic planning for developing future in-demand skills, ensuring that learning investments are targeted toward the areas that will have the greatest impact on the organization's long-term success.

As a result, in recent years, major companies across industries have announced their investment in upskilling and reskilling initiatives. *Upskilling* refers to training employees in specific roles on the new skills needed to do their jobs effectively, while *reskilling* refers to training employees on new skills for new roles, typically when a certain role is no longer needed in the business or has been made obsolete by technology.

Skills data plays an instrumental role in designing upskilling and reskilling programs because the goal is to build the skills that employees need for the work that must be done. By providing a clear understanding of each employee's current skills and the skills required for future roles, skills data helps L&D teams create tailored learning pathways that address both immediate needs and longer-term goals. This ensures that employees are not only prepared for their current roles but also equipped for future responsibilities, creating a dynamic workforce that can grow alongside the organization.

Analyzing patterns in skills data can allow L&D teams to identify emerging skills that are growing in demand, such as digital literacy, advanced data analytics, or sustainability practices. By analyzing industry trends and other sources that provide predictive data and aligning them with internal skills data, L&D professionals can pinpoint the skills their employees need to develop to stay competitive. This proactive approach allows organizations to build training programs that prepare employees for the challenges of tomorrow, positioning the workforce to meet new market demands and seize emerging opportunities.

Skills data provides organizations with the agility they need to adapt to shifting industry demands. With a continuous stream of data about employee skills and learning progress, L&D teams can quickly identify gaps or changes in required competencies and adjust training programs accordingly. This ability to pivot ensures that workforces remain aligned with their organizations' strategic directions, even as external conditions change, helping companies stay competitive in rapidly evolving industries.

Skills data also enables L&D leaders to forecast trends and align their efforts with the organization's broader goals. By understanding which skills are likely to become more valuable, L&D can proactively build programs that ensure the workforce is prepared. This alignment helps L&D teams become strategic partners in their organizations' growth, ensuring that their initiatives directly contribute to future success.

Conclusion

The integration of skills data into L&D strategies is reshaping how organizations develop talent, fostering a culture of continuous learning and data-driven decision making. By making learning more personalized, transparent, and aligned with strategic goals, skills data empowers L&D teams to transform training from a traditional cost center into a driver of competitive advantage. As the future of work continues to evolve, L&D's role will become increasingly predictive, personalized, and data driven, creating an environment in which employee growth and business success go hand in hand. Embracing the potential of skills data is not just a shift in practice; it's a transformative opportunity to redefine L&D's influence on a skills-based organization's future.

PREskilling: The Secret Advantage in the Quest for the Future

Contributed by Gina Jeneroux, Future Work and Skills Strategist, AETHEON

Imagine holding a treasure map that clearly shows only part of the path. The rest? It's a bit fuzzy. You can't see all the twists and turns ahead, but you know that hidden treasures await.

The map is a lot like the landscape in front of us, as we prepare for the future of work.

In my mind, "PREskilling" is the key to surviving and thriving in an uncertain world. We don't need to wait for the entire map to appear. We can start developing skills now to navigate the unknown.

The Future Is Already Here

The world is already facing a tremendous skills shortage. Experts predict that nearly half of the skills in every job will change in the next few years, and skills demands will continue to outpace supply.

Eighty-seven percent of companies don't have enough future-ready talent to meet current business needs (McKinsey 2021). By 2030, experts predict a global shortfall of 85 million skilled workers, and this gap could drive more than $11.5 trillion in unrealized economic potential (WEF 2020).

The good news: It's more of a skills and work mismatch than a shortage of great talent.

Effective skill development must focus on both today and tomorrow:
- **UPskilling** enhances existing skills and builds targeted new ones to stay current in an existing job or field.
- **REskilling** enables individuals to acquire entirely new skills to transition into a different job or field. This is especially important when roles are becoming obsolete.
- **PREskilling** equips individuals to build skills that will be critical in the future, starting now.

PREskilling gives you the tools you'll need to tackle the future. Strong preparation keeps you nimble.

Put another way, each skill you develop gives you a new building block. The more you learn, the more blocks you have, and the more you can build. As new work and opportunities emerge, you can assemble and reassemble your blocks to create whatever you require to survive and thrive. PREskilling puts you ahead.

The PREskilling Journey

Successful PREskilling relies on five steps, which are important for both organizations and individuals:

1. **Identify critical skills.** Prioritize which skills will matter most in the next few years within the context of your organization and industry.

2. **Assess where you are today.** Determine your current proficiency level so you have a realistic picture of your starting point. Assessments could be subjective (for example, self-assessments) or objective (for example, observed or tested assessments).
3. **Prioritize learning through targeted development.** Set specific goals and map out learning activities that will move the dial on your prioritized skills.
4. **Engage in active learning.** Build skills and apply them in action through hands-on experiences. This could include a range of options, from immersive boot camps, to project-based learning, to on-the-job rotations.
5. **Measure and refine.** Regularly evaluate progress, adjust your approach as needed, and celebrate achievements along the way.

This approach equips individuals to become capable, confident, and ready for the future.

Businesses that embrace PREskilling can stay ahead of the competition, innovate faster, and build resilient teams capable of flourishing in any landscape.

PREskilling in Action

PREskilling isn't just an idea. It's already transforming institutions, companies, and entire nations. Consider these examples:

- **Higher education.** Universities such as Purdue Global, Western Governors University, and International Business University are embracing flexible, competency-based education and skills-based credentials. They're also forging deeper relationships with governments and employers to equip students with the skills, hands-on practice, and work experiences they need to be more employable, meet job demands, and make a business impact.
- **AETHEON.** I'm one of the founders of AETHEON, a startup that's bringing business and individuals together through

skills. Our goal is to celebrate each person for the strengths and experiences they already have and empower them to unlock their potential through skills. We're focused on opening doors to opportunity through skills-based academies, social learning accelerators, dynamic communities and credentials, and using AI-fuelled insights to predict future potential.
- **Singapore's AI-driven skill strategies.** Singapore has integrated more than a decade of job data into its educational system. These insights are informing all levels of education, as well as corporate learning and career development programs, and providing guidance for individuals to make informed choices about learning and careers.

Which Skills Are a Priority?

I think about skills in three broad categories:
- Technical and digital skills
- Human ("power") skills
- Higher cognitive skills

Within these categories, the following skills will be essential for everyone:
- **Technical and digital skills**
    - Digital fluency (including AI fluency and prompt engineering)
    - Data and analytics
    - Business and financial acumen
- **Human ("power") skills**
    - Empathy
    - Resilience
    - Communication
    - Collaboration
    - Leadership
- **Higher cognitive skills**
    - Critical thinking
    - Creativity

- Innovation
- Problem solving

There is (rightly!) a significant focus on helping people navigate the world of AI. Generative AI in particular is already a game changer, with the power to create and capture new value in new ways. In fact, in a recent study by Ernst & Young, 99 percent of CEOs confirmed they are already investing in AI or are in the midst of planning large investments.

Effective AI skills include more than AI fluency and prompt engineering. Individuals also need to embrace the human skills that set them apart from technology and the higher cognitive skills that help them critically assess the quality, accuracy, and bias of the responses they receive from AI models.

Your Future Starts Now

Like the treasure map, the future is crystallizing before us, full of possibilities. PREskilling gives us the tools and confidence to rise to the challenge.

The skills we build today are the keys that will unlock the doors to tomorrow's opportunities. Whether you're an individual looking to stay ahead or part of an organization striving to build talent to drive strategies and results, the time to act is now!

Let's set out on this bold quest together. The path to PREskilling starts now, and the treasures are yours to discover.

CHAPTER 10
Implementing Skills-Based Talent Management

In this chapter, we'll cover:
- Strengthening teams with diverse skills
- Offering flexible career trajectories based on skills development and personal growth
- Shifting from traditional appraisal methods to skills growth and application
- Facilitating internal movement based on skills matching

Whenever I think of people management, I think of the phrase *leading from the middle*, which is also (maybe not coincidentally) the title of numerous books on leadership. It's no wonder because the roles of leadership and management have fundamentally changed. As businesses navigate a dynamic landscape characterized by technological advancements, shifting workforce demographics, and changing employee expectations, the way organizations manage, develop, and engage their talent must adapt. People managers are no longer just responsible for overseeing day-to-day operations and taking orders from the C-suite; they are strategic leaders on the front line of organizational culture, shaping employee experiences and aligning team capabilities with the broader goals of the business. To do this effectively, managers need new tools and approaches that can keep pace with the complexity and rapid changes in the workplace today.

One of the most significant shifts in people management is the growing reliance on data-driven approaches to managing employees. As organizations collect more data on employee performance, engagement, and development, they gain a deeper understanding of what drives productivity and satisfaction within their teams. These insights allow managers to make more-informed decisions about hiring, training, and talent allocation, moving beyond intuition-based practices to strategies backed by measurable evidence. Data-driven people management not only enhances transparency but also enables managers to proactively address challenges such as skills gaps, employee turnover, and uneven team dynamics, leading to better overall outcomes for both individual employees and the organization.

Skills data, a powerful tool that offers a more precise and dynamic view of employee capabilities, is at the center of the data evolution for people managers. Skills provide a more nuanced, detailed, and accurate understanding of what an employee can do, empowering managers to align talent with business needs more effectively. Leveraging skills, organizations can identify hidden talent, recognize potential in unconventional candidates, and build teams that are more diverse, agile, and capable of adapting to change. And when people managers adopt the skills-based approach, they can infuse skills across the business.

This chapter will explore how skills data can revolutionize people management, detailing its impact on critical areas such as team diversity, career flexibility, performance reviews, talent mobility, and succession planning. With modern managers leading organizational success "from the middle," skills data better prepares them to manage their teams, connect their performance to the business, and more effectively communicate to executive stakeholders in a skills-based organization.

Building Diverse Teams

Building effective teams is one of the main functions of organizational leadership. A core characteristic of effective teams—and thus organizational innovation, productivity, and overall success—is diversity. A team that brings together individuals with different backgrounds, perspectives, and experiences is better equipped to tackle complex challenges and develop creative solutions. Research consistently shows that diverse teams are more likely to explore a wider range of ideas and approaches, leading to higher levels of innovation (NLI Staff 2021). This diversity of thought enables organizations to anticipate market needs, connect with a broader range of customers, and adapt to changes more effectively.

The value of diversity extends beyond surface-level characteristics such as race, gender, or ethnicity; it includes diversity in background, thought, and skills. When team members bring different ways of thinking and problem solving to the table, they enrich the collective intelligence of the group. For example, a team composed of members with varying expertise—such as a data analyst, a creative designer, a project manager, and a software developer—can leverage its unique strengths to approach problems from different angles, making the team more resilient and adaptable. Such a blend of skills and perspectives enhances the team's ability to solve problems creatively, think critically, and innovate in ways that homogeneous teams struggle to achieve.

Building diverse teams is not without its challenges. Many organizations continue to rely on traditional selection criteria (such as education, past roles, or years of experience) when forming teams. Traditional approaches can lead managers to overlook the unique skills and competencies that individuals may bring, especially those who have developed their abilities through nontraditional career paths. When this happens, organizations risk missing out on potential talent that could bring fresh perspectives and valuable skills to their teams. Skills data can play a critical role, shifting the focus from traditional criteria to a more inclusive and effective way of building diverse teams.

Skills data helps overcome the challenges of building diverse teams by providing a clear and detailed picture of the skills that individuals bring to their roles. Skills data allows managers to see the specific capabilities and strengths of each team member, regardless of their background or past roles. This skills-centric approach helps identify complementary skills among team members, enabling managers to form teams that leverage each individual's strengths for maximum effectiveness. For instance, rather than assembling a team based solely on previous job titles, managers can use skills data to ensure the group includes a mix of technical, analytical, creative, and interpersonal skills—a combination that is crucial for well-rounded problem solving.

By focusing on the actual skills that team members possess, skills data can bring together individuals who might not have been considered under traditional hiring or team building practices. For example, a candidate without a formal degree in computer science may have gained coding expertise through hands-on projects or self-study. Similarly, an employee with a background in customer service might possess valuable communication and empathy skills that are critical for roles involving user experience or client relations. Skills data makes these strengths visible, allowing managers to see beyond conventional qualifications and build teams that have diverse skill sets and can tackle a wide range of challenges.

If you're creating cookie-cutter profiles based on roles, skills data can help you avoid homogeneity by encouraging a more balanced distribution of skills within teams. By analyzing the skills profiles of existing team members, managers can identify overlaps or gaps and adjust their team-building strategies accordingly. For example, a team that is heavily focused on technical expertise might benefit from adding members with strong creative-thinking or problem-solving abilities. This approach ensures that no single perspective dominates the team, fostering a more collaborative environment for diverse ideas to flourish. It also helps prevent the formation of siloed teams that think and act alike, which can stifle innovation and hinder the ability to adapt to new challenges.

In addition, skills data can better support project-based businesses, such as consulting organizations, helping managers identify employees who can contribute to different teams or projects based on their unique skills rather than their job title. Project-based internal mobility is particularly valuable for developing diverse teams because it allows managers to tap into hidden talent within the organization. Employees who have previously been overlooked for certain roles may find opportunities to thrive in new contexts, contributing their skills in ways that align with their strengths and interests. This not only promotes a more inclusive approach to team building but also empowers employees to develop their careers in dynamic and fulfilling ways.

Ultimately, using skills data to build diverse teams is about shifting the focus from who people are to what they can do. By looking beyond traditional criteria and embracing a more data-driven, skills-based approach, organizations can build teams that are more inclusive, adaptive, and innovative. This leads to a culture that not only welcomes different perspectives but actively seeks them out, and gives every employee the opportunity to contribute meaningfully to the organization's success.

Rethinking Career Paths

For decades, career progression in most organizations has followed the traditional ladder approach—a linear path that employees move up through a series of predefined roles and titles. This model is rooted in the idea that success is defined by promotions within a single department or function, with each step up the ladder representing increased responsibility, a new title, and greater compensation. While this approach has provided a clear and structured path for advancement, it is also inherently one-size-fits-all, failing to account for the diverse skills, interests, and potential of individual employees.

The limitations of the ladder model have become increasingly apparent as the nature of work and employee expectations have evolved. Many employees find themselves reaching a plateau as opportunities for upward movement become scarce. The emphasis on vertical progression can also mean that promotions are based more on tenure or time served rather than on the development and application of relevant skills. This can lead to disengagement and stagnation as employees feel constrained by a lack of opportunities to grow in directions that align with their interests and strengths.

At the same time, the modern workforce is seeking more flexibility and personalization in career growth. Employees today value opportunities to expand their skill sets, explore different roles, and take on new challenges—whether or not these moves involve a traditional promotion. This shift reflects a desire for career growth that is as dynamic and multifaceted as the challenges facing today's organizations. To meet these changing expectations, companies must rethink their approach to career development, moving beyond rigid structures and embracing models that allow for more diverse and adaptable career paths. This is how skills data comes into play, offering a new way to support career progression that is driven by capabilities rather than job titles.

Skills data offers a foundation for more flexible, nonlinear career paths by focusing on what employees can do and the skills they bring to the table rather than simply how long they have been in a particular role or what the next predictable step in a traditional career ladder would be. Instead of following a fixed path up a ladder, employees can now pursue a range of career trajectories that align with their skills and interests. Skills data allows organizations to identify which employees have the potential to excel in different areas, even if those roles fall outside the traditional path of their current position. This approach emphasizes continuous skills development, allowing employees to grow horizontally, move across departments, or engage in project-based roles that offer new challenges and learning opportunities.

With skills, career pathing is fluid, based on the needs of the business and the interests of the employee. For example, a marketing professional with a strong interest in data analysis might move into a role on the data science team so they can apply their analytical skills while learning from technical experts. This flexibility benefits both the employee, who gains new skills and experiences, and the organization, which can leverage talent across different parts of the business.

Skills data also facilitates cross-departmental roles and project-based career growth because employees can take assignments or roles based on their unique skills rather than their job title. This model is particularly valuable in agile and fast-paced industries that value the ability to quickly deploy the right talent to the right projects as a competitive advantage. By using skills data to match employees with opportunities where their skills are most needed, organizations can optimize team performance while giving employees the chance to develop in new and rewarding ways.

Additionally, skills data allows for personalized career development plans that are tailored to individual strengths and interests. Rather than being funneled into a one-size-fits-all progression plan, employees can work with managers to identify their skills, interests, and potential career paths based on their unique profile. This enables employees to self-assess, track their skills, and visualize potential career opportunities within the organization. For example, an employee who is interested in transitioning from a technical role to a leadership position can use skills data to identify the leadership competencies they need to develop, access targeted learning resources, and set goals for acquiring those skills. This skills-based approach transforms career planning into a more dynamic and empowering process, which gives employees a clear vision of how they can shape their own career journeys.

Career pathing is one of the key opportunities for organizations to engage with employees in a way that directly affects retention of key talent. Skills data allows people leaders to more objectively evaluate someone's skills in relation to organizational opportunities and connect employees to opportunities that support their career growth and address the needs of the business.

Shifting to Skills-Based Performance Reviews

Traditional performance appraisals have been a standard practice in many organizations for decades, but they come with significant limitations that can hinder both employee growth and organizational success. One of the most critical issues is the overemphasis on subjective opinions, biases, and ratings. Traditional performance reviews often rely heavily on a manager's personal perspective, which can introduce various biases, whether conscious or unconscious. These biases may relate to an employee's communication style, work habits, or perceived enthusiasm rather than their actual contribution or skill level. This subjectivity can lead to inconsistent evaluations because the same performance might be rated differently depending on the manager, leading to frustration among employees and a lack of trust in the review process.

Another challenge with traditional performance reviews is frequency. Typically conducted annually or (at best) twice a year, these reviews provide feedback that is often too delayed to be actionable. When feedback is given only once or twice a year, it becomes difficult for employees to make timely adjustments or improvements. This lack of real-time progress tracking means that employees might not know how they are doing until it is too late to change course. Moreover, it often leaves managers without the opportunity to address issues promptly, potentially allowing underperformance to continue unchecked.

Last, traditional performance appraisals tend to focus mainly on past performance, with little emphasis on future growth or potential. The review process often revolves around recounting what an employee has done over the last review period, which limits the discussion to achievements or mistakes that may no longer be relevant to the employee's current role or the organization's needs. This retrospective focus can stifle growth because it does not encourage employees to think about how they can develop new skills or prepare for future challenges. As a result, performance reviews become more of a historical record than a tool for development and career advancement. To address these challenges, many organizations are turning to skills-based performance reviews as a more effective alternative.

Skills-based performance reviews represent a shift from traditional, subjective evaluations to a more data-driven, objective approach that focuses on skills growth, proficiency, and practical application. This approach uses skills data to assess how employees are developing key competencies and how effectively they are applying those skills in their roles. By focusing on measurable aspects of an employee's skill set, managers can provide a more accurate and fair assessment of their progress and performance.

One of the core benefits of skills-based reviews is the ability to continuously track skills development. Unlike traditional reviews, which occur at fixed intervals, skills-based reviews leverage real-time data to monitor how employees are advancing in specific areas. This allows for dynamic reviews so feedback can be given throughout the year, enabling employees to adjust their focus and efforts as needed. For example, if an employee is working on improving their project management skills, a manager can track their progress over the course of a few months, offering targeted feedback as they take on new projects and responsibilities. This ongoing feedback loop makes performance conversations between managers and employees more interactive and ensures that employees are always aware of where they stand and how they can improve.

Skills data also enables a more objective and forward-looking evaluation process. Instead of relying on general opinions or broad categories like communication or teamwork, managers can use specific metrics tied to skills. For instance, managers can assess an employee's ability to analyze data by looking at how they have applied data analysis skills in recent projects, the accuracy of their insights, and the improvements in their analytical thinking over time. This data-driven approach allows managers to recognize strengths, identify areas for growth, and have constructive conversations about how the employee can continue to build their skills in alignment with the organization's goals. By focusing on future potential and skills growth, skills-based performance reviews help encourage employees to think about their development rather than just look back at past performance.

Skills-based reviews shift the emphasis from job titles and roles to the practical application of key skills. In many traditional reviews, an employee's role or job title often dictates what is expected of them, which can lead to narrow assessments based on predefined criteria. However, skills-based reviews allow managers to look at how employees use their skills across various projects and tasks, regardless of their official job title. For example, a software developer might be assessed not only on their coding skills but also on their ability to lead a team or mentor junior staff, even if their title does not formally include a leadership role. This shift encourages employees to apply their skills more broadly and seek out new challenges, contributing to a more versatile and capable workforce.

Encouraging Development Over Critique

A significant advantage of shifting to skills-based performance reviews is the opportunity for leaders to move away from punitive evaluations toward a focus on growth-oriented feedback. Traditional performance appraisals often feel like a judgment, with employees fearing negative ratings or critiques. Focusing on evaluation can create a defensive mindset if employees are more concerned with justifying their past actions than with identifying ways to improve. Skills-based reviews, however, emphasize development, encouraging employees to see feedback as a valuable tool for upskilling and enhancement rather than a critique of their shortcomings. Because providing difficult feedback is also challenging for managers, being able to offer feedback throughout the year and focus on performance and skills growth gives managers and employees a common language about skills to center performance conversations, making the conversation more focused and less subjective than a yearly performance review.

Skills-based reviews help employees approach performance discussions with a growth mindset. Employees are more likely to take an active role in these conversations if they see them as opportunities to gain insights into how they can develop new skills and advance their careers. This perspective not only benefits individual employees but also supports a culture of continuous improvement within the organization so learning and growth are seen as ongoing processes.

Aligning skills-based reviews with the company's strategic goals further enhances their value. By identifying the skills that are critical for the organization's success, managers can use skills data to guide conversations about how employees can develop those competencies. For example, if a company is focusing on expanding its digital presence, managers might encourage employees to develop skills in digital marketing, data analysis, or user experience design. This approach ensures that individual development is closely tied to the organization's priorities, making the review process more relevant and actionable. It also enables managers to link an employee's skills data to specific organizational objectives, creating a clear connection between personal growth and business outcomes.

For instance, a sales representative might be encouraged to develop their negotiation skills if the company is targeting larger, more complex clients. The manager can use skills data to track improvements in this area, such as success rates in closing deals or client feedback on negotiation effectiveness. A targeted development approach not only supports the individual's career growth but also contributes directly to the company's growth metrics, making performance reviews a strategic tool for both the employee and the organization.

Providing Actionable Feedback

Skills-based performance reviews facilitate actionable feedback that is directly linked to measurable data, with a baseline and the ability to measure change over time. With access to detailed skills data, managers can provide feedback that is not only specific but also rooted in real-world performance. For example, rather than giving vague feedback such as "improve communication skills," a manager can point to specific instances when an employee demonstrated strong communication and suggest ways to build on those strengths. This makes the feedback more relevant and actionable, helping employees understand exactly what they need to do to improve. When examples are included as skills signals, managers can use that data specifically to tie performance feedback with data used to validate skills, providing transparency and consistency in how data is being used.

Skills data also allows managers to identify specific areas where employees have opportunities for growth. If an employee has been working on enhancing their data analysis skills but still struggles with interpreting complex datasets, their manager can recommend targeted training or mentoring sessions to help them bridge that gap. This type of feedback is much more valuable than general statements because it directly addresses the skills gaps that are most relevant to the employee's role and future career path.

By linking feedback to skills data, managers can create development plans that are tailored to each employee's needs and directly tied to measurable progress. These plans can outline the steps an employee should take to build specific skills, set goals for improvement, and track their progress in developing proficiency over time. This structured approach ensures employees have a clear road map for their development, making it easier for them to stay focused and motivated, while ensuring that they are aligned with their managers on expectations.

By using skills data as the basis for feedback, organizations can transform performance reviews into a powerful tool for empowering employees and driving continuous improvement. This shift from evaluation to development creates a more engaged, capable, and future-ready workforce. As we'll explore in the next section, skills data can also play a pivotal role in facilitating talent mobility, ensuring that employees have the opportunity to apply their skills in new and exciting roles across the organization.

Powering Talent Mobility

Talent mobility, or the ability for employees to move into new roles or teams within a company, is one of the main drivers of employee retention, providing a chance for them to grow professionally by connecting them to opportunities that don't follow a linear career path. As we discussed earlier in this chapter, flexible career paths are a talent management benefit of skills-based organizations. While career paths look at mobility from an employee perspective, talent mobility looks at how an organization has set up systems and processes to facilitate employee movement within the organization to meet the needs of the business.

For many organizations, talent mobility has been a challenging process because of the rigidity of traditional internal promotion and transfer systems. Internal mobility has historically followed a linear path, closely tied to hierarchical structures and based on tenure, predefined job levels, personal networks, or a manager's discretion. This approach often limits employees' opportunities to move laterally or explore roles outside their immediate function, leading to a narrow view of career advancement. And it can lead to inefficiencies in talent placement if the right person for a position is overlooked because they are newer to the organization or less visible to decision makers. Such practices can stifle innovation and contribute to employee disengagement because many believe their career progression is restricted by factors unrelated to their actual abilities.

A further challenge is the limited visibility into internal talent pools. Many organizations lack a centralized and up-to-date view of the skills possessed by their employees, making it difficult for managers to identify candidates for roles outside their current department. Without insight into the full range of capabilities within the workforce, companies often look outside for new hires, even when the skills they need exist within their own ranks. This not only increases hiring costs but also contributes to turnover, as talented employees leave in search of opportunities that they perceive as unavailable internally. Addressing these challenges requires a more flexible and data-driven approach to talent mobility, so skills can take center stage in matching people to roles.

Skills data can enable more effective and dynamic internal mobility by allowing HR and managers to evaluate how an employee's capabilities align with the needs of various roles. Skills databases or talent platforms that aggregate and share a transparent view of employees' skills across the organization make it easier for managers to identify potential internal candidates for open positions or new projects. For example, if a manager is looking for someone with advanced project management skills for a cross-functional initiative, they can quickly identify employees who have demonstrated those skills, even if they are currently working in a different department. Transparency democratizes access to opportunities, helping to break down barriers that previously limited internal mobility.

Skills data makes internal talent more visible and accessible for new opportunities, allowing employees to take a more proactive role in their career progression. Some organizations have implemented internal talent marketplaces where employees can explore new roles or projects that align with their skills. These platforms function like internal job boards but are driven by skills data, matching employees to opportunities that may not have been visible to them otherwise. For example, a marketing professional might discover an opening in product development that aligns with their strategic-planning skills, or a customer support agent might find a fit in the training department based on their strong communication skills. Such marketplaces empower employees to navigate their careers within the organization, fostering a sense of ownership and engagement. Internal marketplaces also provide hiring managers with internal candidates who have not only the right skills for, but also interest in, open roles and projects.

Finally, skills data can help with building temporary project teams, short-term gigs, consulting assignments, and cross-departmental task support, encouraging employees to apply their abilities in new contexts. By identifying transferable skills that are valuable across different functions, organizations can create opportunities for employees to contribute to projects or roles outside their primary department. This approach not only broadens an employee's career possibilities but also helps break down silos within the organization, fostering collaboration and innovation.

A company might use its internal skills database to identify employees in the IT department who possess strong analytical skills and could contribute to the marketing team's new data analytics initiative. This allows the organization to leverage existing talent in new ways, reducing the need for external hires and ensuring that knowledge and expertise remain within the company. Employees benefit from the opportunity to broaden their experience, form and develop connections with a larger internal network, and develop skills in different areas, making them more versatile and better prepared for future roles.

An example of this in action can be seen in companies that use skills-mapping software to match employees with temporary projects or cross-departmental task forces. By analyzing employees' skills profiles, the organization can quickly assemble teams with the right mix of technical, creative, and leadership skills for specific projects. This approach not only ensures that projects are staffed with the right talent but also encourages knowledge sharing among departments. It allows employees to apply their skills in new ways and gain exposure to different areas of the business, inspiring innovative solutions and fostering a culture of continuous learning.

These examples show how organizations can use skills data to create talent mobility frameworks that benefit both the business and its employees. Implementing skills-based talent mobility not only reduces the cost and time associated with external hiring but also builds a more agile and adaptable workforce that's capable of responding to changing market needs. For organizations looking to remain competitive in a dynamic business environment, skills-driven talent mobility is an essential strategy for maximizing the value of their existing talent and fostering a culture of growth and innovation to weather the ever-evolving dynamics of the global market.

Supporting Career Development and Succession Planning

Career development (the processes to support employees moving to the next step in their career path) and *succession planning* (the preparation of future leaders to fill vacated leadership roles) are often underdeveloped in organizations, leading to employees leaving when they are ready for their next career move and to organizations having gaps in leadership when tenured leaders leave. Career development and succession planning require proactive planning and data, and skills-based organizations are uniquely positioned to support both efforts. By leveraging skills data, companies can create a more transparent and dynamic approach to career progression, identify high-potential employees, and ensure a steady pipeline of future leaders. This approach not only supports individual growth but also aligns with the strategic needs of the business, ensuring that talent development efforts are directly tied to organizational success.

Supporting Career Progressions

One of the most valuable aspects of skills data is its ability to support career progression by offering managers a clear view of each employee's strengths, areas for improvement, and potential career paths. Many traditional approaches to career development rely on general job descriptions and standardized training programs, which can be too rigid to accommodate the diverse talents and ambitions of the workforce. In contrast, skills data allows for a more personalized approach because employees can understand precisely which skills they need to develop to reach their next career milestone and managers can be more effective coaches in helping their employees achieve their career goals.

By using skills data to create skills-based development plans, managers can guide employees in setting realistic goals for their growth. For example, if a software developer aspires to move into a project management role, skills data can pinpoint the key competencies they need to acquire, such as leadership, communication, and strategic planning. This data-driven approach ensures that employees have a clear road map for their career advancement, empowering them to take charge of their development and pursue opportunities that align with their aspirations.

Identifying High-Potential Employees and Future Leaders

Skills data can also help identify high-potential employees who have the capability to take on greater responsibilities within the organization. By analyzing skills data across the workforce, companies can spot individuals who consistently excel in critical competencies, such as problem solving, strategic thinking, or team leadership. Managers can also see which employees develop new skills quickly and who is invested in ongoing skills development. These insights help organizations recognize emerging leaders early, providing opportunities for targeted leadership development and mentorship.

For example, an employee in a midlevel role who has demonstrated strong analytical skills and a track record of leading successful projects may be identified as a candidate for future leadership. Using skills data, managers can tailor development programs that prepare this individual for advanced roles, such as participating in cross-functional leadership training or taking on more complex strategic initiatives. Managers can also look for high-potential employees to develop any missing skills required of leaders, such as coaching, people management, or budget management. This proactive approach to talent identification ensures that the organization is continuously developing a pool of potential leaders who are ready to step up when the need arises.

Designing Customized Leadership Development Programs

With high-potential employees identified, and an understanding of the skills that are most important for leadership roles, companies can develop targeted training programs to fill potential leadership gaps. This approach ensures that succession planning is based on measurable competencies rather than subjective assessments or favoritism.

Using skills data, companies can design leadership development programs that focus on building the skills necessary for success at higher levels of the organization. For example, a potential successor for a senior leadership role might participate in a structured program that includes advanced communication training, strategic decision-making workshops, and hands-on leadership experiences. By tracking the individual's progress in these areas through skills data, the organization can assess their readiness for a leadership transition, making the process more transparent and effective.

Skills data can also enable organizations to identify the skills that will be critical in the future. This insight helps L&D teams create, and managers recommend, customized training paths that equip high-potential employees with the competencies they will need to lead the organization through future challenges.

For instance, as digital transformation reshapes many industries, a company might focus on developing skills such as digital literacy, data analysis, and innovation management among its future leaders. By aligning these development efforts with long-term strategy, the company can ensure that it is building a leadership team that is capable of guiding the company through evolving market dynamics. This skills-based approach to leadership development creates a robust talent pipeline, ready to meet the demands of both today and tomorrow.

By using skills data to guide career development and succession planning, organizations can create a more agile, prepared, and motivated workforce. This approach ensures that talent development not only aligns with business needs but also creates clear and rewarding pathways for employees to grow into the leaders of tomorrow.

Conclusion

Skills data can be a transformative force in skills-based organizations, reshaping how they understand, develop, and deploy their talent. By gaining a more granular understanding of the skills each employee has, organizations can take a more tailored approach to managing their workforce. Unlike many traditional management practices, which rely on static job titles and hierarchical structures, a skills-driven approach enables a more nuanced and flexible view of mapping talent to the work, focusing on what employees can do rather than just their roles or past experiences.

The integration of skills data into talent management will help organizations build diverse, flexible, and agile teams. By leveraging this data, organizations can create personalized development paths for employees and ensure that each team member is in a position that maximizes their strengths. This approach not only benefits individual employees by aligning their career growth with their skill sets but also drives the organization toward sustained success in a competitive landscape. Ultimately, empowering people managers with skills data allows organizations to create a dynamic, future-ready workforce, capable of thriving in the face of continuous change.

Skills-Based Promotions at the London Stock Exchange Group

Contributed by Asi DeGani, Director, Skills and Talent Development, London Stock Exchange Group

In 2021, the London Stock Exchange Group (LSEG), a business with more than 320 years of history, merged with Refinitiv, a three-year-old financial data and platform provider. This created one of the world's leading financial-markets infrastructure and data providers. The resulting organization was made up of more than 25,000 employees and focused on three major areas:

- **Data and analytics**—delivering data-driven insights, indexes, and products to customers

- **Capital markets**—supporting customers across the end-to-end capital markets' workflow, providing them with access to liquidity across multiple asset classes and regions
- **Post-trade**—supporting customers' clearing and reporting obligations, providing risk, balance sheet, and financial resource management solutions

Becoming a Skills-Based Organization

While the economic potential of the new, bigger entity was clear, a doubt did sneak into the hearts of the people function leaders: The nature of the two organizations was so different that there was a risk that the people coming from one would not bond well with those coming from the other.

To mitigate this risk, the people team at LSEG took a unique approach. Instead of rolling out a new employee engagement program, the team started working on a construct—called the "career framework"—that would simplify the merging of the organizations and standardize roles and career stages. The framework reduced 25,000 roles to 1,029 job profiles, each with a description, key responsibilities and accountabilities, and the skills needed to succeed in it. With extreme transparency, the team built the framework to include every role in the organization, all the way to CEO.

To make the framework more approachable, it was coupled with a talent marketplace in late 2022. This meant that every employee could see beyond their current role and use their skills to plan a way forward to the next role, or to plan a complete career. By mapping the employees' skills, LSEG was able to provide better development plans, realistic career conversations, and longer-term career opportunities.

The benefits delivered by skills became clear as they were woven into more organizational processes. In late 2023, it became clear that the organization could, and indeed should, go all in on the skills-based approach.

Bringing Skills to Promotions

In 2024, as part of the drive to become a skills-based organization, LSEG started testing a skills-based promotion process. People leaders had access to skills data for each of their team members. This included a 360-degree skills assessment that highlighted gaps in the skills that employees relied on daily and how those skills would position the individual once promoted.

The methodology ensured the following:

- The process is straightforward, consistent, and led by data, ensuring that people leaders make objective decisions that are easy to explain and justify.
- The promotion process is data driven, which means those promoted are more likely to succeed in their new roles because the skills gaps are smaller. This also translates to a faster time to competency.
- Employees who are not promoted receive a data-led explanation for the decision, as well as a development plan that will help them bridge their skills gaps.
- Employees are consistently measured against the skills they need in their existing (and future) roles. This ensures a transparent approach to talent across the organization and the ability to draw on needed skills at any time.

The skills-based promotion methodology was developed in close collaboration with the business. The key element behind the methodology is objectivity, which is possible only if it is led with data. Tools were developed with the business and informed by the human resources information system (HRIS) and talent marketplace.

The process followed these steps, giving employees control of and access to the data throughout:

1. The employee assesses their own skills, asks stakeholders to assess them, and receives an assessment from their people leader.
2. The people leader and employee get access to a promotion dashboard showing the resulting scores. This dashboard shows how the individual rates against their current role, as well as against the future role they may be promoted to. The people

leader reviews the results using a dashboard that highlights assessment inconsistencies—these are proficiency levels that the employee and people leader do not agree on.
3. The people leader and employee meet with the objective of agreeing on the scores—this is critical for next steps and for the promotion decision. With agreed-upon skills proficiencies, the people leader can review them against those needed for the role the employee is in and the role they may be promoted to. Skills proficiencies are detailed in the career framework, which uses job profiles to detail the skills needed in every role in the organization.
4. Once agreed, the people leader makes a decision. If they are certain that the gap is nonexistent or easily bridged, they can recommend promoting the individual. If promotion is not advisable, then a development plan is put in place to support the individual through the needed improvement.

What Happened Next

Following the first skills-based promotion cycle, a few things became apparent very quickly:

- **A more objective process.** Out of 159 promotions, 117 relied on skills while 42 (26 percent) did not. This shows that LSEG people leaders were eager for a data-led process to rely on.
- **Reduction in rejected promotions.** Only 14 percent of the promotion recommendations were rejected. In most cases, this was based on the skills gaps that individuals had when the future role was assessed.
- **A more transparent process.** Of people leaders and team members, 74.3 percent saw the new process as transparent.
- **A process perceived as fair.** Of people leaders and team members, 67.6 percent saw the new process as fair.

The team at LSEG believes that basing promotions on the skills that an individual possesses (and actively applies) increases the employee's chances of succeeding in a new role. When a gap exists, a development plan can help the employee bridge the gap.

Systems Thinking in Talent Management: Designing Skills-Based Programs for the US Space Force

Contributed by Emily Anderson, Jennifer Tucker, Allison R. Suerdieck, and Katie Gunther, United States Space Force, Enterprise Talent Management Office

Disclaimer: The views and opinions expressed or implied in this book are those of the authors and should not be construed as carrying the official sanction or official policy position of the Department of Defense, United States Space Force, Enterprise Talent Management Office, or other agencies or departments of the US government.

Building the USSF Culture: "Semper Supra"

The United States Space Force (USSF) was established to protect US interests in space, a domain increasingly vital to national security and daily life. Early in its formation, the Space Force introduced the Guardian Ideal, a framework defining the core values of its service members, known as Guardians, while outlining strategies for developing and managing talent in alignment with mission objectives. This framework serves as a road map for recruiting, training, and cultivating a highly skilled workforce prepared for the complexities of space operations.

The Guardian Ideal emphasizes adaptability and collaboration, encouraging Guardians to approach challenges from diverse perspectives. With space operations growing more complex, the ability to remain flexible is key to overcoming emerging challenges. The Space Force is committed to enhancing its personnel's skills, particularly in digital fluency and future readiness, to meet these demands.

The Guardian Spirit operationalizes the values expressed in the Guardian Ideal, translating character, connection, commitment, and courage into daily actions. It provides clear expectations for behavior and leadership, ensuring alignment between personal conduct and the Space Force's strategic goals. This focus on actionable values helps build consistency across the service and reinforces its mission-driven culture.

Decentralized leadership is central to the Guardian Spirit. By empowering Guardians at all levels to take initiative and collaborate, the Space Force promotes faster, more responsive decision making. This flexibility is essential in space operations when real-time adaptability is critical. Teamwork is emphasized over individual achievement, ensuring collective focus on mission success. The motto "Semper Supra" ("Always Above") captures this collective ethos, symbolizing the pride and unity of current and future Guardians in their commitment to excellence and service.

As this cultural framework takes root, it is shaping the foundation of talent management within the Space Force. By integrating personnel management with technological advancements, the USSF is optimizing its workforce to meet current and future mission demands. This comprehensive approach ensures that Guardians are prepared to take on various roles, fostering a ready and capable force.

Developing USSF Talent Management Processes

The USSF talent management program was designed to increase talent permeability into and within the Space Force and improve responsiveness to current and future needs. These processes aim to present ready forces to operational units, capitalize on existing personnel systems, and ensure inclusivity of both military and civilian personnel. By increasing permeability, Guardians are given more control over their career pathways, allowing them to transition between different fields throughout their careers. Personnel structures that track Guardians' knowledge, skills, abilities, and other characteristics enhance job matching and improve career flexibility.

As part of this approach, the USSF continually reviews the capabilities and skills needed for successful performance, adjusting them as mission requirements evolve. If new capabilities are identified, they are added through targeted job analyses, ensuring that positions are filled with the right talent at the right time.

The USSF's talent management program has progressed through three distinct phases. In the initial phase, the USSF conducted strategic job modeling to align personnel processes with the vision of the service (Sanchez and Levine 2009; Schippmann 1999). This helped establish foundational capabilities applicable to all career fields and identified critical skill sets needed for successful job performance. Leaders actively participated in shaping these capabilities, embedding them into personnel processes such as selection, training, and development.

As the service moved from organizational formation to program execution, more granular job-level information was required. In the second phase, the USSF employed traditional job analysis methodologies to gauge Guardians' proficiencies in specific capabilities and skills. These analyses benchmarked job requirements against industry and government standards, providing detailed information for creating assessments and offering targeted developmental opportunities.

The USSF recognizes the need for greater synchronization between personnel management and training processes and has entered a third phase, which takes a systems thinking approach to talent management. This shift emphasizes the importance of integrating and providing feedback between high-level structures and day-to-day processes to drive skill development (Bronfenbrenner and Evans 2000; Bronfenbrenner and Morris 1998). By integrating previously disparate personnel and training systems, the USSF enhances its ability to track Guardian skills and proficiency levels, both in support and independent of required job-specific certifications. This approach fosters career pathing by recognizing and providing feedback to Guardians who demonstrate initiative and develop expertise beyond current job-specific requirements.

Understanding system dynamics allows the USSF to anticipate and manage the broader organizational impacts of meeting emerging skills requirements caused by environmental changes. By designing systems that support cross-training and career path flexibility and track upskilling outcomes, the Space Force can mitigate potential disruptions related to workforce adjustments by having a broader bench of Guardians with diverse skill sets. By targeting leverage points and critical interconnections within subsystems, talent management processes can be more responsive to personnel needs and maximize person-job fit, ultimately better supporting mission objectives in Space Force units and organizations.

Reaching for the Stars—Next Steps for USSF Talent Management

The USSF's future talent management efforts focus on creating a culture of assessment and using AI to develop adaptive, skills-based assessments that will be integrated into routine procedures, providing Guardians with regular feedback to refine their skills and ensure that their growth aligns with mission needs. This continuous feedback loop will help prevent skills decay and enhance performance, contributing to mission readiness.

The implementation of these assessments will also enable leadership to proactively address operational challenges. By providing early insights into skills gaps and development needs, the system will support real-time decision making and allow for timely adjustments to training and personnel assignments.

One of the defining features of this assessment system is its focus on fostering leadership behaviors while also promoting comprehensive development across all capabilities and skills. Guardians will receive targeted feedback on leadership, technical expertise, and operational skills, ensuring they continually advance in their roles. The system reinforces accountability and alignment with the Guardian Spirit values, providing a clear path for professional development across multiple dimensions.

As the Space Force continues to face shifting mission priorities, the adaptability of its assessment system will prove essential. The unpredictable nature of space operations demands that assessments evolve in real time to remain relevant and responsive to changing needs. This flexibility ensures that the force remains agile and ready to meet future challenges.

Data analytics tools will play a crucial role in this process, offering leadership deeper insights into Guardian skills, performance, and development. These tools allow for more informed decisions on training, personnel placement, and team composition. With real-time data at their disposal, leaders can address gaps, spot trends, and make strategic adjustments to maintain the agility of the force. The integration of these analytics ensures that decisions are not only timely but also based on a comprehensive view of performance across the organization.

As the culture of assessment matures, it serves as a foundation for continuous improvement within the Space Force. Routine feedback ensures that Guardians have the tools necessary to enhance their capabilities and skills, while leadership can feel confident that the force remains aligned with mission objectives. This data-driven, dynamic approach supports proactive decision making, enabling the Space Force to refine its strategies and ensure that Guardians consistently meet the evolving demands of their roles.

CHAPTER 11
Empowering Employees

In this chapter, we'll cover:
- Enabling employees to own their skills (and skills data)
- Mapping employee experiences to their skills
- Driving employee career pathways
- Identifying opportunities for employees to develop skills for the future

If the world is moving toward being more skills-focused, then we need to understand our own skills in a way that can be shared with others. Do you know what you're good at? Do you know what your areas of expertise are, where you are just beginning to develop skills, or what skills you used to be really good at but haven't used in a while? How do you communicate your skills to others, particularly in a work context? Being able to answer these questions is important. And empowering everyone in your organization to have deep insight into their own skills is critical to supporting the evolution to a skills-based organization.

> **Skills Tip**
> While we are going to discuss the employee value of skills within the context of a skills-based organization, the reality is that people need to also understand their skills and expertise outside a particular role in a particular organization. This way, they can understand how their skills map to their employer's needs within their organization, across organizations, and in the market overall. While no universal standards have been set for skills or skill data, employees do need to think about how their skills evolve throughout their careers in relation to different roles and employers.

Within any organization, the ability to understand, market, and develop one's skills has become a cornerstone of professional success. As job roles evolve and the demand for specialized competencies grows, employees must take an active role in managing their skills and leveraging data about their abilities to navigate their careers. Skills data provides employees with the insights needed to identify growth opportunities, market their abilities, and plan strategic career moves.

Consider an employee working in customer support who has developed an interest in user experience (UX) design. They can use skills data to understand the competencies required for such a role. By identifying their current skills and the gaps they need to address, the employee can pursue relevant online courses, workshops, or mentorship opportunities provided by the organization. Over time, they can build a skills portfolio that makes them a strong candidate for UX-related projects or roles, allowing them to pivot into a new career path without needing to leave the company. This approach not only retains valuable talent but also fosters a culture of internal mobility that encourages employees to grow within the organization.

By making skills data visible to employees, organizations empower them to set personalized development plans that align with both their career goals and personal aspirations. This could mean developing technical skills that align with future industry needs or focusing on soft skills, such as leadership or communication, that support long-term growth. L&D teams can use this data to design learning initiatives that address individual skills gaps, offering targeted training that supports employees' development goals.

The result is a collaborative approach to career planning, with employees, managers, and L&D working together to ensure that career growth is not only about moving up but also about expanding one's capabilities and exploring new possibilities. By integrating skills data into the process, organizations create an environment that allows employees to navigate their careers more fluidly, transitioning into roles that align with their evolving skills and interests. This flexibility is particularly valuable in a business landscape because adaptability and continuous learning are key to staying competitive.

This chapter explores how employees can take charge of their skills data to enhance their professional journey. It covers the fundamentals of understanding and owning one's skills, the nuances of marketing those skills effectively, and using skills data to drive career progression. Moreover, it delves into the critical importance of continual skills development to stay competitive in an ever-changing job market. For skills-based organizations to survive and thrive, employee ownership of skills is critical to leverage skills data to its fullest advantage.

Enabling Employees to Own Their Skills and Skill Data

Helping employees own their skills begins with educating them about what skills data is and why it matters. Skills data includes measurable information about an individual's proficiency in various competencies, gathered through performance reviews, skills assessments, project feedback, and even self-assessments. This data helps employees recognize their strengths, identify areas for improvement, and understand how their skills align with their current roles or future career goals.

For employees, having access to this information is like holding a map of their professional capabilities. It allows them to make informed decisions about which skills to develop further and where they can add the most value in their organization. It gives substance to conversations with managers and mentors about opportunities for development. It provides insight into readiness for the next stage in their career. With skills data, employees can approach their careers more strategically, setting realistic goals and identifying the steps needed to achieve them.

Understanding and leveraging skills data starts with education. Employees need to learn how to interpret skills data and understand the different proficiency levels associated with each skill. Organizations can support this by providing workshops, training sessions, and resources that explain what skills data is and how it can be used for personal growth. For example, sessions might focus on understanding skills rating systems, using data to identify skills gaps, and setting development goals based on skills assessments.

Educating employees about the value of skills data empowers them to take an active role in their professional development. It encourages continuous learning because employees can regularly assess their progress and seek out opportunities to improve. This education also helps demystify the process of skills evaluation, making it easier for employees to understand feedback from managers and to use it to guide their growth.

Who Owns Skill Data?

Who owns this data? This is a critical question in the discussion of skills data. While organizations typically collect and maintain skills data through internal systems, the question of ownership can be complex. Employees have a vested interest in their skills data because it directly affects their career progression and development opportunities. They should be able to access their data easily, understand how it is used, and have a say in how it is shared or used within and outside the organization.

Organizations benefit when they are transparent about how skills data is collected and used. Clear policies regarding data access, sharing, and privacy can help build trust between employees and their employers. For instance, if an employee wants to use their skills data to apply for internal roles or opportunities, they should feel confident that this information is being used to support their growth. Ultimately, a collaborative approach to data ownership ensures that skills data is used in a way that benefits both the individual and the organization.

> ### Skills Tip
> As organizations grapple with data ownership, basic guidance should be that skills data is collected and analyzed with employees, not without them. Because skills are currently in a gray area in terms of performance improvement initiatives, defaulting to skills data being owned by the individual is recommended.

Understanding Proficiency

Proficiency is a key aspect of skills data because it defines an employee's level of expertise in a particular skill. Proficiency levels can range from basic awareness to advanced mastery, and understanding where an employee falls on this spectrum is essential for targeted development.

Help employees familiarize themselves with the proficiency scales used in your organization's skills assessments and reflect on where they see themselves within these levels. This self-awareness helps identify realistic goals for improvement and relevant training or projects to advance to the next level. It also makes it easier for employees to discuss skills development with managers and mentors, ensuring that everyone is aligned on the employee's growth trajectory.

Expertise Profiles With Isanno

In 2023, just as large language models (LLMs) were becoming part of our everyday interaction with AI, I asked myself, "What if it's not about all your skills, but what you're especially good at? If we could identify someone's strengths, would that empower them to better navigate their career and their skill development?"

I joined forces with two colleagues and we began to experiment with folks in our immediate circle. We collected their information—resume, current job description, personality assessments, and LinkedIn profile—and created an AI-generated expertise profile that included a narrative of their strengths, recommendations for next steps in their career (both linear progression and adjacent opportunities), and a list of their top skills with supporting evidence. It wasn't a particularly polished start, but everyone loved their profile and many asked if they could post it to LinkedIn or use it as a cover letter for their resume. These reactions made us feel like we were on to something.

We also noticed a pattern in peoples' responses. In general, women were hesitant to accept the description of their expertise at face value, whereas men reacted positively and heartily embraced the narrative of their strengths. So, we would encourage folks to share their profile with trusted colleagues, managers, or mentors for validation or suggestions for improvement; this reinforcement from people they respected helped those who were hesitant gain confidence.

Another pattern we identified was how motivated people were to build any missing skills their profiles identified to prepare for their next career step. Some people were excited to explore adjacent career path suggestions, while others were curious about which skills would help them stay current and successful in their current roles.

Once we finished building expertise profiles for a range of individuals, the next step was to explore how expertise profiles might work within a team. We partnered with a regional credit union's L&D team to build individual profiles for the team's six members and leaders. Once again, we saw the same response patterns as in our early testing with gender differences and motivation to explore next steps. What we didn't anticipate was the team leader's need to review the individual profiles before we shared them with the team. In particular, the manager identified some members of her team who were not ready for the next step in their career, despite having expertise profiles that could spike their confidence in being promoted or moving into new roles.

The biggest takeaways from our early product testing were twofold. Individuals need to be empowered to own their skills story. These profiles provided insight into each person's top skills and how those skills align to career opportunities, which became a strong motivator in driving their careers. Second, if taking on a skills strengths analysis for a team, managers must be prepared to have career pathing conversations with their team members and set realistic expectations on opportunities for skill development and career progression. As many organizations and managers are not accustomed to regularly having these types of conversations, it's possible to create a disconnect between employee and manager expectations if employees are given these additional details about their skills.

For now, Isanno Expertise Profiles are still in testing mode, and we've resumed experimentation and refinement for creating individual profiles. As organizations become increasingly skills based, the opportunity for deeper analysis of team strengths and for managers to engage their team members' in more detailed career development conversations could make these profiles an incredibly powerful tool.

Helping Employees Market Themselves With Skills Profiles

If the next evolution of resumes are skills profiles, then individuals need to understand how to build a skills profile that showcases their unique strengths and capabilities. Think of a skills profile as adding to the information contained in a resume; in addition to job history and educational background, a skills profile provides details on skills and proficiencies, highlighting data points that reinforce or build confidence in the accuracy of skill level.

A skills profile is a powerful tool that employees can use to clearly and confidently present their professional expertise and competencies. It acts as a personal branding asset that highlights the unique skills they bring to the table. For many employees, having a well-rounded skills profile can be crucial for standing out within their organization or industry, especially when seeking promotions, applying for new roles, or networking with peers.

Skills Tip

Many skills-focused technologies have developed skills profiles as part of their product. For organizations that have more than one skills-related supplier, they may have multiple skills profiles across the suppliers' platforms. Organizations themselves may develop a standard for skills profiles as well. To simplify the process, employees may want to keep a skills profile, similar to a resume, that they refer to and that can inform the skills profile that their organization uses internally.

Creating a compelling skills profile starts with a thorough understanding of an employee's abilities. Employees should include metrics from skills assessments, results from completed projects, feedback from peers and managers, and certifications that validate their expertise. Practically, a software developer might include details about their proficiency in various programming languages, certifications in frameworks such as Amazon Web Services or Google Cloud, and specific projects that they played a critical role in developing new features for. This approach allows others to see not just what the employee has done but how their skills have evolved over time.

A well-maintained skills profile provides a verified snapshot of an employee's capabilities, making it easier to demonstrate their readiness for new challenges. It also encourages regular reflection on progress, helping employees identify areas where they have grown and where further development is needed. This makes the profile not just a marketing tool but also a valuable resource for personal growth.

How to Talk in Skills-Based Terms

Effectively communicating skills is a critical aspect of leveraging skills data. When speaking to managers, peers, or potential employers, framing conversations around specific skills rather than just job titles or responsibilities can change the focus of conversations in meaningful ways. This involves focusing on concrete examples of how skills have been applied to achieve tangible results.

For instance, instead of simply stating, "I led a team of five people," an employee could frame this achievement in skills-based terms: "I used my leadership and strategic-planning skills to guide a team of five, resulting in a 15 percent increase in project efficiency over six months." This shifts the narrative from generic job duties to clear evidence of skills application and the impact it had on the team or project.

Talking in skills-based terms helps employees position themselves as experts in their field and makes it easier for others to understand their value. It emphasizes their ability to deliver results, making a stronger case during performance reviews and interviews or when seeking out new responsibilities. This skills-focused language also helps build credibility because it demonstrates a deep understanding of how specific abilities contribute to overall success.

Mapping Experiences to Skills

One of the challenges employees often face is translating their past experiences into a clear picture of their skills. Experiences such as leading a project, developing a new product, or managing client relationships all involve a range of skills that may not be immediately obvious. Learning to map these experiences to specific skills is a crucial step in creating a strong skills profile and shifting the conversation from roles to skills.

For example, managing a cross-functional project can involve a variety of skills, including communication, time management, problem solving, and stakeholder engagement. By breaking down a project into these components, employees can more accurately describe their abilities and strengths. This approach helps create a detailed skills profile that reflects the depth and breadth of their experience.

Mapping experiences to skills also prepares employees for conversations about their growth and aspirations. During performance reviews or career discussions, being able to pinpoint specific skills that were developed through key projects can make it easier to articulate future goals or opportunities. It provides a more complete picture of how past experiences have prepared them for new challenges, whether they are seeking a promotion, a lateral move, or an entirely new role.

Driving Employee Career Paths

When it comes to the career paths, some employees find themselves on or drawn to a linear progression, remaining in the same domain of work during their tenure with an organization. Others may seek a nontraditional route to a fulfilling career, changing direction as their interests change or perhaps by necessity. Let's explore both.

Linear Career Paths

For many employees, a linear career path—one that follows a straight trajectory upward within a particular field—is a familiar route to advancement. Skills data can be a valuable tool in this type of progression because it helps employees pinpoint the skills they need to reach the next level within their role or department. For example, an accountant looking to move into a senior accounting position can use skills data to identify which competencies, such as advanced financial analysis or leadership skills, are essential for the promotion.

By using skills data to set goals, employees can plan their progress step-by-step, ensuring that each new skill they acquire moves them closer to their desired role. It also helps them prepare for the skills-based evaluations that many organizations use to determine promotions. This data-driven approach makes the path to advancement more transparent and achievable, providing employees with a clear road map to success.

Typically in a linear career path, employees reach a point when they have a choice to make: Do they want to continue to develop as an expert individual contributor, or do they want to move into people management and leading teams? Let's explore how skills can support either career trajectory.

Becoming a SME

As employees advance in their career, one path to continued growth is becoming a subject matter expert (SME) in their area. For employees with deep expertise or a passion for a specific skill, skills data can help identify opportunities to become the go-to person for that area within their organization. For example, a data analyst might focus on developing niche expertise in machine learning or data visualization, using skills data to track their progress and identify gaps.

Skills data also helps SMEs showcase their value by providing concrete examples of how their expertise has contributed to the organization. This can be especially useful during performance reviews or when negotiating roles with more responsibility or compensation. Becoming a SME allows employees to make a significant impact on their organization while carving out a unique professional identity.

Becoming a People Leader

For those interested in moving into leadership positions, skills data provides insights into what it takes to become an effective people leader. Many leadership roles require a combination of technical expertise and capabilities such as communication, empathy, and strategic thinking. By using skills data to understand where they excel and where they need to improve, employees can focus on developing the competencies required for successful leadership.

For example, an engineer looking to become a team lead might use skills data to assess their current abilities in mentoring, conflict resolution, and project management. Identifying gaps early allows them to pursue relevant training or seek mentorship from current leaders. This proactive approach ensures that when a leadership opportunity arises, they are well prepared to step into the role.

Nontraditional Career Paths

Skills data can also be a game changer for employees interested in exploring nontraditional or nonlinear career paths. Rather than following a standard progression within a single discipline, some employees may wish to explore diverse roles that allow them to use different skills. For instance, someone with a background in finance might be interested in transitioning into a role in data analytics, using their quantitative skills in a new context.

By highlighting transferable skills and capabilities, skills data makes it easier for employees to pivot into new areas. It allows them to build a case for how their existing expertise can be valuable in a different role. This flexibility is especially important in a job market in which new roles are constantly emerging, giving employees the confidence to explore new possibilities without being confined to their current job title.

Lateral Moves

Lateral moves, when an employee shifts into a new role at the same level, can be a valuable way to gain experience and expand their skill set. Skills data helps employees identify lateral opportunities that align with their interests and long-term goals. For example, an HR specialist might use skills data to move into a role in talent development so they can apply their skills in a different context and develop new competencies.

By using skills data to map out potential lateral moves, employees can create a diverse portfolio of experiences that make them more well-rounded professionals. These experiences not only enhance their skill set but also increase their visibility within the organization, positioning them for future advancement.

Reskilling for Something New

In some cases, employees may decide to pursue an entirely new career direction, either within their current company or in a different industry. Skills data plays a crucial role in this process because it allows employees to see which skills they need to acquire to make a successful transition. It also helps them identify transferable skills that can ease the shift into a new field.

Reskilling is often necessary when industries change or when an employee's interests evolve over time. Skills data provides a structured approach to reskilling, helping employees focus on learning the skills that will be most beneficial in their new career path. This makes the transition smoother and increases the chances of success in their new role.

Developing Skills for the Future

As the workplace evolves, so do the skills required to thrive. For employees, maintaining a focus on continuous learning and future skills is key to staying competitive and adaptable in their careers. Skills data provides valuable insights into which skills are likely to be in demand, helping employees stay ahead of the curve. Think transferable or cross-functional skills (such as problem solving, communication, data analysis, and digital literacy) and future-proof skills (such as AI, cybersecurity, and remote team management). This section explores how employees can use skills data to seek out learning opportunities and take advantage of various pathways for skill development.

Seeking Out Opportunities to Build and Practice Skills

Learning new skills is only part of the equation—applying them in real-world scenarios truly solidifies growth. Employees should be encouraged to actively seek out opportunities to use their developing skills in practical settings because this experience helps refine their abilities and demonstrate their skills growth to others.

Within an organization, one approach is to connect employees to stretch assignments or special projects that challenge them to use new skills. For instance, an IT professional looking to build project management skills might volunteer to lead a new software deployment project, gaining hands-on experience while applying what they have learned. Skills data can guide employees to choose projects that align with their development goals, ensuring they focus on areas where they want to grow.

Another approach is coaching and mentoring. For employees, engaging with mentors provides an opportunity to gain insights into industry trends, learn best practices, and receive personalized feedback on their growth. Employees with experience to share may in turn want to coach or mentor less-experienced employees. Skills data can enhance this process by providing a clear starting point for discussions between mentors and mentees, focusing on specific strengths and areas for improvement.

An employee might use their skills assessment data to identify gaps in strategic thinking and then seek out a mentor who has excelled in this area. Through regular mentoring sessions, they can work on practical strategies to improve this skill, using feedback and progress tracking to refine their approach. Structured mentorship can significantly accelerate the development process, making skills data a powerful tool for both employees and mentors.

Building Skills Outside Work

Not all skills need to be exclusively developed within the context of a job, nor perhaps can be. Employees may want to focus on developing skills and capabilities that fall outside their current roles. To think about skills development as something that doesn't just happen at work, employees should consider how they are developing skills not only while at work, but also in the full spectrum of their life's activities.

Volunteer Work

Volunteering is a valuable way to build and apply skills, often in environments that offer different challenges from the typical workplace. For employees looking to develop leadership, project management, or other transferable skills, volunteering for community organizations or industry groups can provide opportunities to apply these skills in real-world situations.

Skills data can help employees choose volunteer roles that align with their development goals. For instance, if an employee wants to improve their public-speaking skills, they might volunteer to lead a workshop or serve as a spokesperson for a community organization. These experiences can then be added to their skills profile, providing evidence of their growth in a way that complements their professional achievements.

Continuing Education

Formal education—such as certifications, degrees, or professional development courses—remains a critical part of long-term career development. Skills data can help employees identify which courses will provide the greatest benefit based on their career goals and the skills gaps they wish to address.

An employee looking to move into a cybersecurity role might use skills data to understand their current level of expertise in network security and identify specific courses that will help them gain the necessary knowledge. Many online learning platforms offer personalized learning paths that align with the skills data employees have gathered, making it easier to find courses that directly support their career aspirations.

Continuing education is especially important for employees working in fields that are rapidly changing because of technological advancements. By focusing on acquiring up-to-date knowledge and credentials, employees can ensure that their skills remain relevant, positioning themselves for future opportunities.

Side Gigs

In the current gig economy, it is not uncommon for employees with full-time roles to take on side projects as a way to make extra money and build new skills and capabilities. Side gigs, freelance work, or part-time projects can be an effective way for employees to build and refine their skills outside their primary job. This type of work often allows employees to take on different types of challenges, providing valuable experience that can be brought back to their main careers. As an example, a graphic designer who takes on freelance web design projects can build new technical skills while expanding their creative portfolio.

Skills data can guide employees in choosing side gigs that align with their long-term goals, ensuring that the time and effort they invest contributes to their overall career strategy. By focusing on side projects that offer opportunities to develop in-demand skills, employees can broaden their expertise and create a more versatile skill set that benefits both their current job and any future career moves they wish to make.

Conclusion

For employees, leveraging skills data is not just about improving current job performance; it's about taking control of their professional future. By understanding their strengths, identifying areas for growth, and actively seeking out opportunities to develop new skills, employees can navigate their careers with greater confidence and clarity. Skills data provides the insights needed to make informed decisions about training, career transitions, and professional development—helping employees stay competitive in a constantly evolving job market.

Through strategic use of skills data, employees can create a personal road map that guides their journey, from marketing their skills to exploring new roles and continuously building expertise. In doing so, they are the drivers of their careers, turning skills into a source of empowerment and opportunity. As the workplace continues to change, individuals who embrace a skills-based approach will be better equipped to adapt, thrive, and achieve their full potential at each step in their career.

As important as empowerment is, employee buy-in and participation in skills-based initiatives is absolutely essential to the success of a skills-based organization. Beyond ownership of and trust in skills data, employees actively speaking the language of skills and using skills to market themselves and target development will shift an organization from a company using skills data to a skills-based organization.

Your Skills Strategy Must Consider People

Contributed by Kristi Bloom, Co-Founder, Rising Tide Cooperative

Everyone is talking about skills. Some folks are talking about the technologies that will drive us into this future. Some are talking about the data. I hear very few talking about people. And that's a problem because what is hard about skills is that they exist within people. And people have emotions.

You see, to get skills data to power your skills strategy to become a skills-based organization, you need people to take action. You need them to assert, or validate, or at least passively agree to name their skills, and then to rate or accept ratings for them.

And unfortunately, that can feel like a reminder of systems and processes that don't always seem great for employees, including school and grading, performance management, and applying for jobs. The organization wants to collect data and to create structure around it to do things with it, but there are many examples of skills data being used nefariously.

So, collecting skills data can be harder than you might initially think. For many of us, messages that promote movement within the organization are motivating. However, for those who are happy in their role, or unhappy in the organization, these messages just don't land well.

Simply put, your skills strategy must consider people. Start with questions like:

- How are other data-related initiatives received?
- What does your engagement survey or net promoter score (NPS) data tell you about employee longevity?
- How many internal promotions have you actually done?
- What is the general sentiment around performance management?
- Do your measurement systems allow individuals time to think about, measure, and update skills on a regular basis?
- How have managers supported previous efforts like this? What do you need to do to empower them to motivate employees?
- Have you considered the "So what?" of the skills data you collect for each employee?

If you can't answer those questions, take the time to dig in. Let's do that together here.

How Are Other Data-Related Initiatives Received?

Think about other times when you have collected data about employees. Maybe the only time you do this is during annual performance reviews. Perhaps you have done other assessments, such as DiSC or Strengths Finder. Maybe it's as simple as asking employees to update beneficiaries or addresses.

In those initiatives, what was your initial completion rate? How many times did you have to follow up? Did you achieve 100 percent data collection?

If data collection was hard for something like addresses or beneficiaries, you will need to do a great deal of influencing to get people to give you updated skills data. Messaging is critical here. People need to trust that the data will benefit them and not just the organization.

What Does Your Engagement Survey or NPS Data Tell You About Employee Longevity?

Most engagement surveys contain a question about employee retention. NPS, by definition, is a vote of confidence for your organization. If either of those numbers is low, you will have a tough time making a case that gathering skills data will help employees with their career at your organization because the data is telling you that your expectations and their expectations for their longevity may not be aligned.

Your first step is to understand why employees aren't staying with or recommending your organization. After you understand that, you can target your skills-data-collection messaging and potentially boost your engagement numbers as well. Or at least, avoid messaging about internal advancement.

How Many Internal Promotions Have You Actually Done?

Speaking of internal advancements, how many have you actually done? If you don't have a strategy for internal mobility, step one is to create one because the cost savings are significant. And if you haven't created or executed well on a strategy, this should not be part of your initial messaging. You'll need to create a different motivator for employees to give you their skills data.

What Is the General Sentiment Around Performance Management?

This is probably the strongest correlator to your efforts to collect skills data. Undoubtedly, many employees will think they are the same thing. You will need to be intentional about your messaging because employees are unlikely to willingly give you skills data if they perceive that performance management has not been kind to them.

I would strongly recommend against correlating skills data with performance management. Skills are a means to achieve performance. They are not the same thing. In fact, I strongly recommend you use a completely different scale for skills measurement than you do for performance measurement. You need to create as many dissociations as possible in the minds of your employees.

Do Your Measurement Systems Allow Individuals Time to Think About, Measure, and Update Skills on a Regular Basis?

Skills data is data, and without regular updates, it will no longer be relevant for your intended purposes. You will need to consider not only initial collection but ongoing collection and refinement. And again, you will need to get data from across your employee population. If employees have autonomy over their time, combined with good messaging and value to them, they are more likely to allocate some of that time to updating their skills data on a regular basis.

How Have Managers Supported Previous Efforts Like This? What Do You Need to Do to Empower Them to Motivate Employees?

This is a big one. Managers have an outsized impact on how employees feel about your organization, so you need your managers to be on board with skills-data collection.

Look at previous people or organization development efforts. What role did managers play? How did you ensure they were bought in so they could incentivize their teams?

Don't underestimate the value managers bring to efforts like this. They may be the exact key to success.

Have You Considered the "So What?" of the Skills Data You Collect for Each Employee?

If you don't get this one right, the rest of the answers don't really matter because here's how this works: If employees don't give you updated skills data on a regular basis, you don't have organizational skills data. And if you don't have organizational skills data, you can't become a skills-based organization. When creating your messaging, you must consider what is in it for the employees. How will they benefit from giving you updated skills data? What, specifically, will change for them as employees of your organization?

It all comes back to the people. You need to find the right emotional connection with them to create the desire to do the work to share their data. But, here's a word of caution: Do not wait until you have the perfect strategy or messaging to get started. Action will help you refine both. Start and adjust along the way.

Skills and User Experience

Contributed by Matthew J. Daniel, Senior Principal, Talent Strategy, Guild Education

In a world where HR and talent professionals argue endlessly about what the definition of a skill is, the fundamental question we should ask ourselves as skilling professionals is this: Why would we expect our employees and learners to know, articulate, and understand the impact of their skills if we can't?

Let's step outside HR and take a moment to think about consumer data. Right now, Google has all kinds of data about you that it uses to tailor your search results, almost none of which it asks you about. The same is true of your social media feeds and a number of retailers that tailor your experience on their websites. They rarely ask you to fill out a form, and they certainly don't ask you to "tag your own profile" with relevant data. They infer based on data they gather along the way. They treat you like a user and design a (mostly) great experience for you.

Another example might be your credit score. For most of us, it's incredibly difficult to understand a credit score calculation. As a result, most major banks and credit card companies have put credit trackers in place. Many of these trackers have features that help you understand how your decisions influence your credit score. You can model the impact on your credit score if you paid off more debt or opened another credit line. Again, you're treated like a user with an experience designed around you, but one that's related to a mound of data.

Both examples stand in stark contrast to how the majority of HR folks think about skills. We nag employees and candidates to tell us their skills. We nag learning folks to tell us the skills associated with content. We nag hiring managers to determine the skills on their job postings. Right now, you'd be hard-pressed to come up with examples of where you're expected to tag yourself in detail with this kind of data as a consumer, yet that's what so much of the world of skills has resolved itself to do. As a field, talent and HR tech professionals try to make the user experience better when they ask for tedious data, but they're still not at the right starting point or mindset regarding skills data.

To crystallize this point, let me share some data from research my team did in 2023 regarding how learners want to receive recommendations on learning. We gave learners the option to receive recommendations based on skills or roles, or those generic to industry. Here's what we found overall: 34 percent wanted skills-based recommendations, 29 percent wanted roles-based, and 37 percent were looking for industry-level recommendations. You read that right; roughly a third of learners wanted recommendations by skill.

Interestingly, there was variation by industry vertical and learner education level. In this instance, 47 percent of learners with a master's degree wanted skills-based recommendations, while 40 percent of those without any degree wanted industry-focused recommendations. We also found variation by industry. In healthcare, 44 percent were looking for industry-based recommendations, with only 26 percent looking for skills-based ones. However, in financial services, 49 percent wanted skills-based, and 38 percent wanted roles-based. In retail, the split was closer to even, but still, skills represented only the way that nearly a third of learners wanted to see recommendations. For my employer, Guild, this means we represent learning in multiple ways so users can navigate it in their preferred version. We show roles-based career pathways with learning tied to them. We show general topic- or industry-level segmentation, and we show skills data inside both experiences.

This led us to do in-depth interviews with a much smaller subset of users (13) across levels and role types (in business, tech, retail, and clinical healthcare) to understand how they defined and used skills data. Here's what we noticed: While nearly everyone could be coaxed into talking about their skills, only three of the 13 actually used "skills" language while describing their skills. When we asked users about skills-based hiring—probably the most mainstream conception of skills-based decision making happening in HR—only three of the 13 were familiar with it, all in retail.

Generally, we found that users just weren't familiar with skills articulation. The majority of users tied that kind of activity to job interviews, and half of the users said they were uncomfortable talking about themselves and their skills, saying it made them "nervous," "embarrassed," or feel like they were "bragging." It's important to note that this divide was starkest by gender; seven of eight women interviewed expressed discomfort with talking about skills, while five of five men said they were comfortable and confident.

In our research, we also consistently found that self-reported skills are defined too narrowly. Consistently, individuals could describe the technical or credentialed skills essential to their roles, but many missed the kinds of people-based and soft skills critical to thrive in most roles. Also, when interviewed in this study, participants almost never listed skills gained outside work. It's common for most of us to maintain activities outside our day jobs: leading sports teams and managing difficult parents; organizing marketing campaigns for booster clubs; becoming "influencers" to our niche followers on social media; or volunteering at a local church or nonprofit. All these things require skills that users rarely report on, even when it would open up numerous opportunities for them.

The implications of this research have been startling. It reveals that some individuals and demographics are clearly disadvantaged when it comes to using skills-based HR systems that require users to get involved in tagging skills data. Although we might hope that HR systems are unwinding systemic biases, our own take on the novel, equity-driving approach of skills actually disadvantages some of the same folks we were hoping to help, such as those without advanced education credentials.

The answer isn't to ignore skills, but it's also critical not to limit navigation of learning, job, and gig opportunities to only skills-based decision making. We've spent years trying to force users to understand how to use skills data in their HR systems, when in fact, we should continue building optionality in how navigation is experienced based on the preferences of our users. We should treat folks more like consumers and layer away much of the data we use for decision making behind the scenes, while still giving users the ability to edit that data when they want.

Let's put a fine point on this. Getting to a skills-based infrastructure is critical for strategic workforce planning. For those of us focused on making better talent decisions, we need to understand how skills are tied to the humans, jobs, projects, and content we have in our organizations. And still, we should be tenacious about wrestling with difficult issues like the data I've presented here until we figure it out. Simultaneously, we should give our users a reprieve from expecting them to understand skills and grapple with how we'll use them to affect their lives. We have to do more of the work for them in the user experience and lower expectations of their ability to understand exactly what a skill is and input that data across our many HR systems.

CHAPTER 12
Measuring Impact and Sustaining Your Skills-Based Organization

In this chapter, we'll cover:
- Setting up metrics for tracking the effectiveness of skills-based efforts
- Maintaining an adaptive approach to your skills-based initiatives
- Building a skills-based HR tech stack that works for your organization and its employees

Becoming a skills-based organization means embarking on a journey, not reaching a destination. Approaching skills and skills data as a focus for continuous improvement means that you will constantly be evaluating what's working, what's not, where and how you can improve, and what new decisions or use cases could benefit from skills data. You'll be constantly evaluating and improving data quality, as well as the systems you use to support your skills-based organization. In short, this is a way of working across every aspect of your business, a language you will develop, and systems you will build up to support your goals.

In this chapter, we'll review key metrics you can use to evaluate progress and the effectiveness of your skills strategy, methods for continuous evaluation of skills processes and frameworks, and markers for technology investment as your skills-based organization matures and grows.

Skills-Based Organization Metrics

Setting up metrics is necessary for tracking the effectiveness of a skills-based model because metrics will enable your organization to gain a clear picture of how data-driven skills initiatives translate into business outcomes. This approach ensures that investments in skills are strategically aligned with the organization's broader goals. Without measurable data, it becomes challenging to assess whether skills efforts are yielding the desired outcomes, such as increased productivity, innovation, or improved employee engagement.

Metrics in a skills-based organization serve as a bridge between skills acquisition and tangible results. They help align the organization's skill initiatives with five core parameters:

- **Skills inventory**—identifying what skills you have and what skills you need to meet the needs of the organization
- **Skills development**—tracking skills growth across the organization
- **Skills utilization**—measuring how effectively these skills are applied in real-world scenarios within the workplace
- **Business impact**—evaluating the direct and indirect contributions of skills-based strategies to the organization's success
- **Employee value**—assessing how skills affect employee satisfaction, engagement, and retention

By focusing on these key areas, it's possible to foster a culture in which skills are measurable and directly tied to the company's success.

Managing Your Skills Inventory

To effectively manage a skills inventory, you should track several metrics that help identify existing skills within the organization and highlight gaps that need to be addressed to meet strategic goals. Common metrics for skills inventory management include:

- **Skills coverage ratio.** This measures the percentage of required skills (based on organizational needs) that are currently present within the workforce. It helps determine how well the existing skill sets align with strategic objectives.

- **Skills gap analysis.** This identifies the difference between the skills the organization currently has and those it needs to achieve its goals. It helps prioritize areas for upskilling or reskilling and informs targeted recruitment strategies.
- **Skills acquisition rate.** This measures how quickly new skills are being acquired through training, development, or hiring. It helps track the progress of upskilling and reskilling initiatives.
- **Critical skills availability.** This focuses on tracking the availability of high-priority skills that are essential for key projects or strategic initiatives. It ensures that the organization is prepared for critical tasks and minimizes the risk of skills shortages.
- **Skills proficiency levels.** This assesses the proficiency of employees in key skills, often on a scale defined by the organization (for example, beginner, intermediate, or advanced). It helps identify areas where deeper training is needed and measures the overall capability of the workforce.

These key performance indicators allow a business to maintain a clear view of its current skill sets and address gaps proactively so it remains competitive and capable of achieving its strategic goals.

Tracking Skills Development

Measuring the progress of skills acquisition is pivotal for a skills-based organization. Metrics provide a standard to track this progress, allowing organizations to understand which skills are being developed, the pace of this development, and how these skills align with business needs. Effective metrics in this context can address various aspects of skills acquisition, from learning outcomes to certification achievements.

Common metrics for tracking skills development include:
- **Rate of skills growth.** This measures the increase in skills proficiency across various domains within a specified period. It provides insight into how quickly employees are advancing in their learning journeys.
- **Completion of upskilling and reskilling programs.** By tracking program completion rates, organizations can assess the

engagement and success of their learning initiatives. High completion rates may indicate that the programs are well designed and align with the learners' needs.
- **Number of certifications or skills badges earned.** Recognizing formal certifications or digital badges provides a tangible measure of skills gained. These credentials can be tied to industry standards, adding credibility to the organization's skills base.

Metrics for skills development require setting a baseline from which to measure change, as well as continuous data collection to demonstrate growth. Depending on your organization's needs, you may also track attrition for skills that employees have but are no longer actively using.

Measuring Skills Utilization

Beyond acquiring new skills, you need to measure how employees apply their skills in their roles. Skills utilization metrics help organizations understand if the investment in training translates into practical, everyday applications that drive performance. This focus ensures newly acquired skills do not remain theoretical but are actively used to benefit the organization.

Key metrics for assessing skills utilization include:
- **Skills application rate.** This measures the percentage of skills learned that employees apply in their daily tasks. It helps organizations determine if training programs are relevant and tailored to the actual needs of the job.
- **Project success based on skills.** By analyzing the success rates of projects led by employees with newly acquired skills, organizations can assess the direct impact of skills application on project outcomes.
- **Cross-functional skills usage.** Tracking how employees apply their skills across different departments or projects provides insights into the flexibility and adaptability of the workforce.

For example, an organization might track how skills gained through a data analytics training program contribute to the success of data-driven projects, such as reducing customer churn or optimizing supply chain processes. These metrics require the organization to map skills to roles or work tasks to effectively track skills needs and skills utilization.

Evaluating the Business Impact of Skills-Based Initiatives

To truly understand the value of a skills-based approach, you must link skills initiatives to business outcomes. This connection ensures that skills initiatives are not just a cost center but a strategic lever for growth. Metrics that track the business impact of these initiatives provide visibility into how upskilling and reskilling efforts translate into tangible improvements in key performance areas.

Essential metrics for gauging business impact include:

- **Revenue growth attributed to upskilled employees.** This examines the revenue contribution from projects or products developed or delivered by employees who have recently completed upskilling programs. It helps assess the return on investment of L&D programs.
- **Innovation driven by diverse skills.** By tracking the number of new ideas or products generated as a result of skills diversification, organizations can measure how upskilling contributes to innovation.
- **Time-to-market improvements.** This measures the reduction in the time taken to launch new products or services after implementing skills-based hiring or training practices. Faster time-to-market can directly contribute to competitive advantage. For instance, a tech company might observe that an upskilling initiative for software engineers results in a 20 percent faster deployment time for new features. This directly translates into a shorter time-to-market period, which can give the company an edge over competitors.

Assessing Whether Employees Value Skills Initiatives

In a skills-based organization, employee perception of their role and the organization is increasingly tied to the skills and competencies they develop. Understanding how skills affect retention and satisfaction is vital for maintaining a motivated and engaged workforce. Metrics in this area provide insights into how well the organization is nurturing talent and creating a culture of continuous skills development.

Key metrics for assessing employees' perception of value include:

- **Employee engagement.** Tracking engagement levels can reveal how skills development opportunities affect motivation and commitment to the organization. Higher engagement often correlates with higher productivity and lower turnover rates.
- **Retention rates.** This helps assess how skills efforts influence employee loyalty. If employees perceive growth opportunities within the organization, they are more likely to stay.
- **Promotion velocity.** This measures the speed at which employees progress in their careers after acquiring new skills. It reflects the organization's ability to recognize and reward skills-based growth.
- **Internal mobility percentages.** This determines how many open roles are filled by internal candidates versus external hires. Higher internal mobility can positively affect employee retention metrics by offering opportunities for employees to grow their careers with the same company.

Conducting employee surveys can provide qualitative data on how employees perceive the value of upskilling and internal mobility opportunities. Survey results showing that a majority think their career progression is positively influenced by skills-based initiatives can indicate that the organization's investment in skills is paying off by fostering a culture of growth.

By setting up a robust metrics framework, you can transform your organization's skills-based strategies into actionable insights, ensuring that both employee growth and business objectives move in tandem. This approach not only enhances the organization's competitive edge but also builds a workforce that is equipped to adapt to the changing landscape of work.

Continuous Improvement of Skills-Based Frameworks

Creating a skills-based organization is not a one-time effort but an ongoing journey that requires continuous refinement and adaptation. Rapidly changing business environments demand that organizations maintain a flexible approach to their skills-based frameworks. Adaptability ensures that the organization stays aligned with evolving market trends, technological advancements, and shifting customer needs. Without ongoing refinement, a skills-based framework can quickly become outdated, leading to inefficiencies and potential talent attrition.

Many organizations invested heavily in the competency model trend that predated skills initiatives, which resulted in them investing heavily in static models that were outdated by the time they were built. To both secure buy-in from decision makers and ensure lasting success, you need to take steps to avoid the same mistakes. Fortunately, skills-based organizations are instead focused on agility, which requires adaptability.

A static skills framework poses several risks to an organization:

- **Misalignment with business needs.** As business objectives shift, the required skill sets often change. A rigid framework can result in a workforce that is not equipped to meet new challenges or capitalize on emerging opportunities.
- **Employee dissatisfaction.** When employees think that their skills are underutilized or that they lack opportunities to develop relevant skills, it can lead to decreased engagement and increased turnover. Organizations must continuously update their frameworks to provide meaningful growth opportunities.
- **Competitive disadvantage.** The failure to keep pace with industry standards can erode an organization's competitive position. Companies that remain agile in their skills strategies can better respond to shifts in the market, while those that do not risk falling behind.

Continuous improvement efforts help ensure that a skills-based organization remains dynamic and capable of meeting the future head-on. The rest of this section focuses on how leveraging feedback, data analytics, and management practices can help you keep skills frameworks relevant and effective.

Using Feedback to Refine the Skills Framework

Employee and managerial feedback is a vital source of information for refining skills frameworks. Gathering input from those directly involved in skills development allows organizations to assess the practical relevance of their frameworks and identify areas for improvement. Regular feedback loops create a culture of transparency and continuous learning because both employees and managers feel invested in the process.

Effective methods for collecting feedback include:

- **Regular skills assessments and data collection.** Conducting assessments and collecting skills signals on a continuous basis helps determine whether employees possess the skills needed for their roles and how these skills align with emerging business priorities. These assessments can highlight gaps or redundancies in the existing framework.
- **Employee surveys.** Surveys provide insights into employee perspectives on the effectiveness of L&D initiatives. They can reveal whether employees think that the skills being emphasized are relevant to their current and future roles.
- **Manager feedback loops.** Managers play a key role in observing how skills translate into on-the-job performance. Their feedback and validation can help refine the skills taxonomy to better reflect the day-to-day needs of the business.

For example, a technology company might revise its skills framework to include new digital skills, such as those related to advanced AI and machine learning, in response to manager feedback and employee input. As automation becomes more integral to operations, including these skills ensures that the workforce is equipped to leverage new technologies, positioning the organization for growth in an increasingly digital market.

Making Data-Driven Decisions

Data analytics provides a powerful tool for identifying gaps and opportunities within a skills framework. By leveraging data, organizations can take a strategic approach to skills development, ensuring that training efforts are targeted where they are needed most. This same data can inform more targeted recruitment practices when upskilling and training aren't possible, bringing new talent and skills into the organization. Data-driven decision making enables more precise adjustments to skills programs, enhancing both their relevance and effectiveness.

Key data sources for continuous improvement include:

- **Skills utilization rates.** Analyzing how often and how effectively skills are used in day-to-day tasks can highlight areas where additional training is needed or where certain skills may be underemphasized. Skills utilization provides a window into the skills currently used and skills needed for project staffing, team development, and more.
- **Performance data and productivity metrics.** By examining correlations between skills and performance outcomes, organizations can identify which skills are most critical to achieving business goals. This insight helps prioritize skills in recruitment and L&D programs.
- **Predictive analytics.** Predictive tools can analyze trends in the industry and workforce to forecast future skills needs. This approach ensures that organizations are proactive in their training efforts, rather than reacting to skills gaps as they arise. Predictive analytics often relies on external data sources to add market context to internal skills data and metrics.

Refining Management Practices

Continuous improvement efforts extend beyond refining the skills framework itself; they also affect how managers support and guide their teams. Effective management in a skills-based organization requires a shift from traditional performance management methods to approaches that prioritize skills growth and application. Getting managers and employees alike to adopt a language of skills will help your organization's culture become skills-based.

Ongoing evaluation of the effectiveness of skills-based management practices includes:

- **Skills-based performance management.** Moving away from purely performance-driven assessments, skills-based performance management focuses on how well employees are applying and developing their skills. This shift emphasizes continuous learning and recognizes the long-term benefits of skill building.
- **Continuous feedback loops.** Instead of relying on annual performance reviews, implementing quarterly or even monthly feedback sessions allows for a more timely focus on skills development. This approach helps managers provide actionable guidance on how employees can apply their skills to current projects.
- **Focus on skills application.** Managers should be trained to observe and assess not just the outcomes of work but how employees leverage their skills to achieve those outcomes. This nuanced perspective helps identify opportunities for further skills enhancement.

Refining these management approaches requires ongoing analysis to ensure that employees receive the support they need to continually refine their abilities, level up their skills, and power their career paths with skills data.

Recognizing and Valuing Skills Growth

Recognition is critical for a successful skills-based framework. When employees believe their skills development is acknowledged and valued, they are more likely to remain engaged and committed to their development. Establishing clear recognition programs ensures that continuous improvement efforts translate into a culture that celebrates skills growth.

Effective strategies for recognizing skills growth include:

- **Skills recognition programs.** Programs that offer certifications, internal skills badges, or peer recognition foster a sense of

achievement among employees. These credentials can be used to signal expertise in a particular domain, providing motivation for further growth.
- **Linking skills growth to career progression.** Connecting skills development to tangible career outcomes, such as promotions or expanded job responsibilities, makes the value of upskilling clear. It creates a pathway for employees to see how their growth can directly affect their careers.
- **Incorporating skills into compensation.** For committed skills organizations, offering performance bonuses or salary adjustments based on skills mastery ensures that employees are rewarded for their efforts. This approach shifts the focus from tenure-based rewards to recognition based on demonstrated competencies.

Skills Tip

Beware of intermingling skills data with performance data. Developing skills is not the only driver for performance, and high performance isn't dependent on skills development. Skills initiatives should be evaluated for impact on performance continuously, as should some more skills-specific metrics like skill development against skill proficiency targets. But organizations should not fall into the trap of mixing the two metrics in terms of impact; instead, they should view skills metrics as a driver of culture change. Organizations should not assume that developing skills is a direct correlation to improved performance, but rather measure skills metrics and performance metrics separately and then gauge correlation.

By embracing continuous improvement, organizations can ensure that their skills-based frameworks remain aligned with evolving business needs, fostering workforces that are both adaptable and highly skilled. Continuous evaluation and improvement of your skills systems drives business success and creates a thriving work environment so employees feel empowered to grow and excel.

Building a Skills-Based HR Tech Stack

The transition to a skills-based organization requires more than just a shift in mindset; it demands the strategic integration of technology to support the management, development, and assessment of skills. A well-designed HR tech stack is the foundation of this approach, enabling organizations to track skills data, deliver personalized learning experiences, and generate insights that drive strategic decision making. It serves as the connective tissue for various skills development elements, from learning and assessment to performance evaluation. By leveraging a cohesive HR tech stack, organizations can more accurately identify skills gaps, deliver targeted training, and align skills development with business goals.

A well-integrated HR tech stack provides several benefits:

- **Centralized skills data.** Technology helps consolidate data related to employees' skills, experiences, and competencies, creating a comprehensive view of the organization's talent landscape.
- **Scalability.** As organizations grow, managing skills data manually becomes increasingly inefficient. Technology enables skills tracking and management efforts to scale across large and distributed teams.
- **Enhanced decision making.** Through data analytics and AI, an HR tech stack offers actionable insights into skills trends, helping organizations make informed decisions about talent development and deployment.

In a skills-based organization, technology not only simplifies skills management but also makes it possible to adapt quickly to changing business needs, ensuring that employees' skills are continuously aligned with organizational goals.

When to Invest in Skills Technology

Throughout this book, I've cautioned against investing in technology to support skills too early, or before you've proved your first use case and successfully shown the potential of skills. But eventually, you will want to invest in technology to support your skills initiatives. Your decisions will revolve around your ability to effectively capture, analyze, and utilize skills data to drive decision making.

> **Skills Tip**
>
> Before investing in any new technology, evaluate what is already available in your existing enterprise systems. While they may not be perfect or a long-term solution, many learning and HR technologies already incorporate skills features. If you do need to buy something new, evaluate which products and platforms can integrate with your existing tech stack to ensure that skills data can be shared across systems.

Here's how an organization might identify the need to start investing in skills technologies:

- **Increasing complexity in skills data management.** As the organization begins to gather more detailed information about employee skills—such as skills assessments, learning records, and proficiency levels—managing this data manually becomes cumbersome. When spreadsheets and basic tools are no longer sufficient to track, analyze, and update skills data, it is a sign that investing in skills management technologies is necessary. These technologies can automate data collection and provide a more structured approach to skills tracking.
- **Difficulty in aligning skills with business needs.** If the organization struggles to match available skills with project requirements or strategic goals, it suggests a need for more sophisticated tools. Skills technologies can provide better visibility into skills inventories, enabling managers to quickly identify skills gaps and align training programs with the organization's strategic objectives. This investment ensures that skills development efforts are more targeted and relevant, contributing directly to business outcomes.
- **Growing demand for personalized learning.** As employees seek tailored learning experiences that align with their career goals, it becomes challenging to provide this level of personalization

without technology. Investing in skills platforms that can recommend personalized learning paths based on an individual's skill set, career aspirations, and organizational needs allows for more effective upskilling and reskilling efforts. This is especially important when the organization aims to foster a culture of continuous learning.

- **The need for real-time skills data and analytics.** When the organization begins to value data-driven decision making around talent management—such as tracking skills utilization rates or predicting future skills needs—it indicates a readiness for investment in skills analytics tools. These technologies can provide real-time insights into how skills are being applied across teams and where future training efforts should focus, helping the organization stay ahead of market trends and technological advancements.

- **Scaling challenges.** As the organization grows, either in size or complexity, scaling a skills-based approach without dedicated technology becomes difficult. For larger organizations with diverse teams and geographies, managing and standardizing skills data can be a major challenge. Investing in skills technologies allows the organization to efficiently scale its skills framework, ensuring consistency in skills tracking, assessment, and development across the entire workforce.

- **Pressure to stay competitive.** If the organization faces external pressures, such as rapid industry changes or increasing competition, there may be a greater urgency to adapt and innovate through skills development. Investing in skills technologies can provide a competitive edge by quickly identifying the skills needed to respond to market shifts, enabling the organization to deploy the right talent in critical areas faster than competitors.

Recognizing these signs allows an organization to make a well-timed investment in skills technologies. Technology will become the enabler and backbone of your skills strategy, so invest wisely to support the needs of your organization. Let's dig further into how technology supports skills-based organizations as they mature.

Skills Tip

Investing in a skills technology likely won't be a silver bullet for a skills-data problem. While different platforms offer different approaches to skills-data inference and measurement, know what your organization wants to work toward for skills validation and map those requirements to potential suppliers before making an investment. Most platforms rely on your organizational data to fuel their features, so make sure your own data house is in order before investing in new technology.

Core Components of a Skills-Based HR Tech Stack

Building an effective HR tech stack involves incorporating a range of systems that work together to support skills development, assessment, and performance management. Each component plays a specific role in fostering a skills-based culture. Here are broad categories of products to consider; note that there is a high variability of types of suppliers and product capabilities within each category (chapter 7 provides a more comprehensive look at the skills technology landscape).

- **Learning platforms and LMSs.** A learning platform with skills incorporated into its user experience is central to delivering personalized, skills-based learning experiences. It allows organizations to create tailored learning paths based on individual skills assessments, providing targeted training that aligns with career aspirations and business needs. A learning platform also tracks progress, offering metrics on course completion rates, learning engagement, and skill acquisition. This makes it easier to evaluate the impact of L&D programs.
- **Skills assessment tools.** These systems are crucial for evaluating employees' current skills and identifying areas for growth. Skills assessment tools can include self-assessments, peer reviews, simulations, labs, and standardized testing to provide a holistic view of employees' capabilities. The data gathered through these

tools helps customize training plans and align skills development with the organization's evolving needs.

- **Skills inventory or analytics platforms.** A centralized skills inventory serves as a repository for tracking all employee skills, certifications, and experiences. This platform helps HR and managers match employees with projects or open roles that align with their skill sets. It also makes it easier to identify skills gaps within teams and departments, allowing for targeted reskilling and upskilling initiatives.
- **Performance management systems (PMSs).** A PMS designed for a skills-based organization focuses on evaluating how effectively employees apply their skills in their roles. By linking performance reviews to skills utilization and growth, a PMS helps ensure that learning outcomes are directly tied to business impact. This approach allows organizations to reward skills application and encourage continuous development.
- **Data analytics tools.** These tools can be powerful for assessing the value of skills initiatives within an organization. Your HR tech stack will generate a wealth of data that can be analyzed to gain insights into how skills affect performance and contribute to business success. By aggregating data from the skills inventory, LMS, and PMS into a unified dashboard, you can monitor skills acquisition and application in real time. Then, using predictive analytics, you can anticipate emerging skills requirements based on industry trends and internal data and plan or adjust learning programs and recruiting efforts appropriately.

As you bring together your skills technology stack, these components create a robust framework for managing and developing skills, making it easier for your organization to ensure that its workforce is equipped to meet current and future challenges.

Integrating Systems for a Cohesive Approach

To unlock the full potential of a skills-based HR tech stack, you'll want your tools and systems to seamlessly integrate. Integrating the learning platform, skills inventory, assessment tools, and performance management systems ensures that data flows smoothly across platforms, creating a holistic view of each employee's skills journey.

Key strategies for achieving effective integration include:

- **Interoperability among systems.** Ensuring that different HR platforms can communicate with one another is critical for creating a unified view of skills data. For example, integrating an LMS with a skills inventory allows for automatic updates to an employee's skills profile as they complete training modules. This reduces manual data entry and ensures that managers have real-time information when making decisions.
- **AI and machine learning for insights.** AI-powered tools can analyze data from across the tech stack to provide actionable insights. For example, AI can identify patterns in skills assessments to predict areas where additional training may be needed or suggest personalized learning paths. Machine learning algorithms can also automate the assessment of skills gaps, enabling proactive planning for future skills needs.
- **Performance feedback loops.** A company that integrates its LMS with its PMS can ensure that learning outcomes are directly reflected in performance reviews. For instance, if an employee completes a data analysis course through the LMS, the skills learned can be automatically considered during their next performance evaluation, highlighting their growth in data-related competencies.

When you're able to integrate these systems, you can create a more dynamic and responsive approach to skills management, ensuring that data is used effectively to drive employee growth and align with strategic goals.

Ensuring Employee Engagement With the HR Tech Stack

An effective HR tech stack is not just about having the right systems; it also requires active engagement from employees. Encouraging employees to interact with the tech stack and take ownership of their skills development is key to building a culture of continuous learning.

Best practices for fostering engagement include:
- **User-friendly interfaces.** The more intuitive and user friendly a platform is, the more likely employees are to engage with it. Simplified navigation, clear dashboards, and easy access to learning resources encourage regular use of learning platforms, skills assessments, and other tools.
- **Real-time feedback and gamification.** Incorporating real-time feedback mechanisms helps employees see the immediate impact of their learning efforts. Gamification elements, such as earning badges or achieving milestones, can make the learning experience more engaging and motivating.
- **Encouraging ownership of skills data.** Providing employees with tools for self-assessment and skills tracking helps them take ownership of their career development. Allowing them to see their progress and identify areas for growth fosters a sense of autonomy and empowerment. Skills profiles are a way for employees to see the full story of their skills.

By focusing on user experience and encouraging active participation, organizations can maximize the effectiveness of their HR tech stack, ensuring that technology supports, not hinders, the goal of creating a truly skills-based organization.

A comprehensive HR tech stack enables organizations to manage skills development more effectively, ensuring that employees have the tools and support they need to thrive. This integrated approach not only supports continuous improvement but also positions the organization to adapt to future challenges, keeping it competitive and resilient.

Conclusion

Maturing a skills-based organization is like being a marathon runner. You start by training and learning about key techniques and skills to make you successful. You begin running longer races; you learn; you buy some better shoes or running gear. You keep training, and then you're ready for a marathon. Now you've learned what it takes; each marathon you run, you're improving and iterating to get better. You never stop training; you never stop learning.

Skills-based organizations, once they hit their stride, still require ongoing investment and continuous improvement. By identifying your organization's success metrics, continuously improving your frameworks, and investing strategically in the technologies to best support your organization, it can become a true skills-based organization.

Precision Skills Management: The Casey-Fink Graduate Nurse Experience Survey at Elsevier

Contributed by Aaron Silvers, Consultant (formerly Elsevier, US National Archives and Records Administration, US Department of Defense, IEEE)

The traditional approach to talent management often relies on broad, generic skill sets and subjective assessments. This method, while sufficient in the past, is increasingly inadequate in today's rapidly evolving business landscape. Organizations are seeking a more strategic, data-driven approach to optimize talent development and utilization. Precision skills management emerges as a transformative solution.

Precision skills management is a methodology that leverages data and technology to accurately define, measure, and optimize skills for maximum business impact. By moving beyond generic labels and vague assessments, organizations can unlock the full potential of their workforces. This approach requires a shift in mindset, emphasizing the importance of clear skills definitions, data-driven insights, and continuous improvement.

The Casey-Fink Graduate Nurse Experience Survey (CFGNES) presents an exemplary case study in the application of precision skills management principles. By focusing on the critical transition period for new nurses, the survey effectively identifies key skills and competencies required for success.

Key Elements of the CFGNES Case Study

- **Clear definition of skills.** The survey identifies core skills areas—such as support, organization, communication, and stress management—as critical for new nurses.
- **Data-driven approach.** The survey collects quantitative data on new nurses' experiences, enabling the identification of patterns and trends.
- **Focus on impact.** By measuring factors contributing to nurse turnover, the survey directly links skills to business outcomes (retention rates).
- **Continuous improvement.** The survey is regularly updated and refined to reflect changes in the nursing profession and healthcare environment.

Applying Precision Skills Management Principles

The CFGNES can serve as a model for organizations in other industries to develop their own skills assessment tools. Key principles to consider include:

- **Identifying critical skills.** Determine the core competencies required for successful job performance.
- **Developing a comprehensive assessment tool.** Create a survey or assessment that measures a wide range of skills.
- **Analyzing data to identify trends.** Use data analytics to identify patterns and correlations between skills and performance.
- **Implementing targeted solutions.** Develop specific programs to address skills gaps and improve employee performance.
- **Measuring impact.** Track the effectiveness of solutions and adjust as needed.

By following these steps, organizations can leverage the insights from the CFGNES to create their own precision skills management strategies.

Elsevier's Transition-to-Practice Learning Product

Elsevier, a global leader in information and analytics, employs the CFGNES as a foundational framework for its transition-to-practice product. The

CFGNES provides a robust blueprint for assessing the challenges faced by new nurses and identifying key areas for support.
- **Survey instrument development.** Elsevier is adapting the CFGNES to create a more comprehensive assessment tool that aligns with specific healthcare settings or specialties.
- **Content development.** After identifying key problem areas for new nurses (such as patient assessment and communication), Elsevier developed targeted educational resources and simulations to address these challenges.
- **Learning platform integration.** The CFGNES data can inform the development of personalized learning paths within Elsevier's learning platform. By understanding a nurse's specific needs, the platform can deliver tailored engagement to supporting staff.
- **Analytics and insights.** Elsevier uses the data collected through its transition-to-practice product to generate insights into nurses' skills confidence, identify trends, and inform support staff of changes in sentiment that may lead to a nurse leaving their job.

Beyond the Survey

While the CFGNES is a valuable tool, a comprehensive transition-to-practice program requires more than just a survey. Elsevier incorporates additional elements, such as:
- **Informal mentoring**—engaging new nurses to journal their experience with their nursing educators (support staff are able to read, comment, and act as mentors to provide guidance and support, if not intervention)
- **Simulation-based learning**—offering realistic practice scenarios to develop clinical skills
- **Performance assessment tools**—evaluating nurses' progress and identifying areas for improvement
- **Career development resources**—helping new nurses build their careers through continuing education and professional development opportunities

Precision skills management offers a transformative approach to optimizing talent development and organizational performance. When organizations focus on data-driven insights, clear skills definitions, and continuous improvement, they can unlock the full potential of their workforces. By combining the CFGNES framework with these additional components, Elsevier created a robust transition-to-practice solution that addresses the complex needs of new nurses.

CONCLUSION
A Skills-Based Future: What's to Come

In this chapter, we'll cover:
- Summarizing the key takeaways for becoming a skills-based organization
- Exploring what lies ahead for skills
- Investigating the potential of AI in a skills-based organization

Organizations continue to shift toward skills-based approaches, and the business landscape is evolving in unprecedented ways. While naysayers may believe the transition from traditional job-focused structures to skills-centric models is a trend, what's becoming clear is it's actually a necessity driven by rapid technological change, evolving market demands, and the growing need for workforce agility.

The path to becoming a skills-based organization involves a fundamental shift in how a business views talent and performance. This is not an HR or L&D initiative; a skills focus is a business-led initiative. Traditional job roles, which were once rigid and static, are being replaced by dynamic, skills-oriented frameworks that prioritize adaptability and growth. Organizations navigating this transition share several key takeaways:

- **Alignment with business goals.** Skills-based organizations align skills development with strategic objectives, ensuring that workforce capabilities directly contribute to business success.
- **Focus on continuous development.** Pervasive learning in every area of an organization is central to a skills-based approach, with organizations continuously upskilling and reskilling employees to remain competitive.

- **Data-driven decision making.** Leveraging systems to track skills data and assess gaps enables organizations to make informed decisions about talent management and development.
- **Employee empowerment.** A skills-based model allows employees to take ownership of their development and career growth, leading to greater engagement and retention.

These takeaways provide a foundation for navigating the future of work as technology, workforce structures, and employee expectations continue to evolve. It is no easy task to embark on this journey, and you and your organization should prepare for ongoing transformation as skills data changes every area of the business, providing deeper insights into the people that drive its success.

So, with these takeaways in mind, let's explore what lies ahead for skills along three major trends: hiring and recruitment, employee management, and workforce management. Then, we'll close with some ideas for how AI can accelerate the movement to becoming a skills-based organization.

Smarter Hiring and Recruitment Practices

As the world shifts toward skills-based organizations, traditional resumes—long the primary tool for assessing candidates—are already beginning to lose their relevance. The future of hiring will be driven by verifiable skills and competencies rather than static, text-based resumes that list past experiences and qualifications. There will be a growing emphasis on real-time skills data, technology-driven talent assessments, and the need for dynamic workforce adaptability. The "fall of the resume" represents a fundamental shift in how talent will be evaluated in the future.

Resumes, by design, provide a snapshot of a candidate's work history and qualifications at a specific point in time. However, as technology and business needs shift at unprecedented speeds in today's rapidly evolving job market, this static representation of a person's skills and experiences is no longer sufficient. Many traditional resumes also fail to capture the full spectrum of an individual's abilities (especially their soft skills, adaptability, and potential for growth), and they offer limited insight into real-world application.

If resumes are going away, how can you evaluate candidates for employment in skills-based organizations? Skills profiles provide a detailed, verified, and up-to-date account of an individual's abilities, certifications, and competencies. They go beyond listing job titles or responsibilities—they offer real-time data on skills acquisition, proficiency, and utilization.

And organizations are increasingly turning to skills-based platforms that allow candidates and employees to build and maintain skills profiles. Many of these platforms integrate with learning and talent platforms and project management tools to ensure that skills data is accurate, comprehensive, and up-to-date.

The decline of the resume also coincides with the rise of AI and data-driven approaches to hiring. Rather than relying on a candidate's past experiences listed on a resume, AI-driven platforms analyze real-time skills data to match candidates with roles that align with their competencies. This process can also reduce biases inherent in traditional resume evaluations.

The future of hiring will be defined by real-time skills data and an emphasis on continuous learning. Organizations that embrace this shift will be better positioned to build a workforce that is adaptable, capable, and prepared for the challenges of tomorrow's economy. The fall of the resume represents the rise of a more transparent, meritocratic, and skills-driven world of work.

Value-Centric Employee Management

As organizations adopt skills-based models, a fundamental transformation in workforce management is coming. Traditional methods of managing employees are being replaced by value-centric employee management, which focuses on the tangible value that employees bring to the organization, particularly through the application and development of their skills. The rise of value-centric employee management marks a shift toward a more agile, merit-based approach that prioritizes employee contributions and impact over static job descriptions or tenure.

As value-centric employee management systems mature, skills and outcomes will become the primary currency by which employees are rewarded and recognized. Organizations can encourage that transformation through implementing clear and transparent recognition programs that make it easy for employees to see how their skills contribute to the organization's success. Employees who develop and successfully apply critical, high-impact skills will see greater rewards in terms of career progression, compensation, and recognition.

For organizations to help drive a culture of continuous learning, they need to reimagine how performance is evaluated. This means replacing traditional annual performance reviews, which focus on job-specific goals and static metrics, with more agile, real-time performance management systems, which are designed to assess how employees apply their skills in day-to-day tasks and projects. They rely on continuous feedback loops between managers and employees on skills development and application and on project-based evaluations (for individuals and teams) that focus on the outcomes delivered through the application of skills.

Employees in value-centric organizations are empowered to take ownership of their skills development. By giving employees the tools and resources to assess and improve their skills, organizations encourage a sense of autonomy and responsibility for personal growth. In some organizations, employees themselves are encouraged to identify areas where they can contribute the most value and proactively seek out projects or learning opportunities that align with their strengths. This ownership means employees also have more flexibility to design personalized career paths based on their skills and interests. Instead of following predefined hierarchies, employees can pursue roles, projects, and specializations that align with their strengths and the value they bring.

Jobless Workforce Management

As organizations increasingly adopt skills-based management systems, they are recognizing that the rigid structure of traditional jobs often limits flexibility and innovation. Therefore, they are shifting to a more fluid, dynamic approach that prioritizes skills and outcomes. This shift toward jobless workforce management is driven by the need to adapt quickly to changing business environments, technological advances, and evolving market demands.

The move to "work without jobs" redefines the relationship between employees and organizations by centering the workforce on skills rather than roles (Jesuthasan and Boudreau 2022). This approach allows businesses to harness the full potential of their talent, deploying employees based on their abilities rather than limiting them to narrow job descriptions. It may be hard to imagine given the current models of work and job architectures, but as more organizations realize the value of focusing on skills, a future workplace without jobs is not just possible, but likely.

Jobless workforce management enables more fluid organizational structures. Instead of departments rigidly defined by job roles, teams can be formed and dissolved as needed, based on the project or task at hand and the specific skills required to address immediate challenges. Employees are evaluated and deployed based on their competencies and expertise, regardless of their formal position within the organization, and can move freely between teams and projects, applying their skills where they are most needed. This dynamic structure promotes cross-functional collaboration, innovation, and a greater sense of ownership among employees while allowing organizations to respond more rapidly to changes in the market or industry with greater workforce flexibility.

Work without jobs will enable organizations to build highly flexible and adaptable teams, while empowering employees to continuously evolve and contribute in meaningful ways. This shift represents a new paradigm for workforce management—one that aligns with the realities of a rapidly changing and increasingly complex global economy.

The Power of AI

AI is set to transform the future of skills-based organizations by powering new ways to manage, assess, and develop talent. As companies shift from traditional job-based models to dynamic, skills-driven approaches,

AI will be at the core of this evolution. AI-driven tools and systems offer powerful capabilities for analyzing workforce skills, predicting future needs, and personalizing L&D. AI will transform every area of the workforce of the future, and it's uniquely positioned to catalyze skills-based decision making by removing current friction in mapping skills to people, jobs, and content.

AI-Driven Skills Assessments and Talent Matching

One of the most significant ways AI will influence skills-based organizations is through its ability to conduct real-time, accurate assessments of employees' skills. Traditional methods of assessing skills—such as annual performance reviews or self-reported surveys—often fall short in capturing an employee's true abilities and fail to adapt quickly to changing business needs. AI offers a more dynamic and continuous solution by automating and enhancing skills assessment.

- **Continuous skills evaluation.** AI-powered platforms can constantly monitor and evaluate employee skills based on performance data, project outcomes, and interactions. By analyzing patterns of work output and collaboration, AI can measure an employee's proficiency in various competencies, from technical abilities to soft skills such as communication or leadership.
- **Automated talent matching.** AI can match employees to roles, projects, or tasks that align with their skills more efficiently and accurately than those mapped by traditional methods. Instead of relying on static job descriptions or managers' subjective decisions, AI systems analyze a variety of data points—such as skills inventories, past performance, and career goals—to recommend the best-suited employees for specific assignments.

Personalization of L&D

AI will revolutionize the way organizations approach learning and development by making it more personalized, responsive, and targeted. Instead of offering generic training programs, AI-powered systems can tailor learning experiences to the individual needs of each employee, ensuring that they acquire the most relevant skills at the right time.

- **Adaptive learning paths.** AI-based L&D platforms can create customized learning journeys for employees based on their current skills, career aspirations, and organizational needs. These systems continuously update learning recommendations based on real-time data, such as completed training modules or demonstrated skills in the workplace. This personalized approach ensures that employees focus on acquiring the skills that are most valuable for their roles and the broader organization.
- **Just-in-time training.** AI can deliver learning opportunities at the exact moment they are needed, integrating training into employees' workflows. For example, an AI system might recognize that an employee is about to start a project requiring expertise in a new software tool. The system could then recommend a relevant training module or tutorial right before the project begins, ensuring that the employee is prepared without the need for lengthy or irrelevant training sessions.
- **Upskilling and reskilling guidance.** As business needs evolve, AI can predict which skills will become critical in the near future and recommend reskilling or upskilling pathways for employees. By analyzing market trends, industry shifts, and internal data, AI tools help employees stay ahead of the curve, continuously adapting their skill sets to meet the demands of a changing workplace.

Predictive Workforce Planning and Skills Forecasting

AI will be instrumental in helping organizations plan for the future by predicting workforce needs and identifying skills gaps. As the speed of technological and market changes accelerates, businesses must become more agile in adapting to new challenges. AI-powered predictive analytics provides organizations with the insights they need to stay competitive by anticipating the skills that will be most in demand.

- **Skills gap analysis.** AI can analyze workforce data to identify skills gaps within the organization. By comparing the company's goals with the skills employees currently possess, AI systems can pinpoint areas where additional training, hiring, or redeployment is necessary. This proactive approach allows businesses to address skills shortages before they become critical issues.
- **Future skills forecasting.** AI also enables organizations to predict the future skills they will need based on emerging trends in their industry or market. Predictive models can analyze vast amounts of data (including industry reports, economic forecasts, and internal business data) to highlight which skills will be vital in the coming years. This allows companies to invest in the development of these skills ahead of time, ensuring that the workforce is prepared for future demands.
- **Strategic workforce planning.** By integrating skills forecasting with workforce planning, AI helps businesses make more strategic decisions about hiring, talent development, and succession planning. AI tools can suggest which employees are best suited to leadership roles based on their demonstrated skills and performance history, helping companies build a pipeline of future leaders.

Reducing Bias and Increasing Fairness

AI offers an important advantage in its potential to reduce bias and increase fairness in talent management processes. Traditional methods of hiring, performance evaluation, and promotion can often be influenced by unconscious biases, leading to unfair outcomes and limiting the diversity of talent within an organization. While AI can reduce human bias, it can itself be biased and should not be used without evaluating whether bias is actually being reduced or new biases are being introduced. That said, AI, when properly designed and monitored, can help mitigate bias by relying on objective data and transparent algorithms.

- **Bias-free hiring.** AI-driven recruitment tools focus on matching candidates to jobs based on their skills, experience, and potential, rather than subjective factors like gender, race, or age. This skills-first approach helps organizations diversify their workforces and ensure that the best candidate for the job is selected based on merit. This matching will only be as good as the data to power it; however, because AI will improve skills-data quality, this aspirational goal of hiring without bias is within reach.
- **Objective performance evaluations.** AI can provide data-driven insights into employee performance, reducing the reliance on human judgment, which can be biased or inconsistent. By analyzing how employees apply their skills in real-world scenarios, AI systems offer more accurate and fair assessments, ensuring that performance reviews are based on concrete contributions and outcomes.

The advancement of AI for skills-based organizations promises to revolutionize the way businesses manage talent, develop employees, and plan for the future. As AI continues to evolve, its ability to deliver real-time insights, automate complex processes, and predict future trends will make it an indispensable tool for organizations that seek to remain competitive and agile in a rapidly changing world.

Conclusion, or Just the Beginning?

Skills-based organizations aren't a fad, but a movement—a movement toward agility, a movement toward data-driven people decisions, a movement toward innovation, and a movement toward empowerment. Bringing skills data into your organization is not a question of if, but when. The potential is clear and already seen in early signals; the earlier you get started, the sooner your organization can begin its own transformational journey.

Remember: Start small, prove business value, focus on data quality, connect all areas of the business, and don't leave employees out of the conversation. If you get stuck, go back to the basics. Learn from others who are also on their skills-based-organization transformation journey.

But do get started, and keep going. Skills-based organizations will lead the way to the future of work.

Acknowledgments

No book is completed without tremendous effort and support from many people. I wrote this book during one of the most chaotic times in my life (ironically, I wrote my first book in another of those times . . .) and the folks I mention here truly made this happen.

My Publishing Crew

Jack Harlow, senior acquisition and developmental editor at ATD Press, was a steady hand in guiding this book in the right direction from step one. When I started working on the book another editor was assigned to me, but I'm so glad I ended up working with him. His feedback was invaluable, and I thought it was funny how apologetic he was when deadlines moved up—little did he know that I'm great under pressure! This book wouldn't be out in the world without the support and guidance he gave it, and I'm deeply grateful for him. I'm very much looking forward to a celebratory toast in person sometime soon.

Melissa Jones, manager of ATD Press, picked up the baton from Jack and really took this book across the finish line. She saw me through the slog of taking the book from draft to printed copies—the part of the process where the excitement of writing has worn off and the important polishing happens. She was patient and persistent, and I definitely needed both! I hope she's as proud of the end result as I am.

Kay Hechler, senior manager of publications and content at ATD, was exceptional in helping me understand the publication and marketing process to get this book out into the world. I say as a product manager that without product marketing, no one will know how great your product is. Kay has been the enabler of all my book marketing efforts, and her knowledge of the unique flows of launching a book has made such a difference to me and ensured it got to more of you.

Justin Brusino, director of content at ATD, took a chance on me as an author more than a decade ago when I wrote my first book, and he was my first call when I decided to take fingers to keyboard for this one. Justin is one of those people who makes things happen seemingly effortlessly; his confidence in me (not once but twice!) in tackling big topics important to the learning and HR industries is humbling. Justin is also one of those people who, no matter how much time has passed since we last talked, is always available to chat, take on a new adventure, or consider an interesting project. This book would not have happened without his early support and feedback.

The Contributors

I had a vision that this book would not just provide foundational knowledge about skills, skill data, and skills-based organizations, but would also include the collective intelligence of people and organizations in the trenches. As I was writing, I was also recruiting—reaching out to folks I know and admire, and getting introduced to folks they knew and admired. In the end, the collective knowledge and experiences of this book's contributors spans a range of organization profiles and geographies. Not only did their content make this book infinitely better, but my conversations with them made my writing better. In no particular order, my deepest thanks to Sandra Loughlin, Dani Johnson, Lori Niles-Hofmann, Kristi Broom, Paul Turner, Gina Jeneroux, JD Dillon, Angela Le Mathon, Aaron Silvers, Asi DeGani, Ellen Beck, Jennifer Tucker, Emily Anderson, Katie Gunther, Rosie Suerdieck, Jeroen Van Hautte, Cedric Vandamme, Matt Hayward, Sarah Mullens, Maria Chrastka, Oli Meager, and Matthew J. Daniel.

I also wanted the book to open with a connection to someone who had done deep thinking about and understood the history of skills and had built the foundations for the movement toward skills-based organizations. There is no one that exemplifies that better than Kelly Palmer. I'll admit I was a bit nervous to ask her to write the foreword for this book, but our conversation bolstered my confidence. It was that conversation perhaps more than any other that buoyed me when the writing got difficult or the deadlines seemed overwhelming. I hope this book lives up to her confidence in me writing it.

The Behind the Scenes Folks

While my name is on the book and the contributors get official credit for their contributions, I have to give extra thanks to Kristi Broom. She not only wrote content for the book, but she wrangled me and all of the other contributors, keeping everything on track and aligned (it really is her super power). I think complementary skills in teams is still underrated; Kristi truly is the "getting it done well" partner to my "I have a crazy idea" persona. Plus, she's a wonderful person who I love. Any excuse to work with Kristi? I'm in.

At the tail end of my writing process and into the editing portion, I started to lose steam. Fortunately, my daughter Violet had some extra time and helped me with transcription, research, and some much-needed conversation so I wasn't so isolated while working from home. It was an unexpected joy to include Violet in my book writing, and it's incredibly gratifying as a parent to see your kids in a professional light. I couldn't be more proud.

While there were many catalysts to this book becoming a book, the very first spark was an invitation from Jane Bozarth to write a research paper on expertise for The Learning Guild. Jane's feedback throughout the process not only made me want to keep writing, but gave me the confidence that I could write another book. Turns out she was right, and as she told me throughout my writing process, she really was my biggest cheerleader.

I would be remiss to not also mention David Kelly, who consistently supported me through his work with The Learning Guild by giving me opportunities to speak and connect with the community. David has not only been my supporter professionally, but also a good friend. His leadership at The Learning Guild and DevLearn specifically made it truly feel like a community that I'm proud to be a part of.

My deepest gratitude as well to Dave Kuntz and Kel Smith, with whom I have been plotting on skills technologies, AI, and products for years now, and who inspired much of this book (without them really knowing). At some point, we'll get the gang back together, it's just a matter of time.

My Personal Support System

Finally, there are some specific folks who had minimal connection to the book itself, but personally supported me through the last year as I was writing the book, launching new ventures, and dealing with . . . life.

Jennifer Solberg, Sarah Mercier, and Julie Dirksen are three badass women with whom I'm honored to be friends. Thanks for letting me skip the painting at the painting retreat to focus on writing, for vetting my ideas, and for inspiring me with your intelligence, humor, and realness. You mean the world to me.

My kids—Max, Arial, Elvis, Violet, Vardan, Sallie, and Rosemary—none of you have grown into who I thought you'd be when you were little. You're all much cooler and smarter than I imagined. The year I wrote this book was a trial, and you (along with our honorary kid, Emily) all supported me with love and grace. I'm so, so proud to be your mom.

John—thanks for making the space for me to take this book on, on top of everything else. You get excited when I'm excited, you push me to follow my dreams, and you always believe that everything will work out (even when I'm really not so sure). I always hoped I'd find a partner who would bring out the best in me, and who I could bring out the best in. What I didn't know on December 2, 2011, was that some people, if they're really lucky, find that person and then go on to have the most glorious adventures, build the most amazing family, and share a breathtaking love. But I know that now, because of you. I love you.

References

America Succeeds. 2021. *The High Demand for Durable Skills*. America Succeeds. americasucceeds.org/wp-content/uploads/2021/04/AmericaSucceeds-DurableSkills-NationalFactSheet-2021.pdf.

Bronfenbrenner, U., and G.W. Evans. 2000. "Developmental Science in the 21st Century: Emerging Questions, Theoretical Models, Research Designs and Empirical Findings." *Social Development* 9(1): 115–125.

Bronfenbrenner, U., and P.A. Morris. 1998. "The Ecology of Developmental Processes." In *Handbook of Child Psychology*, 5th ed., vol. 1, edited by R.M. Lerner. Wiley.

Deloitte. 2017. *Soft Skills for Business Success*. Deloitte Access Economics. deloitte.com/au/en/services/economics/perspectives/soft-skills-business-success.

Dewar, J. 2023. "Career Pathing 101: What It Is and How to Get Started." LinkedIn Talent Blog, April 20. linkedin.com/business/talent/blog/learning-and-development/career-pathing-101.

Guerzoni, A., N. Mirchandani, and B. Perkins. 2023. "Is the AI Buzz Creating Too Much Noise for CEOs to Cut Through?" EY Parthenon, October 23. ey.com/en_gl/ceo/ai-buzz-creating-noise-for-ceos-to-cut-through.

Guerzoni, A., N. Mirchandani, and B. Perkins. 2025. "How Can a Strategic Transformation Mindset Unlock Long-Term Value?" EY Parthenon, January 21. ey.com/en_us/ceo/ceo-outlook-global-report.

Haller, S. 2022. "1/3 of Recent College Grads Are Working at Jobs That Don't Require a College Education." Resume Builder, July 4. resumebuilder.com/one-third-of-recent-college-grads-are-working-at-jobs-that-dont-require-a-college-education.

Intelligent.com. 2023. "4 in 10 Business Leaders Say Recent College Grads Are Unprepared to Enter Workforce." Intelligent.com, August 30. intelligent.com/4-in-10-business-leaders-say-recent-college-grads-are-unprepared-to-enter-workforce.

Jesuthasan, R., and J. Boudreau. 2022. *Work Without Jobs: How to Reboot Your Organization's Work Operating System.* MIT Press.

Kaufman, J. 2019. "Everything I Know About Business I Learned From World of Warcraft." Josh Kaufman, April 18. joshkaufman.net/everything-i-know-about-business-i-learned-from-world-of-warcraft.

Liable, M.-C., S. Anger, and M. Baumann. 2020. "Personality Traits and Further Training." *Frontiers in Psychology.* ncbi.nlm.nih.gov/pmc/articles/PMC7701053.

McKinsey. 2021. "The Skillful Corporation." *McKinsey Quarterly Five Fifty*, January 8. mckinsey.com/capabilities/people-and-organizational-performance/our-insights/five-fifty-the-skillful-corporation.

McKinsey. 2023. *Generative AI and the Future of Work in America.* mckinsey.com/mgi/our-research/generative-ai-and-the-future-of-work-in-america.

NLI Staff. 2021. "Why Diverse Teams Outperform Homogeneous Teams." NeuroLeadership Institute, Your Brain at Work Blog, June 10. neuroleadership.com/your-brain-at-work/why-diverse-teams-outperform-homogeneous-teams.

Peiperl, M. 2001. "Getting 360-Degree Feedback Right." *Harvard Business Review*, January. hbr.org/2001/01/getting-360-degree-feedback-right.

Rock, D., and H. Grant. 2016. "Why Diverse Teams Are Smarter." *Harvard Business Review*, November 4. hbr.org/2016/11/why-diverse-teams-are-smarter.

Sanchez, J.I., and E.L. Levine. 2009. "What Is (or Should Be) the Difference Between Competency Modeling and Traditional Job Analysis?" *Human Resource Management Review* 19:53–63.

Schippmann, J.S. 1999. *Strategic Job Modeling: Working at the Core of Integrated Human Resources.* Psychology Press.

Shah, B. 2024. "The Future of Work Isn't Powered by AI. It's Powered by People Enabled by AI." *Fortune*, March 18. fortune.com/2024/03/18/mpw-summit-guild-ai-future-of-work.

WEF (World Economic Forum). 2020. "Closing the Skills Gap Accelerators." WEF, weforum.org/docs/WEF_Closing_the_Skills_Gap_Accelerator_1pager.pdf.

WEF. 2024. *Putting Skills First: Opportunities for Building Efficient and Equitable Labour Markets*. WEF.

Zahidi, S. 2020. "We Need a Global Reskilling Revolution—Here's Why." WEF, January 22. weforum.org/stories/2020/01/reskilling-revolution-jobs-future-skills.

About the Contributors

Emily Anderson is a personnel psychologist who leads the Command Assessment Program within the US Space Force's Enterprise Talent Management Office, designing assessments that strengthen leadership evaluation and talent development across the force. She specializes in assessment design and talent management strategy, supporting efforts to build a strong leadership pipeline for the future force.

Rosellen Beck is an HR leader with more than 20 years' experience in HR technology, AI transformation, learning strategy, talent development, and business operations. She excels in strategic leadership, innovative solutions, and data-informed decisions, enhancing organizational culture and employee experiences. Throughout her career, Rosellen has held notable roles at complex global companies. She is currently the executive leader of global HR technology and AI enablement at GE HealthCare, where she spearheads AI transformation and strategic HR initiatives. Previously, she served as the executive manager of global learning strategy and operations at General Electric, leading the company's separation into three public entities. Rosellen has also held leadership positions at Luxottica, First Financial Bank, and Citigroup, where she consistently delivered results and drove significant improvements in HR and learning strategies.

Kristi Broom is the co-founder of Rising Tide Cooperative, a management consultancy firm dedicated to guiding organizations through change. With more than two decades of experience in skills development, change management, and leadership enablement, Kristi has partnered with HR and L&D teams to design and implement scalable talent strategies that support business growth and transformation. She brings a practical, systems-level approach to solving workforce challenges—whether building skills frameworks, reimagining learning ecosystems, or guiding culture change during periods of rapid scaling or reinvention. Her work empowers organizations to build the capabilities they need today while preparing for what's next.

Maria Chrastka is a product manager with a passion for education and a track record of delivering successful, innovative products. As a senior product manager at Microsoft, Maria is currently focused on building AI-powered learning systems that use intelligent agents to deliver personalized, real-time skill development.

Matthew J. Daniel is senior principal of talent strategy at Guild Education, where he provides analysis of industry trends, conducts research, and advises Guild leaders on its solution strategy. He also advises HR leaders from Guild's existing and prospective employer partners on workforce transformation, skilling, career pathways, mobility, and inclusive learning. Previously, he's worked both internally as an L&D leader at Capital One and in various talent development consulting roles for several Fortune 100 companies. He also serves on the product advisory board for many learning technology companies. Matthew writes regularly for *TD*, *CLO*, Forbes BrandVoice, *CTDO*, *Training* magazine, and Talentmgt.com. Since 2021, he has also been a member of the Talent and Culture Subcommittee of the Defense Business Board, where he advises the secretary and deputy secretary of defense on the latest in talent practices.

Asi DeGani is an award-winning L&D leader with more than 13 years of experience spearheading digital transformation and talent management initiatives on a global scale. He has driven groundbreaking projects, including pioneering BT Group's Skills for Tomorrow initiative, which empowered more than 10 million UK citizens with essential digital capabilities. At the London Stock Exchange Group (LSEG), Asi architected skills-based career frameworks and innovative digital learning ecosystems to unify diverse L&D approaches, reduce learning times, and significantly boost engagement. His strategic vision and execution have earned his work accolades including Learning Technologies and Brandon Hall awards, and the World Economic Forum has recognized LSEG as a skills-first "lighthouse." Holding an MSc in digital education from the University of Edinburgh, Asi's expertise is built on a strong foundation of academic excellence and an unwavering commitment to redefining how organizations cultivate talent.

JD Dillon began his career on the frontline, managing movie theaters and theme parks. With 25 years of experience leading operations and L&D at dynamic organizations like Disney, AMC, and Kaplan, JD has become a recognized authority on performance enablement and a passionate advocate for improving the employee experience. As the chief learning officer of Axonify, JD develops technology and services that empower more than 4 million frontline workers worldwide to perform at their best every day. A sought-after speaker, author, and advisor, he specializes in ecosystem strategy and AI-enabled practices through LearnGeek. JD's latest book, *The Modern Learning Ecosystem*, offers a personal, practical, and hilarious perspective on L&D's evolving role in today's workplace.

Katie Gunther is a senior manager of global selection and assessment at Walmart and part of the enterprise initiative to implement end-to-end skills-based talent management that creates transparency in job requirements, facilitates career pathing, and encourages talent mobility within the organization. Prior to her current position, she served for 20 years as a civil servant in various assessment and leadership development roles in the US Army, Air Force, and Space Force. Katie holds a PhD in industrial and organizational psychology from Auburn University.

Matt Hayward is the global learning manager for the Medical Protection Society. He has been in learning and development for almost 20 years, focusing on building solutions and frameworks to develop talent across all levels. Over the last two years Matt has disappeared down the skill-focused rabbit hole championing the approach as the future of talent development in organizations.

Gina Jeneroux is on a mission to unlock human potential and shake up how people prepare for the future, with fresh skills, sharp insights and bold opportunities. Through a career spanning more than 30 years in the finance, talent, and learning industries—including five years as chief learning officer at BMO Financial Group—Gina has developed deep expertise in business leadership, human-centered design, and predicting and developing skills for the future. Along the way, she's led award-winning teams, delivered big-picture strategies, and stayed endlessly curious about what's next. Today, you'll find Gina at the intersection of AI, skills, and industry as a chief skills and innovation officer, professor of practice, and future work and skills strategist. She holds an MBA from Dalhousie University and is committed to learning at least one new thing each day—because that's where the future begins!

Dani Johnson co-founded RedThread Research in 2018 with Stacia Garr. Before RedThread she led the learning and career research practice at Bersin and Deloitte, and before that led research at the Ross School at the University of Michigan. Dani holds an MBA, as well as an MS and BS in mechanical engineering from Brigham Young University. Before having a kid, her favorite vacations involved a backpack, a map, and Google Translate.

Angela Le Mathon is the founder and chief AI officer of People Alkemie. She previously served as the vice president of people data and analytics at GSK, where she sat on the HR executive leadership team and led global workforce intelligence initiatives powered by AI. With more than 15 years of experience at the intersection of HR, finance, and technology, Angela brings a systems-thinking approach to people strategy and organizational design. Born in the US and raised in New York and Paris, she brings a cross-cultural fluency that deeply shapes her leadership—balancing precision with empathy, intuition with structure, and strategic clarity with a human touch. Angela is a compassionate vegetarian, a registered yoga teacher, and a devoted lover of all things matcha.

Sandra Loughlin is the chief learning scientist at EPAM Systems, which is a global leader in digital platform engineering and a company with three decades of experience as a skills-based organization. Sandra uses her expertise in learning science and organizational psychology to ensure EPAM's numerous people initiatives work together under one skills umbrella and collectively drive business growth, quality, and results. She also leads the global effort to share EPAM's skills-based experience and insights to help other organizations progress in their transformation journeys and reap the benefits of using validated skills data to make business decisions.

Oli Meager is the co-founder and managing partner of Skill Collective, a fast-growing advisory firm helping enterprises rethink how they build, develop, and deploy talent. A trusted partner to some of the world's leading brands, Oli brings entrepreneurial energy and strategic insight to designing skills-based ecosystems that are built to last. His work bridges real-world execution with bold thinking for a rapidly changing world.

Sarah Mullens is a customer-centered product leader with more than a decade of experience in skills tech. As a senior growth product manager at Skillable, she drives product innovation to shape the future of the performance-based skills market.

Lori Niles-Hofmann is a senior learning strategist with 25 years of experience leading large-scale digital learning transformations across industries including international banking, consulting, and marketing. She advises Fortune 500 CLOs, helping organizations navigate complex change and reposition L&D as a strategic driver. Drawing from extensive EdTech implementation experience, she has developed data-driven frameworks that equip L&D teams for impact. Lori is the author of *The Eight Levers of EdTech Transformation* and the creator of two LinkedIn Learning courses. She also partners with EdTech vendors—from start-ups to scale-ups—on road maps and product strategy and supports PE/VC firms in evaluating investments. With a keen eye for opportunity, she connects vendors with potential acquirers and brings deep insight into the evolving role of L&D.

Aaron Silvers is a pioneering strategist in organizational learning and skills-based talent development with more than two decades of experience transforming how organizations approach capability building. As the human capital practice lead at the US National Archives and Records Administration, Aaron implemented innovative skills-matching systems and Agile methodologies that revolutionized workforce development. Previously, at Elsevier, Aaron architected competency-based learning platforms that mapped professional standards to measurable skills development. A recognized thought leader in learning technology standards, Aaron chaired the IEEE P9271.2.1 xAPI Profiles Working Group and has been instrumental in developing frameworks that enable skills portability across organizational boundaries. His implementation of data-driven approaches to talent development has generated millions in organizational value by connecting skills gaps to targeted learning initiatives. His work developing xAPI has also generated billions internationally.

Allison "Rosie" Suerdieck is the current skills management branch chief with the US Space Force's Enterprise Talent Management Office. She earned a BA in political science from the University of Nevada and an MA in government from the Johns Hopkins University. Rosie has worked in legislative, policy, doctrine, and personnel development-related capacities throughout the US federal government. She is currently a PhD student in Colorado State's organizational learning, performance, and change program.

Jennifer Tucker currently serves as chief of the assessments and job analysis branch with the Enterprise Talent Management Office at the US Space Force. She received a PhD in systems science, industrial and organizational psychology from Portland State University in 2005. Jennifer has led teams of scientists and technical and military experts in the areas of organization development and talent management to assess and develop military leaders and team members. She has led programs to develop innovative methods to assess, track, and provide feedback on critical cognitive, social, and other attributes that are needed to optimize military members' performance across their careers.

Paul Turner has built a career around mastering new industries, markets, and technologies—developing deep expertise across sectors while leading transformative initiatives in product strategy and applied AI. With a strong foundation in cognitive science, Paul has worked extensively in the learning field, where he explores how technology can enhance knowledge sharing, skill development, and human potential. He has led teams focused on everything from taxonomy design to LLM-based applications. Paul lives in Canada with his wife, Melissa, and their four amazing kids, Nolan, Nate, Penny, and Posey.

Jeroen Van Hautte is the co-founder and chief technology officer at TechWolf, where he drives the technology and AI strategy. A top-scoring computer science student at University of Cambridge and Ghent University when he founded the company, Jeroen is one of the leading voices in AI-powered skills intelligence and has been cited in more than 80 peer-reviewed research papers. Forbes 30 Under 30 and the World Economic Forum recognize his leadership in talent transformation.

Cedric Vandamme is the vice president of professional services at TechWolf, where he leads the team responsible for connecting the technology and customers by ensuring seamless implementation and delivering real business value to clients. Before joining TechWolf in 2024, Cedric spent five years at McKinsey & Company as an associate partner, advising public and private sector organizations globally on HR strategy and skills transformation. His work focused on aligning workforce capabilities with long-term business goals, redesigning organizations for agility and efficiency, enabling culture transformation through skill-focused mindsets, and helping companies navigate the future of work.

Index

A
accountability, 149
accuracy, outcome measure, 204–205
achievements, tracking, 207–208
actionable feedback, 227–228
active learning, 213
adaptability, 120, 180, 182
adaptive learning, 24, 199–200, 295
AETHEON, 213–214
agility, 4, 156, 179
AI. *See* artificial intelligence
alignment, xxvi, 56, 57, 155, 186–187, 187, 273, 279, 289
analytical skills, 182
application process, 185
artificial intelligence (AI), 79–80, 283, 293–297
automation, 44, 174, 176, 294

B
badges, xviii, 207–208, 270
baseline data, 48, 92
behaviors, 89–90, 92
bias, 112–113, 120, 178, 296–297
blind reviews, 113
broad strategy implementation, 49
business goals, 186–187, 205, 289
business impact, 56, 204–205, 268, 268–273, 286
business needs, 180, 273, 279
business problem, solving, 47, 286
business process, aligning experimentation with, 56

C
career development, 25, 231–233, 287
career pathing programs, 23
career pathways, xxiii, xxiv, xxvi, 31–34, 162–163, 221–223, 251–254, 277
case studies, 202
Casey-Fink Graduate Nurse Experience Survey (CFGNES), 285–288
centralized skills data, 278
certifications, xvii–xviii, 124, 202–203, 270
CFGNES (Casey-Fink Graduate Nurse Experience Survey), 285–288
change management, 150
change resistance, 71–76, 156
classroom-based training, 10–11
coaching, xxiii, 28–29, 125, 161
collaboration skills, 182
collaboration tools, 124–125
common skills, 44–45
communication, 114, 150, 181, 184–185, 250–251
compensation, 277
competencies, 88–89, 92
competency-based interviews, 203
competency models, xx

competitive advantage, 273, 280
confidence, 90, 107–122
consent, for data collection and use, 150
consistency, data, 118, 121
content delivery, personalized, 25
context-specific skill validation, 120–121
continuing education, 256–257
continuous data collection, 122–127
continuous feedback, 276
continuous improvement, 273–277, 286, 289
continuous learning, xxvi, 120, 209–211
continuous skills evaluation, 294
core capabilities, 179
credentialing, 8–9
credibility, data source, 111
critical skills, 269, 286
critiques, 225–227
cross-functional skills exposure, xxiv, 270
cross-verification of skills, 120
customer service, 182

D

data analysis, 127–132, 160, 286
data analytics, 160, 164–167, 280, 282, 287
data-based approach to skill building, 58–60
data classification, 150
data collection, 111–112, 115–119, 122–127, 150, 158–159, 274
data-driven decision making, xxvi, 259, 275, 286, 290
data-driven recruitment, 174
data privacy, 150
data quality management, 150
data security, 150
data signals, volume of, 117–119

data sources, 63–64, 111, 119–121
data usage policies, 150
decision making, xxvi, 72–73, 117, 127–132, 259, 275, 278, 286, 290
deep learning inference models, 146–147
deep strategy implementation, 49
degrees, xvii
detail, attention to, 182
digital badges, xviii, 207–208, 270
digital skills, 214
diversity, xxvii, 37, 113, 218–221, 271
documentation, 114

E

economic benefits, 7
e-learning, 11
Elsevier, 285–288
employee capabilities, xvi–xxii, 12–13
employee development, 80–81, 126, 225–227
employee empowerment, 3–4, 243–265, 290
employee engagement, xxii–xxiv, 13, 31–36, 206–208, 272, 283–284
employee profiles, 123
employees
  buy-in from, 70–71
  consent for data use from, 150
  mapping skills data to individual, 153
  skill data updates by, 261–262
  skills analysis questions of, 131–132
  skill/skills data ownership by, 245–247
employee satisfaction, 273
employee self-assessments, 23, 123–124, 134
employee surveys, 260, 274

employee value, 163, 268, 272–273
engagement surveys, 260
enterprise collaboration tools, 124–125
enterprise systems, integration across, 149–152
EPAM Systems, xxvii–xxxiii
equity, 5, 9, 237, 296–297
ethical issues, 150
evidence, breadth/depth of, 118–119
executive stakeholders, 48–49, 66–67, 127–128
expense-related objections, 73–74
experiences, mapping skills to, 251
experimentation, xxiv, 55–58
expertise, xviii–xix, 35–37, 118
external benchmarks, 135
external talent acquisition, 16–20

F
fairness, 237, 296–297
feedback, xix, xxvii, 24–25, 114, 125, 134, 186, 203, 227–228, 274, 276, 283, 284
flexibility, 156
formal observation, 134
freelance work, 257
frontline work, 40–45
future skills forecasting, 296

G
gamification, 284
garbage in, garbage out, 117
goal-oriented coaching, xxiii
goals, 29, 33, 35, 186–187, 205, 289
Guild Education, 263

H
half-life, of skills, 103–106
higher cognitive skills, 214–215
high-potential employees, 232

hiring, 171–191, 290–291
  aligning, with business goals, 186–187
  assessing potential in, 179–180
  bias-free, 297
  candidate-sourcing efforts, 175–178
  challenges of traditional, 173–174
  enhancing experience in, 184–186
  evolution of recruitment and, 173–175
  to fill future skills gaps, 187
  interview process for, 181–184
  process improvements for, xxv
  products to assist with, 161
  traditional vs. skills-based, 15–22
human potential, 3–4, 100–103, 179–180
human resources (HR) professionals, 67–68, 127–128
human resources (HR) systems. *See* skills-based human-resources system
human skills, 37, 87–88, 92, 96, 214
hybrid inference models, 147
hybrid work environments, 208–209

I
impact of learning, 27–28, 48, 204–205, 286
inclusivity, xxvi
informal observation, 134
innovation, xxiv, xxvii, 4, 156, 271
integrity, 90
internal (talent) mobility, 20–22, 56, 161–162, 234–237, 260, 272
interoperability, 283
interviews, xxv, 19–20, 181–184, 203
investing, in technology, 278–280
Isanno Expertise Profiles, 247–249

J

job application process, 185
job candidates, 174–180, 184–186
job descriptions, xxv, 16–17
job function, 93–95, 156
jobless workforce management, 292–293
job postings, 184–185
job recommendations, personalized, 184
job role, 93–95, 154, 159
job skills, 37, 87, 92, 96
job trials, 203
just-in-time training, 295

K

key skills, 63
knowledge, 89, 92

L

land and expand strategies, 76
lateral career moves, 254
L&D. *See entries beginning* learning and development
leadership, 29, 217, 233. *See also* line of business leaders
learning. *See also specific types*
　impact of, 27–28, 48, 204–205, 286
　interview questions about, 182
　mindset shift away from, 198–200
　prioritization of, 213
　skill building vs., 25–26
　skills-based targets for, 200–201
　skills development vs., 199
learning agility, 179
learning and development (L&D) strategy, 22–28, 78–81, 155, 196–201, 204–205, 294–295
learning and development (L&D) teams, 68–69, 129–131, 194–200
learning content, 25, 153–154, 206–208, 287
learning culture, 193–215
　engagement and motivation in, 206–208
　and evolution of L&D, 196–201
　measuring L&D impact in, 204–205
　and organizational personas, 194–196
　PREskilling in, 211–215
　in remote/hybrid environments, 208–209
　reskilling and upskilling in, 209–211
　ROI for skills acquisition in, 205
　skill validation in, 201–204
learning management systems (LMSs), 161, 281
learning organizations, 194–196
learning outcomes, measurement of, 204–205
learning paths, tailored, 24
learning platforms, 125–126, 161, 280, 287
level of confidence in skills data, 107–108, 111–113, 115–119, 121–122
linear career paths, 252–253
line of business leaders, 69–70, 74–75, 232, 253
London Stock Exchange Group (LSEG), 234–237
long-term relationship building, xxiv

M

machine learning, 146, 283
managers, 23, 69–70, 128–129, 203, 261, 274–276
mentoring, xxiv, 23, 28–29, 125, 287
meritocracy, xxvi

microcredentials, xviii
mindsets, 91–92, 92, 198–200
misrepresentation, 120
motivation, 206–208, 261

N

needs analysis, 62–66
net promoter score (NPS), 260
networking, 9
nontraditional career paths, 253–254
NPS (net promoter score), 260

O

objective data, 113, 183–184, 297
objectives, defining, 62
observational assessment, 110, 134
ontologies, skills, 141–145, 150, 160
organizational culture, xxvi. *See also* learning culture
organizational readiness, 61–81
organizational resilience, 4–6
outliers, in skills data, 118
ownership, skill and skill data, 71, 149, 245–247, 284

P

participants, needs analysis, 62–63
people management. *See* skills-based talent management
people managers. *See* managers
performance assessment tools, 287
performance data, 275, 277
performance evaluations, 183–184, 297
performance feedback, 134, 283
performance management, xxiii, xxv, 30–31, 260–261, 275–276, 276
performance management systems (PMSs), 282
performance metrics, 205

performance reviews, xxv, 23, 110, 116, 123, 203, 223–228
perseverance, 90
personality traits, 90–92
personalized job recommendations, 184
personalized L&D strategy, 294–295
personalized learning, 22–25, 199, 279–280
planner L&D cultures, 194
PMSs (performance management systems), 282
portfolio reviews, 202
portfolios, skills data from, 126
practical assignments, 203
practice labs, 161
precision learning, 12–13
precision skills management, 285–288
predictive analytics, 24, 160, 275
predictive workforce planning, 295–296
pre-employment testing, 161
presentations, 67, 183
PREskilling, 211–215
prioritization, 37, 75, 213
problem-solving skills, 181
productivity metrics, 275
proficiency levels, 96–100, 247, 269
progress tracking, 206–207
project assignments, xxv
project management, 124, 182
project staffing, 36–38
project success rates, 270
promoter L&D cultures, 194–195
promotion velocity, 272
provider L&D cultures, 194

Q

quizzes, 201–202

R

rate of skills growth, 269
real-time feedback, 284
real-time skills data, 280
reassessment, regular, 115–116
recognition programs, xxvii
recruitment, xxv, 15–22, 173–175, 186–187, 290–291
RedThread Research, 133
Refinitiv, 234–237
reliability, data, 109
remote work environments, 208–209
required skills. *See* skill requirements
reskilling, 209–212, 254, 269–270, 295
resource assessment, 49–50
resumes, 17–19, 123, 176–177
retention, 272
return on investment, 205
revenue growth, 271
reviews of assessment methodology, 114
rewards, 207–208
risk assessment, 76–78
risk comfort, 76–78
risk-trust matrix, 77–78
role-playing games (RPGs), xv–xvi
rubrics, 183–184
rule-based inference models, 146

S

scaling, 278, 280
scenario-based assessment, 110
self-awareness, 90
self-management, 90
self-reported expertise, xviii–xix
side gigs, 257
simulations, 202, 287
Singapore, 214
Skillable, 138–139

skill building, 25–27, 160–161, 205, 255
skill diversity, xxvii, 271
skill logs, 116
skill matching, 7–8, 176
skill requirements, 44, 63, 116, 184–185
skill(s). *See also specific types*
   agreement on prioritization of, 75
   aligning business needs and, 279
   application of, 110–112, 138–139, 276
   approaching, as data problem, 58–60
   behavior and, 89–90
   creating comprehensive view of, 120
   defining, 6–7, 76, 85–87, 155
   half-life of, 103–106
   job recommendations based on, 184
   knowledge as indicator of, 89
   mindsets vs., 91
   ownership of, 245–247
   personality traits and, 90–91
   prioritizing, for project staffing, 37
   seeking out opportunities to practice, 255
   in tech-driven world, 189–191
   visibility of, xxii
skills acquisition rate, 269
skills analytics platforms, 160, 282
skills application rate, 270
skills assessments, 24
   AI-driven, 294
   application of skills in, 110–112
   collecting data from, 126
   and engagement/motivation, 206–207

feedback based on, 186
mapping, to proficiency levels, 99–100
measuring growth with, 180
pre-employment, 161
for PREskilling, 213
recency of data collected in, 115–119
reducing bias in, 112–113
regular use of, 274
skills verification in, 134–135
structuring interviews around, 182
transparent methodology in, 114–115
validation through, 201–204
validity and reliability of, 107–117
skills assessment tools, 159, 281–282, 286
skills-based hiring platforms, 161
skills-based human resources (HR) systems, 135, 262–265, 278–284
skills-based models, xx–xxii
　alternatives to, 8
　continuous improvement of, 273–277
　costs and benefits of, 7
　credentialing and, 8–9
　data relationships in, 92–93
　definition of skills for, 6–7
　equity and networking, 9
　first initiative with, 47–50, 297–298
　foundation for, 54–55
　innovation and agility with, 4
　objections to, 6–9
　organizational readiness for (*See* organizational readiness)
　for organizational resilience, 4–6

skills matching in, 7–8
starting small with, 61–62
unleashing human potential with, 3–4
skills-based organization(s)
　blueprint for, 52–53, 169 (*See also specific components*)
　employee considerations in strategies of, 258–262
　employee engagement in, xxii–xxiv
　EPAM Systems, xxvii–xxxiii
　key takeaways for building, 289–290
　London Stock Exchange Group, 235
　making your case to become, 10
　metrics for, 268–273
　processes in, xxiv–xxvi
　systems in, xxvi–xxvii
skills-based performance management, 276
skills-based performance reviews, 223–228
skills-based talent management, 217–242
　building diverse teams, 218–221
　for career development and succession planning, 231–233
　career pathways in, 221–223
　at LSEG, 234–237
　performance reviews in, 223–228
　talent mobility in, 228–231
　traditional vs., 28–31
　at USSF, 238–242
skills category, grouping data by, 95–96
skills-centric interview questions, 181–182
skills coverage ratio, 268

Index 321

skills data
- analyzing (*See* data analysis)
- bad, decision making based on, 117
- building confidence in, 107–121
- centralized, 278
- codifying, 44
- continuous collection of, 122–127
- defining, 85–106
- determining proficiency with, 100–102
- for employee empowerment (*See* employee empowerment)
- grouping, 93–96
- integrating, across enterprise systems, 149–152
- intermingling performance and, 277
- mapping associations with, 152–157
- measuring confidence in, 121–122
- ownership of, 71, 149, 246, 284
- planning collection and analysis of, 107–139
- predicting potential with, 100–103, 179–180
- predicting proficiency with, 100–102
- real-time, 280
- recency of, 115–119
- in recruitment, 175
- relationships between, 92–93
- resistance to sharing, 71
- in role-playing games, xv–xvi
- for talent management (*See* skills-based talent management)
- trust in, 72, 108–121
- updating, 261–262
- validity of, 109–117

skills-data governance, 149–151
skills data management, complexity of, 279
skills development, xxiii, xxvi, 56, 78–81, 198–200, 254–257, 268–270
skills-focused coaching, xxiii
skills forecasting, 296
skills gaps, 187, 269, 296
skills growth, 276–277
skills inference models, 145–149, 158–159
skills infrastructure, 141–167
skills inventories, xxv, 160, 268–269, 282
skills mapping, xxii–xxiii, 99–100, 152–157, 180, 251
skills ontologies, 141–145, 150, 160
skills pathways, xxiv
skills profiles, 247–251
skills recognition programs, 276–277
skills taxonomies, 79–80, 142–145
skills tests, 201–202
skills-to-jobs databases, 159
skills tracking, 24
skills utilization, 112, 268, 270–271, 275
skills verification, 120, 133–136, 138–139
skills vision statement, 50–51
skill validation, 120–121, 159, 201, 201–204
small-to-medium-sized organizations, 78–81
SMEs (subject matter experts), 252–253
social awareness, 90
social-emotional skills, 90–91
social validation, of expertise, xix
solution proposal, 63–66
source credibility, 111

stakeholders, 62–63, 66–76, 127–132. *See also specific types*
standardization, 113, 156
strategic workforce planning, 187, 296
stretch opportunities, 37–38
structured coaching sessions, xxiii
subjective data, 113, 156
subject matter experts (SMEs), 252–253
succession planning, 38–39, 231–233
success metrics, 47–48, 56–57
suppliers, technology, 158
supply chain approach to skills management, 11–14
survey instrument development, 287
system integration, 149–152, 282–283

T
talent acquisition and development, 67–68, 128
talent alignment, 155
talent management, 291–292. *See also* skills-based talent management
talent matching, 294
talent mobility. *See* internal mobility
talent pools, 21–22, 177–178
task intelligence, 154–157
task rotation, xxv
tasks, defined, 92, 155
taxonomies, skills, 79–80, 142–145
technical proficiency, 181
technical skills, 87, 92, 96, 136–139, 214
technology, xxiii, 157–163, 189–191, 249, 278–284

Telefonaktiebolaget LM Ericsson, 136
Telescope platforms, xxxii
360-degree feedback, xix, 125
three Vs approach, 108–121
timeboxing, 49
time management, 182
time-to-market improvements, 271
timing-related objections, 73–75
training, 10–11, 23, 113, 124, 295
transferable skills, 179
transparency, 114–115, 184–185, 237
trust, in skills data, 72, 108–121

U
unconscious bias, 178
United States Space Force (USSF), 238–242
updates, 116, 261–262
upskilling, 209–212, 269–271, 295
user experience, 262–265
user-friendly interface, 284
USSF (United States Space Force), 238–242

V
validity, assessment, 109–117
value-centric employee management, 291–292
values, xxvi
variety, of data sources, 119–121
versatility, 180
visibility of skills, xxii
vision statement, skills, 50–51
volume, of data signals, 117–119
volunteer work, 256

W
work, mapping skills data to, 154
work allocation, xxv, 36–38

work data, skill verification from, 135
workforce management, 36–40, 292–293
workforce planning, 39–40, 156, 162, 187, 295–296
workload-related objections, 74–75
work samples, 126

About the Author

Koreen Pagano is a globally recognized product executive with deep expertise in learning technologies, skills strategy, AI, analytics, and immersive experiences. She has held leadership roles at Lynda.com, LinkedIn, D2L, Degreed, and Wiley. Koreen previously founded Tandem Learning, where she pioneered immersive learning through virtual worlds, games, and simulations. She is currently an executive advisor for product strategy and skills transformation and is building a portfolio of skills-related products.

Koreen is a seasoned international speaker and author of two books, *Immersive Learning* (2013) and *Building the Skills-Based Organization* (2025). She lives in Carpinteria, California, where she raised her seven (now adult) children with her adventure partner, John. Koreen is a certified Master Gardener and helps run the family business, Night Owl Ciderworks.

About ATD

The Association for Talent Development (ATD) is the world's largest association dedicated to those who develop talent in organizations. Serving a global community of members, customers, and international business partners in more than 100 countries, ATD champions the importance of learning and training by setting standards for the talent development profession.

Our customers and members work in public and private organizations in every industry sector. Since ATD was founded in 1943, the talent development field has expanded significantly to meet the needs of global businesses and emerging industries. Through the Talent Development Capability Model, education courses, certifications and credentials, memberships, industry-leading events, research, and publications, we help talent development professionals build their personal, professional, and organizational capabilities to meet new business demands with maximum impact and effectiveness.

One of the cornerstones of ATD's intellectual foundation, ATD Press offers insightful and practical information on talent development, training, and professional growth. ATD Press publications are written by industry thought leaders and offer anyone who works with adult learners the best practices, academic theory, and guidance necessary to move the profession forward.

We invite you to join our community. Learn more at **td.org**.

www.ingramcontent.com/pod-product-compliance
Ingram Content Group UK Ltd.
Pitfield, Milton Keynes, MK11 3LW, UK
UKHW021843140426
5217IPUK00022B/1567